FAITH
AND THE
FLAG

Also by Jeremy Murray-Brown

KENYATTA

FAITH AND THE FLAG

The Opening of Africa

JEREMY MURRAY-BROWN

London
GEORGE ALLEN & UNWIN
Boston   Sydney

DT
2 8
.M85
1977
Feb-1998

Printed litho in Great Britain
in 11 point Baskerville type
by W & J Mackay Ltd, Chatham

For my mother and my father

'The centuries of past history would have rolled by like empty jars, if Christ had not been foretold by means of them'

Augustine of Hippo

PREFACE

I have tried to write this account of an often misunderstood period of African history from the point of view of one set of principals involved, namely, the European and American pioneers who wanted, more than anything else, to impart their religious faith to the inhabitants of the continent. The context in which they operated gave rise to various expressions nearly all of which would be resented by most black Africans today. They spoke of Africa as benighted and of Africans as heathen. Phrases like 'the degraded sons of Ham' and 'the land cursed for Ham's sake' frequently appear in their writings. But we have to remember that they were using these words within strictly religious and moral terms of reference. Of course their attitude was influenced by their own social and economic background, but they did not in any way believe in the moral superiority of western man on the grounds of colour of skin or range of material achievements. They often used equally forceful language about the civilisation they came from.

Yet because of the controversy that still surrounds the colonial era in Africa it is often forgotten, by Africans as well as others, that Christianity flourished in the northern part of the continent centuries before Augustine brought it to Kent in 597. It is also often forgotten that a form of Christianity existed in Ethiopia long before white missionaries, Catholic or Protestant, ever visited the shores of Africa. A phenomenon which all traditional churches must also reckon with is the unprecedented growth of the African Independent Church Movement, which now claims one-fifth of the entire Christian community in Africa on a broad geographical spread across one-third of Africa's tribes.

Although I have not wilfully departed from normal academic standards in handling the material, this is not an academic study. Rather, I see it as a drama with a set of actors represented by certain historical personalities, each one of whom believed he had a special role to play in the continent. What this role was may not have been in every case, or consistently in all cases, very clear. But they shared in a conviction that God had a purpose for them in their lives, to be revealed in the history of Africa, though they might not live to see its fulfilment themselves. Naturally they looked for a congruity of events which would make that purpose clearer as the years went by. For them, too, history was an unfolding drama.

This theme links the various episodes which make up the book.

Where necessary I have tried to fill in the historical background so as to give a continuous narrative of the period. If I have given prominence to Robert Moffat, it is partly because his life spanned fifty years of African history, but also because he was in my view a giant of a man. I can imagine him as a figure in one of the great windows of Chartres. Because of his stature others were enabled to see even further into the distance.

But I make no claim to completeness. I have excluded West Africa entirely and dealt cursorily or not at all with men and women who deserve better treatment – for example, the French Protestant François Coillard, whose work among the Lozi people at the end of the period was all-important in the history of what is now Zambia. Standing by his grave in the upper Zambezi valley I was struck by the epitaph engraved on it: *Vivre c'est Christ*. These words present a challenge to all secular interpretations of history, as they did when St Paul first used them in the heyday of the Roman Empire.

In this respect mine is a committed approach. It seems to me that if we are properly to understand these men and what brought them to Africa, if we are to understand the age they lived in – now virtually unrecognisable from our own – we have to enter into the spirit of their convictions and see history through their eyes. Whether there is any truly 'objective' history is, of course, very much a matter of opinion. As we can see from our attempts to understand the present, for example in the way we handle news on radio and television, subjective factors always seem to enter into the selection of material and the ordering of its presentation. Is not the same thing true of each generation's attempt to make sense of the past?

I offer this book, then, as an argument only, as a basis for discussion, and not as a technical work, still less as a history of missionary societies or the missionary movement. For this reason I have not included notes or detailed references and have used the commonest or simplest spelling of African names. It is said that over sixteen versions of Moselekatse are extant, Umsiligasi and Mzilikazi being two. Similarly, one finds Kimeri, Kmeri and Kimweri in regular use. I hope specialists will excuse the many liberties I have taken in this matter. Acknowledgements and a brief explanation about sources are at the end of the book.

Someone I must thank here, however, is Mrs Katharine Makower. I could not have attempted this book without the aid of her indefatigable researches, which have provided the material for whatever is new in it. Her clear mind and sure faith have kept me from many errors; those that remain are entirely my own.

Finally, a special word of thanks to Malcolm Muggeridge, with whom I have talked over the underlying theme on many a walk at Robertsbridge, at Carthage and Hippo. I hear him now, reciting the verses of William Blake from which I have taken the title of the first chapter:

> Mock on, Mock on Voltaire, Rousseau:
> Mock on, Mock on: 'tis all in vain!
> You throw the sand against the wind,
> And the wind blows it back again.
>
> And every sand becomes a Gem
> Reflected in the beams divine;
> Blown back they blind the mocking Eye,
> But still in Israel's paths they shine.

The friendship of Malcolm and Kitty has brought constant joy and light to me and my family.

JEREMY MURRAY-BROWN

CONTENTS

ILLUSTRATIONS

MAPS

CHAPTER ONE

ISRAEL'S PATHS

1 *Opening of Suez Canal: Inaugural Banquet*
(Eugénie is fourth from left, facing, Ismail is on the right,
wearing fez)

I

At eight o'clock on the morning of 17 November 1869, the French
imperial yacht, *Aigle*, left her moorings at Port Said and to a terrific
barrage of ships' salutes passed between two tall marker posts to
become the first vessel officially to sail down the Suez Canal. Standing
proudly on her bridge were the Empress Eugénie, wife of Louis
Napoleon of France, and Ferdinand de Lesseps, the man who for the
past fifteen years had been the driving force behind the building of
the canal. It really was *his* canal; and because of him it was France

Tropic of Cancer

Equator

Tropic of Capricorn

ATLANTIC

OCEAN

INDIAN

OCEAN

I   AFRICA: GENERAL

| 0 | | 1000 | | 1800 mil |
0   800   1600   2400 kilometres

that was being honoured in this opening ceremony. '*Vive l'impératrice!*'
shouted the crowds lining the banks, and Eugénie waved decorously
back. Beneath the sailor's cap jauntily perched on her head she was
sick with nerves that something would go wrong. Luckily she did not
know that the previous evening an Egyptian frigate had foundered
somewhere down the canal completely blocking it, nor that the ruler
of Egypt, Ismail Pasha, had responded to de Lesseps' suggestion and
had had the obstructing craft blown up. When the *Aigle* set off that
morning de Lesseps himself had not heard if this operation had been
carried out successfully and the canal cleared.

Three hundred vessels of all nationalities had assembled at the
newly created Port Said for this opening ceremony, with the world's
notables or their representatives on board. For days salutes had
boomed out across the waters of the Mediterranean as each ship in
turn welcomed the newcomers, salvo after salvo greeting the last and
most important personages, the Emperor of Austria, the Crown
Prince of Prussia, and Eugénie herself. The previous day the canal
had been consecrated to commerce by religious officials, Christian
and Moslem, seated in two specially constructed pavilions on the
water's edge, and Ismail's guests in a third pavilion had heard
Eugénie's confessor describe de Lesseps as a new Columbus. At night
Port Said was aglow with rockets and Chinese lanterns and entertain-
ments of all kinds.

The seventeenth was the highest point of the celebrations, a day of
bunting and cheers, of difficult protocol successfully overcome, of day-
dreams for the romantic, and for the worldly-wise bets as to which
ship would run aground first as the flotilla of notables followed
Eugénie and the *Aigle* down the thin strip of water that led through
the desert. Thomas Cook of London was there conducting his clients
on a special Egyptian tour; Théophile Gautier and Emile Zola were
among the sightseers from Paris, and among those from England was
an aristocrat in a private yacht newly acquired for the occasion who
found it all 'very quaint'.

At the centre of it all Ismail Pasha moved confidently in a splendid
uniform of blue and gold, a jewelled scimitar glittering at his side.
Two years before he had been accorded the title of Khedive, or
Prince. On this his day of days he was waiting to receive Eugénie at
Ismailia, a new town named after him which was situated halfway
down the canal on Lake Timsah, and which boasted his new palace,
restaurants with French cuisine, hotels in various mock-European
styles, special swimming facilities, Bedouin encampments, brothels
and many other distractions. At five in the afternoon the *Aigle*

arrived without mishap to meet a flotilla of less important ships sailing northwards from Suez. Crowds of fellaheen, 80,000 of whom had at one time been employed in the construction work, had been ordered to line the banks and cheer, and cynical dragomen shepherded 20,000 visitors about the gaudily decked streets and tents; there was more entertainment that night, another ball and Prussian officers in cavalry boots climbing on the furniture to catch a glimpse of Eugénie, and next day camel rides across the desert, visits to the Bedouin encampments, and exotic views of the sun rising and setting between palm trees. The oceans had joined hands at last, and the journey to India was halved. Africa was an island.

The opening of the canal brought to a climax a process begun more than fifty years before under the genius of Mahomet Ali, an illiterate adventurer of Albanian origin serving in the Turkish army. Profiting from the anarchy that followed the French and English descent on Egypt during the Napoleonic war, Mahomet Ali had established his personal authority in Cairo, killed off the Turkish Mamelukes, and built up an empire in the Near East powerful enough to threaten that of his nominal suzerain, the Sultan of Turkey. At this point European powers intervened, fearing loss to their own interests. Mahomet Ali's rule was confined to Egypt. He remained subject to Turkey with the title of hereditary pasha, or viceroy, but he was given a free hand in Africa and encouraged to consolidate his hold on Nubia and the Sudan and the Red Sea ports which gave access to the upper Nile. Khartoum, founded in 1830, provided a base for further expansion southwards.

Napoleon had appointed as his consul-general in Egypt Mathieu de Lesseps, an expert in Near Eastern affairs who ensured that French influence remained dominant in Cairo under Mahomet Ali and his successors. Frenchmen for their part never lost interest in Egypt after the publicity which followed Napoleon's brief adventure there, many of them becoming Moslems in order to identify themselves more closely with the Levant. De Lesseps' fourth son, Ferdinand, was born in 1805 and followed the same diplomatic career as his father, serving for a time in Cairo, where he formed a close friendship with Mohammed Said, an indolent son of Mahomet Ali. Fretting under the austere regime of his soldier-father, the young prince used to come secretly to the Frenchman's rooms for dishes of macaroni, and so became inordinately attached to the French way of life. Ferdinand de Lesseps was a charming conversationalist, a brilliant horseman, and an accomplished dancer, all of which gave him status in the world. In 1849, however, he had to retire from public service after a disastrous mission to Rome, and with nothing better to do spent his days dreaming of the great Napoleon's plan for a direct canal across the isthmus of Suez. In 1854 Said became Pasha of Egypt and Ferdinand de Lesseps saw a chance of realising his dream.

Said was delighted to welcome back to Cairo the man who had been his friend and unofficial tutor twenty years before. They went out into the desert together and talked about the canal. By executing a spectacular leap with his horse de Lesseps won Said's backing. For fifteen years and with unflagging energy, acting in turn as diplomatist, entrepreneur and business manager, he overcame a succession of obstacles presented by persistent British opposition, Turkish amour-propre, Egyptian inefficiency, commercial rivals and engineering difficulties. Cairo became a new Mecca for European adventurers and adopted a western-style face, and Egypt turned into a prototype developing nation where side by side with the luxury and vice of the Orient could be seen gas and electricity, the telegraph and railways, dockyards, new model armies and schools and health programmes, leather upholstery and French style of living. Said died in 1863 and was succeeded by Ismail who thus enjoyed the prestige of being host at the gala event of the century. His glittering display epitomised Egypt's transformation. As one French observer remarked, it was 'an extraordinary mixture of sumptuosity and barrenness'.

2

A civilised Egypt held out one kind of prospect for Africa. At the same time another set of forces was at work at the opposite pole of the continent, which offered development of a rather different sort. Here too the starting point was the beginning of the nineteenth century when the world war between France and England was at its height.

On 2 January 1806, shortly after the Battle of Trafalgar had given Britain mastery of the sea, an English fleet of fifty transports escorted by five men-of-war came in sight of Table Mountain, on the Cape of Good Hope. The convoy had been four months at sea. It had collected men and supplies at Cork, in Ireland, and followed the trade winds via Madeira and San Salvador, on the coast of Brazil, both possessions of Britain's ally, Portugal. Only when he was well out to sea had the commodore received his final orders, which were to capture the Cape of Good Hope from the Dutch, whose Batavian Republic was an ally of France. On 3 January the troops landed under the guns of the

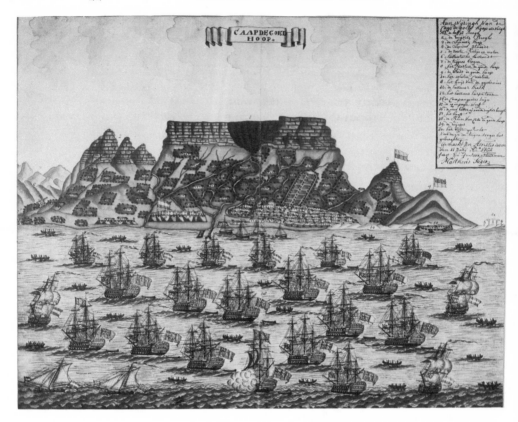

2 *Caap de Goed Hoop:* Painting by Mattheus Sager, 1752

men-of-war and after a good deal of artillery and musketry fire the defenders surrendered. The Cape of Good Hope thereupon passed into the hands of Britain to become her first colony in Africa.

It so happened that on board one of the East Indiamen in the transport convoy was a recently appointed company chaplain, Henry Martyn, whose journal recorded the event in these words:

'About five the commodore fired a gun, which was instantly answered by all the men-of-war. On looking out for the cause, we saw the British flag flying on the Dutch fort. Pleasing as the cessation of warfare was, I felt considerable pain at the enemy's being obliged to give up their fort and town, and everything else, as a conquered people, to the will of their victor. I hate the cruel pride and arrogance that makes men boast over a conquered foe. And every observation of this sort which I hear cuts me to the very heart; whether from nature or from grace I do not know, but I had rather be trampled upon than be the trampler. I could find it more agreeable to my own feelings to go and weep with the relatives of the men whom the English have killed, than to rejoice at the laurels they have won. I had a happy season in prayer. No outward scene seemed to have power to distract my thoughts. I prayed that the capture of the Cape might be ordered to the advancement of Christ's kingdom; and that England, whilst she sent the thunder of her arms to the distant regions of the globe, might not remain proud and ungodly at home; but might shew herself great indeed, by sending forth the ministers of her church to diffuse the gospel of peace.'

Henry Martyn was the finest scholar of his year at Cambridge, the gayest of companions and an ardent admirer of a girl in Cornwall. All these pleasures of the mind and senses he forsook to carry the Christian gospel to the heathen world. His sentiments are generally labelled as the product of the 'evangelical revival', which term is a convenient description of, but no explanation for, the religious upheaval which shook the Protestant world in the second half of the eighteenth century and gave birth, among other things, to the English crusade against the slave-trade and the world-wide missionary movement which spread within a single generation throughout Britain, Europe and America. Both need a brief mention.

The anti-slave trade crusaders were a group of rich and influential men who gathered round the rector of Clapham parish church, a few miles south of Westminster, whereby they became known as the Clapham Sect. They included businessmen, lawyers and members of Parliament, the best known being William Wilberforce, a friend of William Pitt. Meeting together to share their religious experience of the world, they felt called on to realise practical good works in the humanitarian field. Their attention was directed towards the slave-trade, against which the Quakers in America had been the first to speak, and which became a controversial issue in England in 1772, when the Lord Chief Justice declared that English law recognised no man as a slave. The abolitionists succeeded in getting the British trade in slaves outlawed in 1807, and the slaves themselves emancipated in all British colonies in 1833, the year of Wilberforce's death. In this cause they spent much of their wealth and time and reputations, and the impulse that led them into it was very humane – even Christian, as the term is most often understood. Certainly they felt guided by a sense of divine mission. But, as a matter of fact, it is doubtful if they achieved any material improvement in the lot of Negroes, slave or free. If anything, the reverse was the case. Some of the greatest profits in the slave-trade were made after Britain's legislation; and as a result of the American Civil War the position of Negroes in America actually deteriorated.

The abolitionists had the idea of transplanting Negroes from the

New World back into Africa – an idea which, at this distance at least, suggests there was a strong racial element in their thinking. In 1787 they founded the colony of Sierra Leone on the west coast of Africa with a mixture of London prostitutes (white) and Negroes, some of whom had found themselves freed and unwanted in England as a result of the judgement of 1772, others having been granted their freedom after fighting for England in the American War of Independence. The latter had been settled first in Nova Scotia, but found the climate uncongenial. The colony had a vaguely commercial purpose to it, but soon became bankrupt, was sacked by the French in the Napoleonic War, and in 1808 was taken over by the British Crown.

The sudden eruption of the missionary movement throughout the Protestant world was contemporaneous with the English crusade against slavery. First in the field were Baptists, in 1792, inspired by the great William Carey; they were followed by the London Missionary Society (LMS) in 1795 which aimed to be free from all forms of church government, but soon became predominantly Congregationalist. After these came societies in Edinburgh and Glasgow (1796), in the Netherlands (1797), and in England where a powerful body of low church Anglicans formed the Church Missionary Society (CMS) in 1799. The movement spread to America, where the first American Society was founded in 1810, to Basel in northern Switzerland in 1815, and to France and Prussia, where the Paris and Berlin Societies were both founded in 1824.

These societies were all voluntary and originated largely outside the established churches, indeed rather in revolt against them. They were managed mostly by laymen and soon became powerful institutions in themselves, similar to the anti-slavery lobbyists. Indeed the same people were often engaged in both causes, as their human urge to organise themselves in the world and attract support at home drew them together. Individually, many of them were men and women of great faith and piety. Collectively, they tended to put their trust in numbers and power, which they saw as serving a single cause, namely the conversion of the heathen world to Protestant Christianity.

As the nineteenth century advanced, two questions had to be answered; first, what should you do with liberated slaves, and later, what should you do with liberated – that is, converted – heathen. The solution applied to the first, the freed slave colony of Sierra Leone, was then adapted to the second, protection within a Christian empire.

During the short battle which gave Britain possession of the Cape,

Henry Martyn came ashore to comfort the dying, narrowly escaping being killed himself by a drunken Highlander who mistook him for a Frenchman. When the fighting was over he sought out Vanderkemp, the pioneer Dutch missionary who had come out in 1799 at the age of fifty-two after a spiritual revolution which followed the tragic deaths by drowning of his wife and daughter in his native Holland. A highly gifted visionary, Vanderkemp was thought eccentric because he refused to wear a hat, the mark of status among white men at the Cape. Also, because he identified himself with the slaves of the colonists and the semi-enslaved Hottentots who formed the bulk of the indigenous population, even to the extent of marrying a seventeen-year old Malagasy slavegirl, whom Henry Martyn thought too flighty for a missionary's wife. When he was questioned once by Gaika, a famous Xhosa chief, as to who had put the idea into his heart to come among them, Vanderkemp answered that the idea had been formed in his heart alone, but it had not been formed by it. It was as good an explanation of the missionary vocation as any.

Vanderkemp died in 1811, but his colleague, Read, from the London Missionary Society, whom Martyn also met, survived until 1852, a notable figure in South African missionary circles. Read also defied the racial attitudes of the Cape colonists by marrying a Christian Hottentot, and he became involved in a bitter controversy with the colonial authorities over the use of forced labour.

After a few weeks the fleet was released from duty and the East Indiamen made ready to continue their voyage. It was a cramped and tedious way of travelling. Henry Martyn was often humiliated at the interruption of his prayer meetings and Sunday services by rowdy officers or an unsympathetic captain. But at least he was a company chaplain; other missionaries were less fortunate, being obliged to take such passages as were available on whalers, slavers and convict ships.

Before leaving the Cape Henry Martyn climbed Table Mountain to survey the vast expanse of sea and sky that would carry him to the east, where his own destiny lay, first in India, and then in Persia. He was one of the most intensely spiritual men whom the Protestant world has produced, and his short life – he was only 31 when he died in 1812 – seemed to embrace every missionary experience. Like the saintly New Englander, David Brainerd, whose writings and example were a constant encouragement to him, Martyn's life is timeless and hardly to be contained in any history. We can imagine him that day on the top of Table Mountain, no human sound or object to distract him and the whole unevangelised world out ahead, lifting his eyes steadily heavenwards, his thin sensitive face lit with expectation.

'I reflected', he wrote, 'on the certainty that the name of Christ should at some period resound from shore to shore. I felt commanded to wait in silence, and see how God would bring his promises to pass.'

3

A hundred years later, it might seem as though Henry Martyn's vision was fast being realised as Christendom, in the form of western civilisation, took possession of Africa from shore to shore. At the opening of the Suez Canal there was nothing in Africa to suggest this would happen. Yet within a matter of twenty-five years of that event the continent underwent a transformation so rapid and so total as to leave historians uncertain how to interpret it. It is usually described as the scramble for Africa, more or less pejoratively as to the motives of those involved in it. But it was a process which cannot be unwritten, and it is not clear why this particular historical episode should be singled out for such opprobrium.

The fact is, by the end of the nineteenth century Africa had been brought into the modern world in the shape we now recognise, the Africa of Kenya, Uganda and Tanzania, of Zambia and Zaire, of Malawi and Botswana and Lesotho and every other nation-state which finds itself with an independent seat at the United Nations. However much names may be changed, regimes varied, federations broken up or boundaries redrawn, that quarter of a century established the concept of separate political entities, each jealous of its neighbour, each with its own flag and postage stamps, its head of state and central government, its right to a place in history.

Not that the Suez Canal was itself responsible for this transformation, though all parts of Africa were directly affected by the new system of world communications which it brought into being. As it happened, the opening of the canal took place on the eve of a colossal change in the shape of Europe. The very next year, the Prussians who clambered on Ismail's Second Empire furniture to catch a better view of Eugénie would be marching to Paris to send Louis Napoleon and his Empress into exile – for poor Eugénie, one of fifty years, spent at Chislehurst in England. The world after 1870 was a radically different place from what it seemed when the *Aigle* led the way to Ismailia.

So the year in which the Suez Canal was opened is a reference point in the story to be told in this book, providing as it does an appropriate occasion to introduce the principal characters who feature in it. Two of them, Robert Moffat and Ludwig Krapf, were in Africa before the event; two others, H. M. Stanley and Charles Lavigerie, after it. What linked them all was the enigmatic figure of David Livingstone, who at the time the canal was opened had disappeared from view.

The first of them to set foot in Africa was Robert Moffat. He was born in December 1795 at Ormiston in central Scotland, the third son of a petty revenue official who had started life as a ploughman. Moffat's boyhood was spent on the Firth of Forth, at Carronshore and Inverkeithing, where he picked up an education as much by observing life around him as from his parish schoolmaster. At fourteen he was apprenticed as a gardener, a hard but healthy training to which he added on his own account some lessons in Latin, mathematics and violin playing. At seventeen he said goodbye to Scotland and set off to earn his living in Cheshire after promising his mother he would read his Bible daily. The surest way south then lay by sea, an eight-day journey from Greenock to Liverpool, during which Moffat had to lie below decks when a Navy press gang boarded his ship in Rothesay Bay.

Moffat was robust and intelligent and had seen how thrift and honesty had advanced his father in the world. Many thousands of his contemporaries were ready to grasp the material opportunities in life presented by the expanding power and wealth of Britain. These did not, however, appeal to him. Instead his eyes fell on an advertisement for a meeting in Warrington organised by William Roby, a noted evangelist from Manchester. God, Moffat felt, had directed his heart towards missionary work overseas, and was now showing him how to carry his wishes into effect.

Roby recognised in the tall young Scottish gardener an individual of exceptional spiritual strength. In 1816 he introduced Moffat to a post nearer Manchester as nurseryman to a certain John Smith of Dukinfield who was, as it happened, a fellow Scot who had changed his name on coming south. Moffat found his employer sympathetic, and his daughter Mary still more so. Roby was a director of the London Missionary Society and at once recommended Moffat to his colleagues, who drew many of their recruits from this class of pious but independent-minded artisans.

Moffat's inexperience at first told against him, but Roby persevered and gave him private tutoring in theology – the only systematic training in this line he ever received. Within a matter of months of his move to Dukinfield, Moffat was called to London, ordained, and sent on his way. Originally he was chosen for Polynesia, but at the last minute he was switched to Cape Colony, along with three other reinforcements for the new LMS mission there. In January 1817 he first set foot in Africa to begin a long and notable career as a missionary pioneer.

By the time the Suez Canal was a reality, Moffat was on the eve of leaving South Africa, having spent fifty years with Bechuana tribes beyond the colonial frontier. He was their apostle, and Kuruman, his base north of the Orange River, was the most famous landmark for every explorer, trader, huntsman and sightseer from the south. Because of Moffat, Kuruman in 1869 was a place of solid stone houses, stores and workshops; it was a communications centre with its own printing press, a postal address connected by a weekly mail service with the colony and the steamers that called at the Cape, and a meeting place where colleagues gathered to put questions on an agenda. Kuruman, in effect, represented civilisation; it was an institutional symbol of South Africa's development.

In history books Moffat is noted for his role in this development, which is usually described as 'keeping the road to the north open'. It is not, however, primarily because of this that he features so prominently in this narrative, but because his life is the clearest and most single-minded expression of the Christian requirement to be in this world, but not of it. As he put it himself, he simply did the work of the day in the day.

Moffat presided over one stream of missionary activity flowing northwards into Africa. At the same time, and unknown to him, another stream was flowing in from the Indian Ocean, directed by an obscure German pastor, Johann Ludwig Krapf.

Krapf was born in January 1810 in the southern German state of Würtemberg, an area noted for independence in religion as in politics. His father was a farmer. The kindly widow of a local vicar paid for his studies, in the course of which Krapf caught the fever of adventure by reading Bruce's travels in Abyssinia. At first it seemed he would become a sea-captain, but his father could not afford the training, and the boy then grew interested in missionary work through a chance lecture at school. Krapf's father was dismayed at the prospect of losing his son to this profession. At the age of seventeen Krapf went to the German missionary college at Basel, founded in 1815. But almost immediately the young recruit turned to mysticism and became what today would be termed a drop-out. To the indignation of his parents, who had sacrificed much to send him to the college, Krapf broke off his studies and adopted the life of a farm labourer. He grew even more unhappy and came to see that it was pride which had made him feel he could dispense with the outward regulations of the world. Unable to return to the missionary college, he studied theology instead, becoming a Lutheran pastor in 1834. But once again he felt dissatisfied with his lot, and when he was rebuked for preaching too positively the imminence of the end of the world, he resigned and earned his living as a private tutor. God, it seemed, would not let him rest in an ordinary job in the world; it was the unconverted overseas who called him. He applied to the English Church Missionary Society and was readmitted to the Basel college, being chosen in 1837 for Abyssinia.

Like many Protestants at that time Krapf's imagination was fired by mysterious references in scripture to a land of whirring wings that sends its ambassadors down the Nile in vessels of papyrus, a land which would one day hold out her hands to the Lord and herald Christ's return to earth. Ethiopia was the fabled Christian kingdom of Prester John which the Portuguese had saved from Islam in the sixteenth century by sailing round the Cape of Good Hope, and which James Bruce had reached in the eighteenth by way of the Nile and the Red Sea, returning via the Sudan to write one of the most celebrated travel books of the day.

The first Protestant missionary to enter Abyssinia was Samuel Gobat (1799–1879), a remarkable Lutheran from the French-speaking Swiss canton of Berne, who was also inspired by Bruce's travels. With Mahomet Ali's conquests in Egypt, access to these regions had become more feasible. Gobat was an early student at the Basel Missionary College, and he too was recruited by the Anglican Church Missionary Society. In 1830 he spent six months at Gondar, the ancient religious capital of Ethiopia, where he found the people to be intensely jealous of their own religious customs but desperate for technical help from their fellow Christians in the west.

Gobat returned to Abyssinia in 1835 with this wife, intending to reside there permanently, working for the conversion of the black-skinned Hamitic Jews, known as the Falashas, and distributing copies of the Bible in vernacular translations. But he was immediately crippled by ill-health and forced to leave. Later, as Bishop of Jerusalem, he retained close ties with Abyssinia, writing of an Abyssinian convert who accompanied him when he left that he was 'the most consistent, sincere, humble, and zealous Christian I have ever known'. A revealing comment from someone who knew most of the leading churchmen of his time.

Like Gobat before him Krapf travelled first to Cairo, a raw city compared with the Cairo of Ismail Pasha. Krapf was appalled by the open-air slave market and the plight of its wretched victims. Even so, Cairo represented the hope of civilisation for Africa north of the Equator, a base where Arabic could be learned, recruits met from Europe (Krapf met his wife there some years later), and stores collected, including the hundreds of Bibles which the missionaries distributed.

For seven years, 1837–44, Krapf laboured in Abyssinia itself and in trying to reach the neighbouring Galla tribes, where he believed a vestigial and hitherto undiscovered Christian community existed; but in the end he and his German colleagues were expelled. The country was rent with civil wars and subjected to various external religious and political pressures. The experience left him chastened but un-defeated. Ethiopia, he wrote later, had to reject him so that he should be free to go to the Gentiles – the pagans of East Africa, where his real work belonged.

But he twice returned to the ancient Christian land which had originally attracted him. The first occasion was in 1855, when a new ruler, calling himself Emperor Theodore II 'King of Kings', gained control and sent an urgent appeal to Gobat in Jerusalem for technical aid, including a gunsmith. Theodore, as it happened, was the son of a man Gobat had once cured of fits of madness by drastic bleeding, and again it seemed as though God had opened a door for the Protestants. At Gobat's request Krapf and a fellow-German, Martin Flad, visited Theodore and returned to Cairo via Sennar, Khartoum and the Nile, as Bruce had done, a gruelling journey which nearly cost Krapf his life, but which made him an advocate of the Nile route into inner Africa.

Krapf then went to Europe, and Flad to Jerusalem, to find technicians for Theodore. But in the following years the king grew increasingly tyrannical, and perhaps insane, and began to maltreat the Europeans at his court, Flad included. It was this that brought Krapf back a second time to Ethiopia, and for his last mission to Africa, when in 1868 he joined Sir Robert Napier's military expedition as official interpreter. 'Rather elderly for a campaign,' Stanley found him, and the climate indeed defeated Krapf, forcing him to leave before the Battle of Magdala, which ended Theodore's reign.

By then, it was generally held by sensible folk that Krapf's efforts in East Africa were premature. In ten years he knew only two East African Christians, one a cripple and the other a man whom Burton assumed was a lunatic. But Krapf had an answer to all accusations of failure. 'If all Missions should fail', he once wrote, 'and fail at the same time, so completely that no trace of them should

4,000 miles entirely alone, apart from his Makololo escort.

On returning to England Livingstone was acclaimed everywhere and wrote a best-selling account of his travels entitled *Missionary Travels and Researches in South Africa*. But his missionary society had reservations about an enterprise which, they said, was only remotely connected with the spread of the gospel. This so stung Livingstone – perhaps he felt there was some truth in it – he resigned from the Society.

His next assignment was to command a government expedition to investigate the possibility of a cotton-growing colony in the region he had just traversed. As most people saw it, he was a missionary turned explorer, albeit one with a philanthropic purpose. He summarised this purpose in a famous visit to Cambridge University, where he concluded two lectures with these words: 'My object in labouring as I have in Africa, is to open up the country to commerce and Christianity. This is my object in returning thither. . . . My object in Africa is not only the elevation of man, but that the country might be so opened that man might see the need of his soul's salvation.'

These were enigmatic words, and many volumes have been written in explanation of them, but they soon passed from notice as the public turned to other sensations. By the time the Suez Canal was open Livingstone was a forgotten man, having disappeared in Africa. In October 1869 a short report appeared in *The Times* claiming that a party of Arabs had seen him some months before at Ujiji, on Lake Tanganyika, and everyone was content to leave it at that. Everyone, that is, except an American newspaper proprietor who, reading *The Times* report in his Paris hotel, commissioned a bumptious young journalist named Stanley to find him. This proved to be a turning point in African history, and a turning point also in the life of the journalist, who was anxious to bury his past.

Stanley was the illegitimate son of a Welsh farmer called John Rowlands. His mother was a sixteen-year-old girl, Elizabeth Parry, the daughter of a local butcher, and he was born in January 1841 at Denbigh, north-east Wales. He was christened John and bore his father's name, being boarded with various relatives and neighbours until the age of six, when he was deposited in the workhouse at St Asaph, where he remained until he was fifteen. It was a stern and unimaginative regime, but John Rowlands came away with a funda-mental belief in the existence of God and of a moral law from which, however much he might contravene it, there was no escape. He later wrote a grim account of these nine formative years, parts of which appear quite fictitious and based on the novels of Charles Dickens, but at least he learnt to read and to pray, and thereafter he was never without a Bible in his pack. 'Where I have been earnest, I have been answered,' he confessed at the end of his life.

In 1856 he left the workhouse to board again with relatives, and in December 1858, when in Liverpool, he took a step which changed his life. John Rowlands signed up on a packet boat bound for New Orleans, the greatest port in the American south, and there jumped ship to embark at the age of eighteen on that murky period of his life which he tried so hard to disown later on.

He first took a new name, from Henry Hope Stanley, a kindly immigrant from Cheshire. 'Morton' was added later. The elder Stanley befriended him for a time but found him too unruly and they quarrelled. When the American Civil War broke out, Stanley senior returned to England, but Stanley junior, then living in Arkansas, felt obliged to join the Confederate Army, and was captured at the battle of Shiloh. He had no feelings about the issues over which the war was fought, so to escape the horrors of prison camp he transferred his allegiance to the Federals and was almost immediately discharged on health grounds. Various escapades followed in which he lied and cheated his way around America, revisited Wales, and posing as a newspaper man went on an expedition to Turkey with an effeminate youth called Lewis Noe. Though emotionally immature, he was ambitious, self-reliant and never at a loss for a story.

But it was not until 1867 that Stanley began to realise his true métier, when he reported on the Indian wars for a Missouri newspaper. In December that year, with his eye always on the main chance, he came to New York to try his luck with the *New York Herald*, whose sensational brand of news coverage had brought an immense fortune to its ageing proprietor, Gordon Bennett. Stanley had already posed as his representative in Turkey. Gordon Bennett junior was then taking over the management of the paper, a prima donna of a man Stanley's own age. He agreed to give Stanley credentials to cover the British military campaign against Theodore of Ethiopia, provided he paid his own expenses. He would be paid by results, Bennett said.

Stanley had saved enough to pay his way and he accepted the offer. Although he cut a rather incongruous figure in the British army camp, he earned his newspaper laurels by bribing the Egyptian telegraphist at Suez to secure an advantage over his rivals in the transmission of his copy. Fortuitously the line then broke down so that for days the *New York Herald* was the only paper that carried the story of the battle of Magdala, Napier's official despatches having been held up along with every other newspaper report. Bennett took Stanley on as a regular correspondent in charge of a bureau in Spain. In October 1869 he sent for him from Paris to give him a wide-ranging brief to cover, among other things, the opening of the Suez Canal due to take place in a month's time, a tourist's guide to the Nile, various locations in the near East and possibly a visit to China. In amongst it all Stanley was told to try and find out what had happened to Livingstone.

The Roman Catholic Church has not yet entered the story, as her prestige was at its lowest when the Protestant missionaries began moving overseas. But in the long and turbulent reign of Pope Pius IX, 1846–78, political disasters brought spiritual renewal. A Vatican Council opened in December 1869, the first since the Council of Trent 300 years before, which drew 700 bishops to Rome for a historic debate about the nature of papal authority. By the time Leo XIII became Pope in 1878, to inaugurate a reign of twenty-five years which would bring the Papacy into the modern age, Rome was a church in the process of becoming more truly catholic than Roman, one that in losing her temporal interests in Italy gained new life, and in suffering humiliation by the powers of the world rediscovered her concern for strangers and outcasts and the poor. She was once again a missionary church, and she found one of her greatest champions in a Frenchman who burst onto the African scene at the same time as Stanley.

Charles Martial Allemand-Lavigerie was born in the Basque country of southern France, the son of a minor revenue official. He was a pious but unruly boy in a revolutionary Europe. In 1848, the year of Europe's revolutions, his patron the Archbishop of Paris was shot dead by the Paris mob and Lavigerie himself narrowly escaped with his life. He was ordained priest the following year. 'I hope that you amount to something,' his mother chided him as she lay dying, and for a time he seemed to want nothing more than to be a pastor of souls in rural France. He could not hide his brilliance, however, and the world of ecclesiastical preferment claimed him, at the Sorbonne, at the Vatican, and in 1863 as Bishop of Nancy. Then in 1867 he was offered the see of Algiers, considered in church circles to be an ecclesiastical backwater. After spending a day in prayer Lavigerie accepted. He would become a missionary to a continent. 'France is calling to thee, oh Africa! For the last thirty years she has been summoning thee to come forth from the tomb!'

No sooner had Lavigerie arrived in Algiers than the colony was smitten with cholera, followed by famine, followed by a visitation of locusts. Feeling God's hand was on them, the native population displayed a fatal apathy which aggravated their misery. Hundreds of thousands were reported dying. Could a civilised power remain indifferent to their sufferings? Could the church? Lavigerie threw himself into relief work, opening his arms to the sick and starving children who had been abandoned by their parents. In no time he had a thousand on his hands, and with great energy he organised them in special orphanges under the care of his religious orders.

What Lavigerie undertook spontaneously as an act of charity suddenly struck him as a door opened by God through which the Christian gospel might pass to the Moslem population of North Africa. The Arab and Berber children who flocked to his orphanages now had no father or mother but the Archbishop and the church. Brought up as Christians they would be the first fruits in their country of Christendom's world mission.

His idea brought down on the Archbishop the wrath of the military government of Algeria, headed by General MacMahon, a descendant of Irish Catholics and hero of the Crimea. French policy in Algiers was to practise through the *Bureaux Arabes*, as they were called, absolute cultural separation between the native Moslem and immigrant European populations. It was a legacy of the first Napoleon's descent on Egypt when French intellectuals in his entourage had helped revive the famous school of Koranic studies in Cairo. With a fanaticism they would have been the first to condemn in their own country, these French ideologues actively promoted the religion of Islam. The conquered people, it was thought, would acquiesce more readily with French rule if France was seen to support the moral and religious basis of North African culture. Mosques were rebuilt at government expense, the teaching of the Koran encouraged, Moslem schools subsidised and pilgrimages to Mecca facilitated. French soldiers stood on guard outside Algiers cathedral to turn Arabs away, and any Roman Catholic priest who spoke Arabic was refused entry into the colony. Heavy fines, even imprisonment, were imposed on Frenchmen who contravened these edicts, and Lavigerie's two predecessors had been broken by them.

The new Archbishop attacked the policy head-on. It was madness, he said, to expect the native people of Algeria, Arabs and Berbers, to assimilate themselves to European civilisation through the Koran, for the Koran would always teach them that Christians were dogs deserving only to be killed and flung into the sea. Not only madness, but intolerant, as the Berbers were not true followers of Islam, being descendants of the people who inhabited North Africa in Roman times. They had indeed been Christians, and it was the Arabs who had driven them into the Kabylia mountains, where a Christian remnant might still exist.

MacMahon began to regret his choice of Lavigerie before his new Archbishop had even crossed the Mediterranean. At the last minute he attempted to divert him from Algiers with the offer of the see of Lyons, where Lavigerie would have been Primate of France and certain of a Cardinal's hat. Lavigerie was unmoved. 'It would be nicer to live at Lyons', he reportedly said, 'but easier to die in Algiers.' MacMahon then accused him of disloyalty to France. Lavigerie returned across the Mediterranean in a passion and confronted the Emperor Louis Napoleon with his own words about France's mission of civilisation. France's only manifest destiny, said Lavigerie, was to spread her religion.

Fifty years earlier a French bishop who defied his sovereign would have been threatened with the galleys; but Louis Napoleon was a cardboard emperor and he needed the support of French Catholics. Lavigerie had the backing of the settlers in Algeria, and France, he told Napoleon, could scarcely deny the church the same freedom she enjoyed in the dominions of the Sultan of Turkey. It was a shrewd point, and Napoleon gave way.

Lavigerie went straight to Rome to inform the Pope. His victory was of momentous importance for the future of Catholic missions in Africa. A first attempt to penetrate the interior had already been made in the wake of Mahomet Ali's conquests. Travelling up the Nile under Egyptian protection a party of brave priests had brought Christianity back to ancient Nubia after an interval of almost a thousand years. They reached Khartoum in 1848 and Gondokoro in 1850, where they were within five degrees of the Equator and in striking distance of Uganda, anticipating by a decade Baker's first appearance in that region. But the cost was terrible: some forty deaths all told in little more than ten years. The Bari and Dinka were friendly at first, but then turned against all outsiders thanks to the attention of slave-traders seeking new sources to replenish the diminishing supply of white slaves. By the time Baker reappeared on the scene as Ismail's Governor, at £10,000 a year, the mission had withdrawn to Khartoum, apparently a heroic failure.

They had come mostly from the dominions of the Emperor of Austria, who gave them his patronage and established a consulate at Khartoum, a Catholic version of Livingstone's 'commerce and Christianity'. Now France, in Algiers since 1830 and thanks to de Lesseps the dominant influence in Egypt, would provide a base for another assault on Africa. Prompted by Lavigerie, the Vatican at once reorganised its missions, giving him responsibility for the western Sudan, a huge area stretching from Senegal and Guinea on the Atlantic to Fezzan, and containing those African states of Islam which in the middle ages had formed the Almoravid Empire, a power which reached into Spain and at one time threatened to encircle the entire Mediterranean. It was known to civilisation only through accounts of isolated explorers such as Mungo Park, Denham and Clapperton from Britain, René Caillié from France, and Heinrich Barth from Germany. This huge, untamed, region was entrusted to the Archbishop of Algiers, and the Propaganda – the Vatican's department of missions – prepared for a new offensive against Islam, instructing its missions in the East to work now for the conversion of Moslems.

Lavigerie announced his new task in unmistakable terms:

'With a delicacy which will be universally appreciated, the Sovereign Pontiff has entrusted those vast regions, situated on the borders of our two great African possessions, to a French Bishop. Can this be a prophecy of the future conquests of France in those countries so little known and for the most part plunged, in spite of their riches, in such profound barbarism? God only knows. But I cannot help believing that Providence has established our settlements on this land of Africa to make us, again, the missioners of civilisation and of the Christian faith. I cannot refrain from considering our colonies of Algiers and of Senegal as the two great gates which the Divine mercy has opened to this numerous population, by which they can enter into charity and Catholic truth, the only means through which they can be gradually Christianised and humanised.'

4

The year 1869, then, is a turning point in the story, of the kind historians use to sign-post their interpretation of events. In Africa, particularly East Africa, it marks the beginning of a new era of communications which coincides with rapid advances in technology, from sail to steam, from muzzle-loading muskets to breach-loading rifles, smokeless powder and Maxim guns, in the preparation of tinned foods, in medicine and many other ways directly related to western man's ability to survive away from his home environment. Then 1869 is a watershed in European history, midway in the hundred years which separate the end of the Napoleonic War from the war of 1914–18. Over the opening of the Suez Canal falls the shadow of the Franco-Prussian war, which means that what happens in Europe will come to have increasing importance in Africa. It may

3 *Opening of Suez Canal : Procession of Ships*

be thought of, too, as a date at which the lives of the principal characters in this book intersect. Moffat is about to leave Africa, and Krapf has paid his last visit; Lavigerie and Stanley have just arrived, and Livingstone awaits his apotheosis in one of the most famous scenes in African history. But the man who will bring the curtain down on the story has not yet appeared. He is at this time at Gravesend, distributing tracts, visiting the sick and the dying, and feeling miserable because he has been passed over in the command of the Abyssinian campaign.

Finally, there is the opening of the Suez Canal itself and what it signifies in terms of what men thought about it at the time. Stanley, for instance, travelling down the Canal in the twenty-first ship behind Eugénie, spoke of the events of that day as 'the greatest drama ever witnessed or enacted in Egypt'. To put it at its highest, the Suez Canal represented the hope of western civilisation that as technology improved, as new discoveries were made and new markets opened, there would be room for everyone to trade freely in the world; an ideal of world order in which peace, progress and prosperity would be assured for all mankind. The great Christian bishop of Hippo, Augustine, writing at the beginning of the fifth century in Roman North Africa, described this ideal of world order as the proper end of the earthly city. In his day it was ruled by Caesar, and in one form or another a Caesar always wields power in the world, commanding the respect and obedience of the citizens of the earthly city. Furthermore, wrote Augustine, citizens of the heavenly city in their pilgrimage through time must necessarily make use of the peace of the earthly city, must indeed seek and preserve it in all that relates to human nature, provided only that their duty towards God is not thereby hindered.

In this formulation of the proper ends of the two cities, the earthly one which belongs to time, and the heavenly one, or City of God, which is eternal, Augustine gave expression to the underlying drama of all human existence. History is the relationship of one to the other, for man has to live in his earthly city even while he longs for his citizenship in Heaven, and Christians should feel ashamed, he said, if they do not show in the service of God qualities which can stand beside those the Romans showed in the pursuit of the glory of their earthly city. What better words, then, to close this introductory chapter than Augustine's own:

'The Heavenly City outshines Rome, beyond comparison. There, instead of victory is truth; instead of high rank, holiness; instead of peace, felicity; instead of life, eternity.'

CHAPTER TWO

WASTE-HOWLING
WILDERNESS

4 Vignette from *Travels in the Interior of Southern Africa*, by
William J. Burchell, 1822: 'Travelling over a plain
abounding in ant hills'

I

At the opening of the year 1818 Robert Moffat found himself making
his way painfully by ox wagon across the wilderness of Little
Namaqualand, some hundreds of miles north of the Cape of Good
Hope, where the Orange River flows through an empty plateau
before falling into the Atlantic Ocean. Six feet tall, slim-built, with
dark curly hair and a strong open face well tanned by the sun, he
walked with an athletic, military, step. A few guides trailed along
beside him and they were joined from time to time by the natives of
the wilderness, a race of nomads who spoke with a peculiar clicking
of their tongues.

It was Moffat's first missionary journey. He had just celebrated

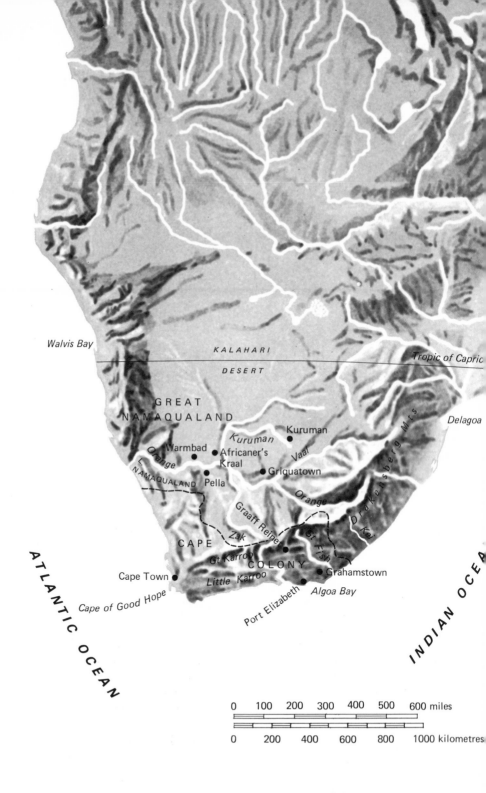

Walvis Bay

KALAHARI

DESERT

Tropic of Capric

GREAT
NAMAQUALAND

Delagoa

Kuruman

Kuruman

Warmbad

Africaner's
Kraal

Orange

Vaal

NAMAQUALAND

Pella

Griquatown

Drakensberg Mts

Orange

Graaff Reinet

Zak

CAPE

Gt Karroo

Gt Fish

D.

Kei

Cape Town

COLONY

Little Karroo

Grahamstown

Cape of Good Hope

Port Elizabeth

Algoa Bay

ATLANTIC OCEAN

INDIAN OCEAN

| 0 | 100 | 200 | 300 | 400 | 500 | 600 miles |

| 0 | 200 | 400 | 600 | 800 | 1000 kilometres |

his twenty-second birthday and was still new to Africa. On the long trek northwards from the Cape friendly farmers had shaken their heads over his intended destination. *They* knew all about the desert. 'What is it like beyond?' he had innocently asked one of them. 'Sir', the kind man replied, 'you will find plenty of sand and stones, a thinly scattered population, always suffering from want of water, on plains and hills roasted like a burnt loaf.'

It was no exaggeration. The heat had sucked all life out of the earth leaving its surface caked with saltpetre, in places so thick it crackled under foot like hoar frost. All around were granite rocks sparkling with quartz whose glare was merciless. Moffat found he was unable to raise his eyelids long enough to survey the route ahead. They had to do most of their travelling by night.

An occasional thunderstorm passed overhead in a terrific display of electric power, but without rain. Moffat's small party had dragged their way across dried-up river beds where moisture could only be found by digging down twenty feet or more. In places the aboriginal Bushmen had made pits to reach this moisture, but it was barely enough to refresh the oxen and took so long to draw up the beasts

5 *Robert Moffat in December 1819, age 24*

were thirsty again by the time the job was done. It reminded Moffat of stale bilge-water in a ship, but he and his men gulped it down avidly. A more miserable, destitute, dreary country could scarcely be imagined.

The little group provided the only sign of life in this desolate setting of rocks and sand. By and by they too were obliged to stop, men and beasts alike being unable to put another foot forward. They were trapped in a plain that was as hot as a frying pan, their water gone, their supplies exhausted, the low hills on the horizon offering neither shade nor comfort. After a time, the oxen grew frantic and bolted off back the way they had come; the natives covered their faces with skins and waited for death; and to Moffat, lost in the wilderness, it also seemed like the end. God, he thought, must have cursed this land and if the purpose of his journey was to reveal this to him, then His will be done.

2

There was snow in England at this time of year, and ice along the sea-shore at Inverkeithing where Moffat's father, the retired customs official, watched the new steam tugs on the Firth of Forth; but in southern Africa it was the hottest season of the year. In London there was talk of reform, which many called revolution; mobs were said to be organising secretly in Manchester; the old mad King George III was dying, and scandal surrounded the affairs of his heir, the Prince Regent; peace in Europe had brought unemployment; landlords agitated for protection; new cities drew more and more families to their factories. In the new year of 1818 the young Robert Moffat had little hope of seeing his native land again, and little to hold him to it; Mary Smith, the daughter of his former employer at Dukinfield, near Manchester, and the girl he wanted to marry, had apparently turned him down, persuaded by her parents that his station in life was beneath and his profession beyond their expectations for her. 1818 was still the age of Jane Austen, and England was another world from the wilderness of Namaqualand.

At Cape Town, 600 miles away, Lord Charles Somerset was Governor – dictatorial, quarrelsome, a good judge of horses and suspicious of missionaries. He was an elegant man, with an aristocratic disdainful face. His twelve-year rule saw Cape Town grow from a military garrison into an imitation Regency city and the capital of an expanding English colony. When he arrived in 1814 the few Englishmen in South Africa looked out to sea with their backs to the continent; when he left in 1826 all eyes were turned inland to the wide champaign which was for the taking if the natives could be tamed.

Lord Charles Somerset ruled Dutch and Rhenish farmers, whose ancestors were the original settlers, French Huguenots, who were descended from refugees from Louis XIV and loyal to any regime at the Cape that was Protestant, 4,500 English soldiers stationed in the garrison, Scottish traders, East India Company officers on leave, dockyard workers and naval storekeepers, their wives, their whores and concubines, and their bastard offspring, together with their slaves (some 40,000) and their semi-enslaved Hottentot neighbours (some 30,000).

Most of the farmers lived in the delectable hinterland of Cape Town itself, where their vineyards and homesteads created a pleasing pattern of European agriculture; but an adventurous few were scattered further on, some northwards along the trail Moffat took to reach Namaqualand, some eastwards towards the Fish River. The ragged boundary of the colony stretched for 600 miles west to east, at a depth of 200 miles from the Cape.

Within this territory Dutch influence was uppermost. Civil law was based on Dutch practice and Dutch was the commonest language, essential for church services, business transactions and communicating with natives. The Dutch farmers ('*boeren*' in their language) numbered some 26,000. Most of them were illiterate and owned slaves (though not for plantation work as in the southern states of America and the West Indies), but they understood their Bibles well enough to know that their religion had nothing to do with secular rights in any political, social, racial, or economic system, but was something that distinguished believers (the elect) from the heathen (for which the Dutch used the word '*kafir*' from an Arabic word meaning infidels).

Christianity had first been preached to the Hottentots by Moravians, those exemplary Protestant missionaries, as early as 1737 and, despite some difficulties with the Dutch Reformed clergy and suspicious colonists, missionaries to the heathen were welcomed, many farmers encouraging Christian teaching for natives on their farms. Holland sent devoted men for this task, the best known being Vanderkemp, and Moffat had prepared for his vocation by learning Dutch, the *lingua franca* of the interior, and in studying the lives of his predecessors. But there could be no question in the eyes of the farmers of equality in this world between themselves and natives, any more

than there was between the Indians of North America and European
settlers in the newly constituted United States Republic, nor for that
matter between rich and poor in England.

The Dutch colonists thus preserved an expression of Christianity
which had seen notable service in the seventeenth century, and which
had safeguarded their separateness on the tip of that vast continent
for several generations. But in 1820 5,000 new settlers arrived from
England, old soldiers mostly from the war against Napoleon who
were subsidised by a grant of £50,000 from Parliament. They filled
up the territory along the eastern frontier, in what was called the
Albany district of the colony, with a new centre at Grahamstown
and served by the growing Port Elizabeth on Algoa Bay.

The idea of separateness had hitherto been of rather simple interpretation, as befitted a simple, fiercely independent agricultural
people. But now the Cape was to be an English colony, and the
Dutch faced a more complicated future ordered by an English parliament 6,000 miles away. Though they did not much concern themselves with the political and cultural changes which the English
introduced, they would come to see that their idea of separateness
was the league and covenant on which their way of life was based,
and they would come to look to Scotland instead of to Holland for
ministers to uphold it.

Lord Charles Somerset also governed missionaries. There were not
many of them in southern Africa when he arrived – perhaps a score
at the most – but they were among the most troublesome of his subjects. In 1811 they had created bad feeling by accusing certain
colonists of criminal ill-treatment of natives, twelve of their number
in the end being proved guilty; and then some of them had scandal-
ised the white community by marrying native women, while there
were charges of immorality against others. Their stations were
said to afford asylum to cattle thieves and runaway slaves, and the
missionaries were themselves confused about what they should do
with their own slaves.

Lord Charles did not much mind the scandals, nor missionary
institutes in well-settled areas where useful training was given to
natives for work in the colony as farm labourers or domestic servants.
It was the ambiguous status of missionaries outside the colony that
troubled him. Missionaries, he felt, should properly be treated as a
class of government official and be subject to colonial rule wherever
they worked. Teaching natives to read or write had been forbidden
by the old Dutch East India Company, the founding fathers of
European settlement at Table Bay, for fear of disturbing relations

between the races, and in 1806 the Cape Government (then British) extended this prohibition to missionaries working outside the frontier. Lord Charles took the same line. Like the trading company before it, his colony was a purely secular enterprise to be run for the benefit of England and the colonists themselves. The colonial state had no moral obligations towards natives; nor was it certain what rights, if any, natives within the colony actually possessed.

The Governor therefore expected missionaries to act as his agents, and he discouraged new stations beyond the frontier, unless they were located away from the direction of colonial expansion.

For this reason when he landed at Cape Town in January 1817 Moffat was made to wait eight months for permission to move out of the colony, and it was only granted then because his destination was Namaqualand, where the colonists had no interest. An earlier group of Dutch missionaries in the service of the LMS had attempted to work in this field and their sufferings had been fearful. They left a touching record of their faith in the names they gave their resting places – Stille Hoop, Silent Hope; and Blyde Uitkomst, Happy Deliverance. 'Their Silent Hope, however,' wrote Moffat, 'was long deferred; and, indeed, could scarcely be said to be fully realised, till their Happy Deliverance from a succession of disappointments, mortifications, and hardships, which brought the Albrechts (two brothers, Christian and Abraham) and Mrs Albrecht (Christian's wife) to a premature grave.' In Namaqualand, the men at the Cape assumed, the young enthusiast would soon perish. If the country did not destroy him, then assuredly Africaner, the Hottentot brigand, would.

3

Out on the Namaqua plain Moffat spent three days waiting for death beside his stranded wagon. He was saved by a group of horsemen who suddenly appeared with water bottles and strips of mutton tied onto their saddles. The missionary Bartlett had heard of his plight and ridden at once to find him, with fresh oxen. He brought him to his station at Pella and after a few days of rest set him on his way across the Orange River.

The Orange River was itself 200 miles beyond the borders of the colony, but it represented a kind of natural frontier to civilisation in those parts. South of the Orange River no great natural obstacle prevented communication with the colony; but the Orange River itself was a mighty barrier, measuring 500 feet across when in flood, and with great rocky banks which might hold up the passage of wagons for weeks. Once a man crossed to the north of the Orange River he entered the territory of Africaner and was lost to the world.

Africaner had a price on his head. An able Hottentot leader, he had once been in the service of a Dutch farmer who put him in charge of cattle-stealing forays against natives who had scattered before the white farmers' advance from the Cape. While Africaner was away on these raids his employer began meddling with his women. There was a show-down on the farmer's porch and one of Africaner's brothers shot him dead. Whereupon Africaner seized the farmer's guns and powder and fled with his people across the Orange River. The farmers tried to punish Africaner by bribing a band of half-caste freebooters to bring him in, dead or alive, but Africaner's men held their ground. In a rough bush warfare which ranged along the banks of the Orange River he had established himself as emperor of the wilderness, driving out the timid Albrechts from their station at Warm Bath for fear they would betray him to the farmers.

Among outlaws news of a stranger's approach travels fast. Although he was suspicious of all white men ('hat wearers' the Hottentots called them) Africaner had sent word that he would receive an Englishman to teach his people, but not a Dutchman. His men were now waiting for Moffat on the far side of the river.

No sooner had Moffat reached Africaner's village, or kraal, than he found himself once again quite alone when the colleague who introduced him quarrelled with the chief and departed hastily across the river. They had intended to call the mission Jerusalem, but with a characteristic touch of irony Moffat suggested that Mount Gilboa 'on which neither rain nor dew was to fall' would be more appropriate. He had brought little with him except clothes and the few provisions that could be packed into the wagon, together with an old violin, once the property of Christian Albrecht, on which he liked to practice the tunes of his boyhood. He had no supplies of food and the natives never offered to share the little they had with him. It was a bleak prospect.

Africaner ordered his women to put up a hut for their visitor, which they did in half an hour, but it was full of fleas, and proved too hot by day, too dusty when the wind blew, and too fragile to offer any security at night against dogs, snakes or wild animals. Unable to confide in anyone, Moffat was much troubled to find himself in this difficult situation at the end of his long journey. It was not fear of death – he never knew fear – but an anxiety to know for certain that he was following God's purpose for his life.

He turned for guidance to his Bible, his never-failing recourse in times of danger or perplexity, and in the evening, when the heat left the ground, he retreated to the low hills above the village where he could sit alone among the granite rocks, play his violin and meditate. 'The sure word of promise was my stay,' he wrote later, 'and I was enabled to adopt the language of one of old: "In the multitude of my thoughts within me, thy comforts delight my soul."' It was an experience which never left him to the end of his days; God's presence in his life was more real than any danger or trouble the world could show. As he put it in a phrase echoed by many who came after him: 'Man is immortal till his work is done.'

For twelve months Moffat shared every hardship alongside Africaner and his people; he literally tightened his belt, as they did, to deaden stomach pains brought on by hunger; he took the same risks with lions, scorpions and cobras; he went with them when they set off on a gruelling search for better land. There was one occasion when Moffat and Africaner were caught in the open in a thunderstorm so violent their horses turned tail to the wind and refused to

6 *Africaner*, as portrayed in Moffat's *Missionary Labours*

move. There was nothing else to be done but to sit on the ground until the deluge passed, leaving them drenched and shaken for the night. They would go for days without food or water and the intense heat would set up such a thirst their mouths would swell and the only way they could raise a little spittle was to share a pipe of tobacco.

Physically Moffat was completely in Africaner's power. But after a short time together in the Namaqua wilderness it was the wild outlaw who became the young missionary's prisoner. Perhaps his soul was tamed by the plaintive notes of Moffat's violin, so strange a sound in those harsh surroundings; perhaps it was because of Moffat's youth and transparent honesty of purpose. Whatever the outward reason, Moffat's message of love overwhelmed Africaner. 'I see men like trees walking,' he exclaimed when he first understood that hearts as tainted as his could be made pure. He began attending Moffat's Bible readings, seizing upon the words as a bee gathers honey. The day being too hot for thought, they sat up together all night discussing the ways of God, finding peace of mind and refreshment of spirit under the stars, nature's cathedral. Africaner sent messengers to his rivals telling them he was now a man of peace; he introduced order and cleanliness to his village, and his people began sharing their livelihood with Moffat. When Moffat fell ill Africaner nursed him tenderly; when he thought Moffat would die, he inquired anxiously how he should bury him. Just as you bury your own people, Moffat reassured him. After his recovery, Moffat once looked at Africaner with unusual intensity. The chief asked him why. 'I cannot imagine you as a firebrand,' was the reply, and Africaner, the scourge of Namaqualand, burst into tears.

4

In April 1819 Moffat caused a sensation among the colonists by re-appearing in Cape Town with Africaner by his side, disguised as his servant. The once sceptical Governor was impressed with the young missionary and invited him to work as an official church minister in the east of the colony. But Moffat would have none of it. To work for the government, he believed, was unscriptural and corrupting, like going into trade; he was determined, he wrote to his parents, to return 'to the heathen beyond the limits of the Colony' with or without the permission of the Governor.

Meanwhile he was overjoyed to learn that Mary Smith had at last won her parents' consent to their marriage and was ready to join him.

She was the same age as Moffat and shared his faith in the guiding truths of scripture. An independent-minded girl, outspoken when occasion demanded, she was a pioneer of a woman's right to serve her fellow human beings, to be, as she put it, 'of some little use in the world'. They were married in Cape Town in December 1819, and she brought practical good sense to their partnership: 'European constitutions require tolerable good living in this climate. I am convinced there is a necessity for missionaries to have wives to provide comfortable food for the support of their bodies under hard labour, and to enable them to set before the heathen an example of cleanliness and decency.'

'A missionary in this country without a wife is like a boat with one oar' Moffat wrote to his father when he knew Mary Smith would marry him. For fifty-one years they pulled together in enviable rhythm.

In Cape Town Moffat also met two new arrivals in Africa who had parts to play in his life. John Campbell and John Philip had been deputed by the London Missionary Society to sort out the difficulties into which their brethren in Africa had fallen. Campbell had been out before in 1812–14, when he explored a little outside the colony and made contact with Bechuana tribes north of the Orange River. He is the clown of the piece, a small man always ready to strike a pose, an indefatigable traveller armed with umbrella, snuffbox and endless stories – and too free in Moffat's eyes with 'Mr Wine, or Mijn Heer Brandy'. But it is often thanks to such men that missions get started. A message sent by Campbell to Africaner after the withdrawal of the Albrechts had prepared the way for Moffat's journey to Namaqualand.

John Philip was very different. He was forty-four years old when he arrived in Africa, in January 1819, on loan from a congregation in Aberdeen. A tough, self-assured man who had worked for a living from the age of eleven, at twenty he had given up a good job in protest at the use of child labour. In Cape Town he found his vocation' as a propagandist of missions, and he devoted the rest of his life to this work, dying in 1851 at the age of seventy-seven.

Philip was spokesman for the militant, political side of missions. He was a man with a programme – easily recognised in our day – expert in pamphlets, lobbying and protests. He had good contacts with the formidable Clapham Sect and his role became an extension of theirs in Africa, with colonial politics his speciality. For thirty years he campaigned relentlessly for civil rights for natives within the colony and for justice for those outside it. Everything to do with the

London Missionary Society stations in Africa went through Philip's hands, and he was instrumental in the decades ahead in bringing in French, German, and American missionary societies and guiding their men to fields all over southern Africa.

Moffat and his wife were critical of Philip's political activities and perhaps they did not much like him as a person. At one time they accused him of vanity and intolerable interference in their affairs. Much of this arose from Moffat's determination to walk through life by faith and not by human calculation. 'To submit to any Ruling Resident Director or Superintendent in the world is what I will never do,' he warned his directors in London. For all that, he agreed to the plan put to him by Philip and Campbell that he should not return with Africaner to Namaqualand, but move instead to the Bechuana tribes, to the mission which Campbell had first promoted in the valley of the Kuruman River, some 700 miles north-east of Cape Town. Here he would replace the missionary Read, whose personal misconduct was under investigation, and join a Scottish artisan, Robert Hamilton, working in great difficulties.

It meant abandoning Africaner and his people, among whom Moffat had proved his missionary faith and where his home, such as it was, and his few possessions lay. Africaner promised to take good care of them. He had a recurring dream, he once told Moffat, that he was climbing a narrow path over a pit of fire which led to a green mountaintop, where a human figure waited silhouetted against an unusually bright sun. But he always woke before he could speak to the stranger. So this African Pilgrim returned alone from the town of Carnal Policy with gifts from Mr Worldly Wiseman, the Governor, to his isolated domain beyond the Orange River. He reappeared briefly in Moffat's life when, true to his promise, he brought Moffat's belongings across country to his new home among the Bechuana. For the first time in twenty years Africaner sat down beside his former enemies, the men the farmers had bribed to kill him. They too were now Christians and it affected Moffat to see these wild men kneel together in prayer before going their separate ways.

Philip was unable to replace Moffat in Namaqualand, which rankled somewhat with the younger man, and within a short while Africaner died and his people dispersed, many of them returning to banditry. 'I feel as one deprived of a near relation,' wrote Moffat when he heard of Africaner's death and in years to come he would look back with nostalgia on 'the many happy hours' he had spent in his company. Despite its privations his time in Namaqualand had been an exhilarating experience.

5

In January 1820 Moffat set off with his bride for the north, the ebullient Mr Campbell trailing along, although the Governor's permission to work beyond the frontier was not yet forthcoming. 'We walk by faith,' Moffat wrote home, 'not by sight.' As he saw it, the missionary must be ready to become an outlaw – 'God's bandit' – in order to break out of man-made restraints on the gospel. Moffat was determined to reach the myriads of souls who, in his eyes, lived in darkness and perished without hope.

But how was the colonial frontier to be defined? To Lord Charles Somerset it was not so much a boundary line as a concept. 'All is colony to us where we can find a good spring of water and pasturage for our cattle,' one farmer answered Philip. It was defined therefore by physical convenience rather than by law, by the mountains which separated the Cape from Namaqualand, by the desert of the Great Karroo (a Hottentot word meaning 'waterless'), and by the rivers beyond which were the Bantu tribes.

In the north-east, beyond the Orange River, lived the Bechuana, distributed under different chiefs on a broad front from the Drakensberg to the Kalahari. They were pasturalists and constantly shifting from one place to another in search of 'fountains' of water for their cattle. Theirs was a healthy enough climate, but hot and dry, and they needed the space of those vast plains.

In the east, between the Fish and Kei Rivers, were the Xhosas, whose migration southwards had been halted by the inward movement of the farmers. Here the colonists had their eyes on new land. It was the principal scene of the violent cattle-raids, reprisals and outright war which so roused Philip, and which, on and off, lasted for most of the century.

As far as the colonists were concerned the huge central plateau between the Orange River and the Zambezi, whither Moffat was heading, was like a vast natural history reserve. It was the world of the solitary trader and the East India Company officer on leave and of the gentleman travel-writer whose tales were welcomed by a public ever looking for adventure and discovery, and some of whose books, like Burchell's, were to become classics.

Beyond the frontier, too, was the world of runaway slaves, outlaws and the half-caste progeny of Dutch farmers and Hottentot women. 'Bastards' they were called in the eighteenth century, but Campbell persuaded them to adopt the name of Griqua from the Hottentot tribe, the Grigriqua, from which most of them were descended. The Griqua were expert horsemen and shots, hunters of game, skins and ivory, interpreters of native languages, ever on the look-out for cattle the vultures of tribal wars. Outside the frontier they carved out baronies for themselves in the sparsely populated Bushman, Koranna and Hottentot country, over whose scattered remnants they held feudal sway. Berend Berends, the Koks, Peter David, Andries Waterboer – these were names important in South Africa's history as the outriders of civilisation. Among them were the men who had been bribed to capture Africaner and who now, under the influence of Christianity, had settled down to more orderly ways.

Perhaps there were 5,000 Griquas all told. They were significant enough for the government to station an agent at Griqua Town, their headquarters close to the junction of the Vaal and Orange Rivers, in an attempt to bring them under some sort of political control. It was a role the missionaries flatly refused to undertake after a first move in this direction had ended in disaster. Kuruman lay 100 miles beyond Griqua territory, and while Philip redistributed his missionary forces and worked on getting permits out of Somerset, the Moffats waited at Griqua Town where, in April 1821, their first child, Mary, was born. In May Moffat took up his post at Kuruman.

To come at last upon the source of the Kuruman River in that open, thirsty country – the 'fountain' or 'the eye' of Kuruman as writers called it – was a strange experience, as though one was discovering a secret of nature. 'The most beautiful water that ever I saw' was Mary Moffat's description; and Philip's 'the finest spring of water I have seen in Africa'.

On a stony mountainside the water gushed from an outcrop of greenish-coloured rock, veined with quartz, which formed a cavern thirty feet deep in the hillside. In this mysterious recess bats flitted about and the water could be heard rumbling through a series of subterranean vaults, fed, no doubt, by springs deep in the earth and extending for a great distance. Thick reeds surrounded the entrance to the cavern where according to legend a monstrous serpent had taken up residence. The stream then fell away into a broad valley, the territory of the Batlapin tribe of the Bechuana whose chief's name was Mothibi. When missionaries first made contact with Mothibi at the beginning of the century his headquarters were thirty miles distant, at what was known as Old Lattakoo. Since then he had moved his town nearer to the Kuruman, and the site finally chosen by Moffat for his station involved a further move eight miles up the valley to a location no more than three miles from the spring itself.

The missionary's immediate need wherever he settled was food. Supplies from the south took a long time to reach Kuruman and were expensive, too expensive for Moffat's salary of £80 a year; and native grain was sparse, the soil being too light and sandy to sustain regular crops unless it could be irrigated.

Moffat's first step, therefore, was to dig a channel two feet deep and six feet wide to bring water from the river to the site he had chosen, a distance of two miles. His water-course required constant attention to begin with, as the Bechuana broke into it hoping for instant results themselves, often on land that was higher than the river. When Moffat protested they attacked his dam out of spite. Often Moffat and Hamilton had to take it in turns to repair the ditch in the heat of the day, and then sit up guarding it all night, to ensure enough water flowed in to keep their produce alive.

Manure was Moffat's next requirement. There was any amount of it in the cattle folds, but the people were reluctant to let him touch it, fearing sorcery. Cow-dung was the Bechuana's soap; they 'washed' their hands with it before eating, to remove other impurities, and they scoured their floors with it, as Mary Moffat learned to do. But to use cow-dung for anything else would disturb the habits of centuries and might place a curse on their cattle.

Once outside the colony Moffat was in the territory of a rival priesthood. The rain-maker was so influential a person that often the chief of the tribe took on the job himself. Innovations like diverting river water and using manure for gardens were a challenge to his authority. The rain-maker derived his power from the fact that instead of being masters of nature, the people were slaves to it. Their lives depended entirely on cattle, and their cattle required pasture, which in turn depended on rain. Mothibi's rain-maker had been brought in from a more distant tribe and his skill during a prolonged drought lay in making his demands steadily harder to meet – first, it had to be an unblemished baboon, then a lion's heart, and finally, when the sky remained dry, the expulsion of the white man.

Neither reason nor prophetic denunciation could discredit the rain-maker's claims when the rains came, nor his explanations when they held off. This particular rain-maker had come secretly to Moffat for medicines to cure his sick wife and admitted his fraudulence, but in public it was for each of them a matter of life and death. Tension mounted, everyone's nerves were excited by the drought and the spiritual forces engaged, for which it seemed there must be a blood-letting. Moffat refused to be intimidated into leaving and challenged Mothibi to kill him. The rain-maker now found his threats rebounding onto his own head, since the elders decided that, if it was a matter of putting someone to death, he could be sacrificed with less risk than the white man. Moffat had to intercede for his life, and the duel ended when the rain-maker made off hurriedly back to the north.

'It is not conferring with flesh and blood to live amongst these people,' Mary Moffat wrote of the men and women with whom she was to spend the rest of her life. The Bechuana appeared to be a nation of liars, beggars and thieves, totally lacking in normal affection for each other. They went almost naked but for furs and skins slung around bodies which were smeared with animal fat and red earth. To Europeans their physical degradation seemed near complete. Only the Bushmen were worse off, and the Bechuana had almost exterminated these aboriginal hunting folk. Mothibi's people, it seemed to Moffat and his wife, showed no concern to help them but were only waiting for death or despair to remove them from their midst. Hamilton once spent half a day laboriously grinding corn between two handstones, enough for a week's bread. When he returned from evening worship, it had all gone. If Moffat left his tools for a moment, they were sure to be 'borrowed' never to be seen again, or perhaps returned twisted and scorched by the attentions of a native smith. The people had no respect for privacy and would

7 *Mary Moffat in December 1819, age 24*

jostle Mary Moffat in her kitchen and threaten her with sticks if she asked them to leave her while she nursed her baby. They hung around, ever curious, ever grasping, and spreading dirt and grease on her clothes and furniture.

'It requires some little fortitude to live at rest in such a tumultuous land,' Mary Moffat continued. 'If we will allow ourselves to reflect on the train of miseries which such a mode of life brings with it, how conclusively we argue against that vain philosophy which declaims against the efforts of missionaries in such a country by saying that the natives live a quiet, harmless, and peaceable life, attending to their flocks and herds, and know nothing of the miseries of refined society. Oh how futile are such reasonings!' And how often were they to be repeated a century or more later!

For Moffat, of course, victory over the rain-maker was the victory of faith over superstition; but for the Bechuana, his superiority as a magician was proved by the actual results of his irrigation and manure. With their own eyes they witnessed the truth of his assertion that nature was beneficent and not malign, that all things in it were provided for man's use by a generous Creator and were not the property of greedy and capricious spirits, and that all creatures were to be respected out of love for that Creator and not cruelly and despitefully treated. This alone was enough to turn their view of reality upside down. Helped by his nurseryman's training, with nothing but his hands and his knowledge of the natural properties of earth and water, Moffat in effect revolutionised the Bechuana world. He had no advanced technology at his disposal (iron ploughs were not yet available), and he was plainly not there to make a trading profit or gain political influence. In short, it could not be said that he was impelled by the ulterior human or cultural motives which critics would later attribute to missionaries. He was simply realising by being there the truth of his religion, which was his mission, and he brought about this potential for development, as we should call it, because he triumphed in the world of the spirit; that is, because he showed love and not hatred, peace and not violence, humility and not retribution. As he put it, it was a victory which 'neither the policy nor the might of an Empire could achieve'.

Even so, it was ten years from the time Moffat showed his bride the beautiful spring of water at Kuruman until they saw their first Bechuana convert to Christianity. They were ten years of non-stop manual labour. Moffat and Hamilton had to work at everything themselves, often in temperatures which rose to 120 degrees in the shade – in the saw-pit, treading clay for bricks, at their home-made

forge, in the vegetable plots or repairing the water-course, and always
ready to improvise as they went along. So much physical activity was
a blight on the spirit and there were moments when Moffat regretted
becoming a missionary. Several times during these ten years he was
driven to retreat to Griqua Town to escape from bandits who appeared suddenly on the hills in the distance. There were money
troubles, too, and moments when Philip questioned the value of the
mission, which added to Moffat's trials. In addition the Moffats
had the sadness of losing a five-day old baby boy, whose body was the
first to be committed to the new graveyard.

To appreciate how Moffat survived these ten years, it is necessary
to read his account of them with a Biblical concordance at hand.
What kept him sane, gave him courage, humility and hope, was the
Bible's realism. Every experience he lived through, every sight that
met his eyes, was illuminated by a passage of scripture applicable to
his own situation; so that, however desperate that situation might
seem, he could always find reminders in it of the promises of God
contained in his texts. Nature in South Africa supplied the same
illustrations of the omnipotence of God as were recorded by the
writers of the Old Testament. There were cattle on the veld which in
times of drought 'snuffed up the wind like dragons' to locate the
direction of water, antelopes which calved prematurely in violent
thunderstorms in terror at 'the voice of the Lord', to give the
Bechuana who followed hurriedly after them some much needed
food, and locusts that 'have no king, yet go they forth all of them by
bands' to descend suddenly and give nourishment when eaten with
wild honey. When robbers appeared in the twilight on the hills beyond Kuruman Moffat and his wife would spend all night in prayer
that the new mission would not be christened in blood; by early
morning they had gone, frightened by noises around them in the
night. So 'do the wicked flee when no man pursueth' was Moffat's
comment, quoting Leviticus, 'and the sound of a shaken leaf shall
chase them'. As he viewed his labours, taking a gardener's pride in
the young willows he had planted along his watercourse, he often
imagined himself to be in Babylon, in bondage like the Psalmist, and
was tempted to hang up his harp fearing he would never hear the
song of triumph in that strange land.

Moffat's God was not a God of the philosophers, of anthropologists,
or of writers of theses about culture-conflict, he was a God who spoke
in the spirit to say 'as thy days, so shall thy strength be'. He might
shroud himself in clouds and darkness – and what could be darker
than heathen Africa? – but He could be trusted in all things. Gloating

over his sufferings, the Bechuana might taunt him one minute to prove his God, and the next, bored and disappointed, mutter viciously, 'Away with him! Away with him!' But truly they were the greater sufferers, living in the condition described by St Paul to the Romans – men without God, without hope. Moffat was never dismayed at the magnitude of the task before him, knowing that Christianity would create a new man, rising free from the centuries-old slavery of dirt, idleness and superstition. In the words of St Paul, of whom Moffat said, 'He who takes the first propagators of Christianity as his models cannot err', 'if any man be in Christ, he is a new creature: old things are passed away; behold, all things are become new'. God would make a people of those that were no people, as the prophets had foretold and the apostles had repeated. He would put 'a new spirit' within them and give them new hearts in place of their hearts of stone. And though the vision would tarry, maybe ten years, maybe a hundred, it would eventually be realised. 'I will be exalted among the heathen,' was the promise of history.

Founding the mission, Moffat said later, was as if an ant set out to climb a mountain; and at the end of this period, like Moses at the bank of the River Jordan he looked back on it as on a 'waste-howling wilderness'.

6

Men living outside the colony faced physical danger at every turn. Lions were common in the bush; scorpions and deadly snakes found their way into huts, hid in the rafters and even in beds and sometimes could be heard slithering across the floor in the dark. Bushmen concealed poisoned stakes in pits to catch game, there was always the risk of a mishap with weapons, or gunpowder, or wagon wheels, or lunatics. The missionaries could not help remarking that fatal accidents were rare and deliverances many, which strengthened the faith of their calling.

But Moffat had no sooner arrived at the scene of his life's work when something happened which threatened not only his own life and station, but all southern Africa. In the early months of 1823 reports were heard of an immense number of savages, more war-like than the Bechuana, who were moving southwards, devastating everything in their path. From the scanty information available it appeared they were ruled by a woman, Mantatisi, more blood-thirsty than any man. The invaders were therefore called Mantatees. No one knew for certain if the reports were true (Moffat was inclined to disbelieve them), but if they were, it was a threat to everyone living north of the Orange River, and possibly to everyone living south of it as well. Did it mark a new wave of migrations which would end by destroying the colony itself?

We know, of course, that this did not happen and that the migration of the so-called Mantatees was part of a vast upheaval of Bantu tribes, the repercussions of which were to be felt for many years and for thousands of miles towards the far north. There must have been many similar upheavals in Africa's past of which there is no record in history and which swept away whole tribes, and even races, without leaving a trace of their existence as members of the human family. The thought often struck Moffat and whenever he stumbled across a pile of bones or ruined stonework, which told of previous inhabitants of the country now possessed by the Bechuana, he would brood on the melancholy idea that their physical extinction was an allegory of their spiritual fate. Conversely, acceptance by the survivors of Christianity would assure their place in history. As Waterboer, the Griqua chief, put it on his conversion, the Griquas had become a people who were no people.

On this occasion, however, three white men were on the scene: Moffat, Melville, the government agent at Griqua Town, and Thompson, a sightseer from Cape Town. In its way, therefore, the Battle of Lattakoo, as it came to be called, is a highlight in African history; to follow it is to lift the veil a little on those obscure millenia.

Let Thompson, the reporter from outside, begin. On the afternoon of 10 June 1823 he and Melville were chatting on the verandah of Melville's house when they saw a wagon approaching from the direction of Kuruman. 'Presently Mr Moffat jumped out of it, . . . dressed in a jacket of leopard skin, and with a black bushy beard, about eight inches long. I was the less surprised at this Jewish fashion, as I had found Mr Melville wearing a beard of similar dimensions; – for beards, it seems (probably from those of the natives being so scanty), are objects of no small respect in this part of the world.'

Moffat confirmed that there was a horde of savages – 'Goth-like' people he called them – moving south. They were said to have destroyed twenty-eight tribes already. Ten days ago he had run into signs of them no more than sixty miles north of Kuruman, whence he had returned to warn Mothibi's people, who in turn begged him to get help from the Griquas.

They put the facts to Waterboer and he went off at once to consult with other Griqua leaders. All agreed that the Mantatees had to be stopped as far to the north as possible. Moffat rested the night at Griqua Town and returned on horseback next day, accompanied by Thompson. They covered sixty miles that afternoon, spent the night at a Griqua farm and after another hard ride reached Kuruman the following evening.

Here they found Mothibi's people in a frenzy of excitement about to hold their tribal assembly, called a *pitso*. The white men were invited to attend. 'Is this our *pitso*?' one speaker asked. 'No, it is the *pitso* of Moffat; therefore we must speak like white men!' All day they harangued each other about what they should do and how they should fight. Mothibi leaped into the arena himself wearing an old chemise Mary Moffat had given his chief wife. 'The cause is a great one – it involves our very existence as a people,' he told them. Dressed in feathers and war paint the warriors shook their spears in the direction of the enemy. They spoke defiance, but their hearts were water. Everything turned on the Griquas; and as the days passed and the Griquas did not appear, it looked as though Kuruman would have to be abandoned.

Thompson went out to explore with a runaway slave, Arend, who was lying up in the veld, out of reach of the colonists. They came upon the Mantatees no more than thirty miles away, at Old Lattakoo.

At this news the Bechuana panicked. All the brave words of the *pitso* were forgotten; possessions were hidden; the cattle, women and children were sent down the valley and the men made ready to follow. Their only escape route led westwards to the Kalahari desert, where they would certainly perish. Reluctantly, Moffat also packed and buried his things, while Hamilton prepared the wagon for a quick get-away with Mary Moffat and their two infant daughters, of whom the younger, Ann, was only three months old.

They passed a tense night, the missionaries on their knees in prayer, the Bechuana nervously watching them, and Thompson preparing to leave for the colony, to give warning, he said, of the danger.

The next day, 22 June, was Sunday and Moffat was determined to keep it as usual, even if it was to be his last. At first light a cloud of dust was seen in the distance and shortly afterwards a party of Griqua horsemen rode in at full gallop, firing their muskets into the air as they came. They had camped for the night close by, they said, thinking Kuruman was already in the hands of the Mantatees.

Moffat held his service, preaching to the newcomers from the text: 'Some trust in chariots, and some in horses: but we will remember the name of the Lord our God.' The church was then turned into a barracks and next morning preparations for the battle began in

earnest. Waterboer was placed in command and all stocks of powder
and shot were collected. When Moffat and Thompson added theirs,
the Griquas found they had enough for only a dozen rounds a man.
Thompson thereupon took himself off to the south as Melville rode
in with the remaining Griquas, bringing their total strength to about
a hundred horsemen.

Early on Tuesday, after further prayer, the Griquas and their
Bechuana allies moved out of Kuruman. Moffat went with them,
hoping that as a white man he might be able to intervene to avoid
bloodshed. Melville went along too, as an observer. It was strictly
not his affair, as the colonial government undertook no responsibilities for the tribes living beyond the Orange River. But he did not like
to think what would happen if the day went badly, and unofficially
he helped direct the action.

That night Moffat, Waterboer and a few scouts rode on ahead and
waited in a patch of thorn trees for daylight. It was bitterly cold. As
the sun rose they finally caught sight of the enemy on the opposite side
of the valley, close to where Thompson had seen them. All they could
make out at first was what seemed like a large area of scorched grass
where many small fires were burning. But to their astonishment what
they thought was blackened grass turned out to be an immense con-
centration of black bodies crowded together on the straw-coloured
hillside. They seemed to be split into two sections, one occupying the
village of Old Lattakoo, the other out foraging. All told, they numbered at least 40,000 people.

Moffat was appalled. It was no organised army, but an entire
tribe on the move, old men and warriors, cattle, women and children,
with all their belongings, cooking pots, weapons, charms and ornaments. Their appearance was very menacing. The men were tall and
strong, with jet-black skins smeared with a greyish mixture of char-
coal and grease, and they wore a circular band of black ostrich
feathers on their heads. There had been rumours of white men being
with the Mantatees, but Moffat saw no sign of them. Also of cannibalism, and Moffat now understood why. Most of the people were
shockingly emaciated. Some were too weak to move; others had died
at the water pools, their bodies mere skeletons. The Mantatees
were being driven onwards by a frenzy of hunger.

Moffat rode forward to make contact, and was shaken by the
violent reaction. 'They broke out in a hideous yell (probably like the
Indian war whoop) which stunned our ears and I just called out "be
on your guard, they are preparing to attack" when the armed men
rushed on us in a most furious manner. They threw their weapons

with great velocity and one of our men narrowly escaped being knocked from his horse. We quickly retreated, only a few hundred yards, and stood astonished at their savage barbarity.'

Anxious to avoid bloodshed Moffat dismounted, unsaddled his horse, and with the utmost coolness shot and cooked two wild turkeys. Since the Mantatees appeared to speak a dialect of Sechuana there was a chance he might win their confidence. They spent the rest of the day on the hillside quietly eating their meal, in full view of the enemy. In vain; nothing in the experience of the Mantatees made it possible to avoid fighting.

Moffat and the Griquas spent another tense night in the open, saddling up in the dark to be ready at dawn. And so on Thursday, 26 June 1823, the Battle of Lattakoo began.

The Mantatees had never seen horses before nor met with gunfire, but as soon as they caught sight of the Griquas, in Moffat's words,

'they commenced their howl and threw out their right and left wings discharging from their hands some of their savage weapons. Their black dismal appearance and savage fury was calculated to daunt, and the Griquas, on their first attack, wisely retreated a few yards and again drew up. Waterboer commenced firing and levelled one of the warriors to the ground – several more shared the same fate when the wings retired with their shields on their backs crouching as the muskets were discharging. According to the plan, the firing was slow but extremely regular from a most irregular and undisciplined corps. It was expected that their courage would be daunted when they saw many of their warriors levelled by an invincible weapon – it was hoped that this would prevent further bloodshed by either alarming or humbling them. Sufficient intervals were afforded them to make proposals but all was ineffectual. They sallied forth with renewed vigour so as to oblige the Griquas to retreat, tho' only to a short distance, for the enemy never attempted to pursue above one hundred yards from their cattle.'

Three hours passed in this skirmishing and the Griquas were using up their ammunition with no apparent effect. They had to change their tactics to bring the battle to a crisis, which they achieved by charging into the Mantatee ranks to break them up into smaller groups. The battle now became wild and confused, as a body of Mantatees in the village set fire to the huts and others tried to escape through them, with the Griquas wheeling through the smoke and dust, shooting as they went. The din was fearful with gunfire, yells and horses' hooves mixing with the shrieks of women, the cries of abandoned infants and terrified bellowing from cattle trapped in the smoke. Isolated struggles were taking place all over the hillside – in one instance a single Mantatee warrior defied fifty Bechuana who had surrounded him, fighting on with his legs broken and a dozen spears in his body. Elsewhere groups of Bechuana cut down women for their ornaments, hacking brutally at arms and necks to grab whatever took their fancy.

Moffat took no part in the fighting (never in his life did he use a weapon against a man), but he was sickened at the indiscriminate killing which followed. He and Melville rode among the refugees to bring women and children to safety. Sensing that these two white men were not going to kill or maim them, the Mantatee women rushed up to them, lifting their breasts and screaming 'I am a woman! I am a woman!' They saved many lives this way, but it was dangerous work and it nearly cost Moffat his life when he suddenly found himself facing a Mantatee warrior who seemed to rise in a fury of despair from under his horse's feet, blocking his escape. A Griqua marksman saw the danger and dropped the man just as he raised his spear, the musket ball passing within inches of Moffat's head.

After seven hours of fighting the Griquas had succeeded in driving the enemy eight miles back from Old Lattakoo, and with a thousand head of cattle in their hands, the spoils of war, they gave the signal to retire. None of their own men had been lost, but behind they left 500 Mantatee dead, two chiefs among them. One Bechuana was also killed.

So ended the Battle of Lattakoo. The southward course of the Mantatee migration was deflected, and after several months of anxiety as to the direction of their ultimate move, during which time Moffat thought it prudent to send his family to Griqua Town, they finally disappeared towards the north, where numbers of them were to be discovered by David Livingstone a generation later in the valley of the Zambezi. Because of him they passed into history as the Makololo.

It was not the kind of battle which receives much attention in the history of empires. Not a fight for a flag, or a colony, or a negotiating position, but for a new order in African history, and in this respect it was as decisive as the battles in which British regiments were engaged later in the century, to be rewarded with honours and citations, with dates to be learnt at school and the attention of film-makers.

The Griquas had the advantage in weapons and mobility, it is true, but they were using muzzle-loading muskets which required careful handling in the saddle. What gave them their victory was rather the psychological factor, the sense that history was with them as the presence of two white men indicated. How ironic it is that having saved Cape Colony by their stand north of the Orange River, the Griquas should be dispossessed by the same colony half a century later when the land they had made their own was found to be rich in diamonds.

Though not a combatant, Moffat's presence in that part of Africa had introduced this new factor into tribal experience. Only he had been able to move far enough beyond Mothibi's territory to bring back warning of the approaching menace; and only he had been able to alert the Griquas and convince them of the need to make a stand. His position among the Bechuana was now assured. Some years were still to pass before his teaching produced a change in the spiritual life of the people, but the idea of a mission station and the presence of teachers of God's word was never again seriously challenged. From then on Moffat was welcomed wherever he chose to go among the tribes to the north. Moshete they called him; and with his new

8 *Moffat preaching to the Bechuana*, lithotint from an original drawing by Charles Bell

authority, his black beard and erect bearing, he moved like an Old Testament prophet across the world outside the colony.

Inside the colony too news of the Battle of Lattakoo proved the value of stationing missionaries beyond the frontier. Later, in 1827, Thompson produced a book in which, true to the travel-writer's technique, he repeated many of the unkind things people said about missionaries: that they were 'vulgar and uninformed', 'injudicious', 'immoral' (some of them), ineffective 'whether to civilise or christianise the natives', and that in general they were 'a fanatical class of men, more earnest to inculcate the peculiar dogmas of their different sects, than to instruct the barbarous tribes in the arts of civilisation'. This was hardly fair from travellers who did not know what living among native tribes really meant, but to do him justice Thompson dissociated himself from the harshest of these judgements. Apart from their work in spreading the gospel, he concluded, missionaries should be honoured as 'pioneers of discovery and civilisation'.

Promoters of missions also quoted the Battle of Lattakoo as an argument for missionary undertakings 'independently of all considerations relating to a future state'. In other words, they pointed out how Christianity brought temporal advantages to everyone concerned. Moffat, of course, recognised this all along; though he stressed that material benefits must be seen as of secondary importance to spiritual advance. Or, as he put it, evangelisation must precede civilisation. The dividing line between the two was not always made clear as the century advanced, and in the end they merged into a single idea of a civilising mission for the colonial empire, since in human terms the only solution to dangers like the Mantatee invasion was to move the frontier. Philip, with an eye also on the rewards for British trade, put the point forcibly: 'Missionary stations', he wrote, 'are the most efficient agents which can be employed to promote the internal strength of our colonies, and the cheapest and best military posts that a wise government can employ to defend its frontier against predatory incursions of savage tribes.'

7

For twenty years the backdrop to Moffat's life was the Kuruman valley and its surroundings of low hills and light-coloured grass. Here he had brought the solidity of English buildings and the freshness of an English garden into a landscape of thorn trees and stony outcrops.

There were occasional breaks when he had to trek to the Cape for equipment or, which he much preferred, visit other tribes further north. Travelling in his wagon across the plains was like sailing a ship across the ocean; but Kuruman was the harbour to which he was always thankful to return. It was his only home. Being the sort of man he was, he made it a spiritual, as well as a human, community. As with his own family, so with his embryonic church, God was the head and the Bible the life-blood. The Battle of Lattakoo was an exciting episode in his life, but the real battles were not so obvious nor so decisive: battles of will with opponents of his teaching, battles of influence with chiefs to save lives where killings were taken for granted, battles with the bandits of the frontier whom he met un-armed, a score of muskets trained on him, challenging them to look him in the face before going through with their evil work. In all these, he possessed a hidden power which stilled the fierce spirits threatening him, as though an extra presence stood beside him.

In 1838, however, the scene changed. In July that year Moffat finished his translation of the New Testament into Sechuana, the language of most of the tribes in his part of Africa. It was an extra-ordinary achievement for a man with no formal higher education. His only tools were standard commentaries on the Bible and his ability to compare Dutch and English versions. Hebrew and Greek he picked up as he went along. The effort of producing a true render-ing of the meaning into a language which possessed no written form, with no standardised grammar or vocabulary to aid him, brought on headaches, dizziness and insomnia, the last of which afflicted him for the rest of his life. To learn the language properly he first cut himself off with a section of the tribe some distance from Kuruman and for three months endured alone their noise, dirt, indecencies and insati-able curiosity. Having to live in such daily proximity to, and endure without protest, a way of life which outraged him was a constant torment. Also he was deeply vexed by finding he simply could not get inside their minds in this, their natural, unconverted, state.

Language was another barrier to the gospel which the missionary had to break through. It took Moffat a further twenty years to trans-late the Old Testament, but when it was complete his Sechuana Bible placed him among the half-dozen great translators of the Protestant world, alongside Tyndale and Luther, Martyn, Eliot, Carey and Morison. The great Reformation principle, that the word of God 'is the only food of the soul', was proved in every corner of the globe where the Bible appeared in the language of the people. Typical was its effect on Sechele, a famous Bechuana chief, whose conversion to Christianity, lapses and strange contradictions of character were a running theme of missionary correspondence in the years ahead. He stopped Moffat once and said: 'I cannot cease to wonder at the things written in the Old Testament – strange things. I sometimes stop short, and startle at what I read, and ask, "Is this the word of God?" I go back and read again and again. Yes, there it is, clearer than ever. Who could have prophesied that I should ever read such things in the Sechuana language – things of wonder, things of terror, things good, things bad, everything to teach, everything to warn?' Sechele learnt to manipulate texts to suit his own devious ways, to the embarrassment of his teachers, but he was held by the power of those words.

Moffat brought his New Testament to England for printing, arriving in June 1839 to his first sight of steam tugs and the Britain of the new Queen who would give her name to an epoch. In February 1840 Queen Victoria married Prince Albert of Saxe-Coburg, a supporter of worthy causes, and in June the Prince opened a well-publicised meeting in Exeter Hall, London, to promote these causes overseas. Moffat had returned to a nation of ambitious and serious men seeking a new purpose for Britain in the world. Peel and Gladstone were the rising stars, and behind them were Christian campaigners like Buxton and Granville Sharp. They and their predecessors had succeeded in getting Britain's trade in and ownership of slaves outlawed; now they looked beyond the frontiers of Britain's existing empire to the entire heathen world. Whatever was not civilised was potentially empire to them. The England of Exeter Hall which Moffat saw was the world Philip already knew well, a world of propaganda and speeches, of lecture tours through northern industrial cities and of tactful conversations with the influential and the wealthy. No doubt Philip prepared his colleagues in London to make the most of this authentic pioneer missionary on his first visit to England for over twenty years.

Moffat played his part well, though with a certain distaste. 'I hate that system of raising the wind,' he wrote later of it. He allowed himself to be spruced up, took lessons in speech production, and posed for a romantic portrait of himself, clean-shaven and beautifully dressed, in an arcadian African landscape. He also wrote a book, *Missionary Labours and Scenes in Southern Africa*, dedicating it to the Prince Consort. It was an immediate success.

Many new recruits presented themselves for work overseas, men of a new generation, born into a world where the British Navy ruled the seas and British commerce much of the land. Among them was David

Livingstone, newly qualified in medicine and hoping to be a medical missionary in China. But his imagination was caught by Moffat's vision of the huge expanse of Africa which still lay unexplored beyond the frontiers of civilisation, of the unknown north where it was said there was a great lake with stars on it, famed for the roaring of its waves but unseen as yet by white men. Up there was the fabled land of Monomotapa, where the Portuguese had tried to find an African El Dorado. To the north was mystery and adventure and boundless possibilities.

Livingstone haunted Moffat's meetings and came to see him afterwards. Would he do for Africa? he asked. Yes, replied Moffat, if he looked to the north, to the unoccupied ground, to that grand landscape where the pioneer alone in his wagon 'had sometimes seen, in the morning sun, the smoke of a thousand villages, where no missionary had ever been'. The appeal of the north, of breaking out beyond the frontier, had been Moffat's inspiration for twenty years. Did he sense a similar feeling in the younger man? Livingstone hesitated no longer. Why wait for an end to the abominable opium war in China? A hurried farewell to Scotland and his dear father, ordination in London, and by the end of the year 1840 he was on board ship for Cape Town. In his first letter home from Africa Livingstone wrote that he 'would never build on another man's foundations' but would work 'beyond every other man's line of things'. St Paul's words, Moffat's directions, but who could say where they would take him?

Moffat spent three and a half years doing propaganda duty in England, years which saw also a start made on the new Houses of Parliament at Westminster and the erection of a monument to Nelson on a column at the other end of Whitehall. They were symbols of a new age. Moffat had earned an honourable position in it. He could have remained in it, watched his children marry into a prosperous middle class, and become himself a prominent member of Victorian society.

Never for a moment did he consider it. With his Sechuana Testament he brought with him another world of faith purified by disappointments and sufferings, a private world shared fully only by his wife. Measles had been raging at Cape Town when they arrived there from Kuruman in 1839, Mary was heavily pregnant and the only passage available to England was on a dirty, cramped troopship from China. They had no sooner embarked than Mary gave birth to a girl (Elizabeth Lees Moffat, the future wife of Roger Price), and simultaneously their second son, Jamie aged six, collapsed with the fever. Just out of Table Bay the ship ran into a storm, and for three days Jamie lay dying in his mother's arms in a small cot below decks, an attack of dysentery adding to his misery, while everybody around them was helpless from sea-sickness. He was the third child to date whom God had taken from them.

The world of fame and wealth made no impression on Moffat. Harrowing experiences like these only deepened his commitment to an altogether different view of life. Preaching in a London suburb before returning to Africa, he explained what it was that called him back there: 'I have tried to look upon those hands and those feet streaming with blood. I have tried to look on that thorny crown that encircled the sacred head of the Son of God. I have tried to hear his voice; I have read in the words of eternal truth what he said, and I believed that he was the Son of God, and the Saviour of the world. I believed that what he said was true when, as he left the sacred mount of Olives to ascend his mediatorial throne, he said: "Go ye into all the world, and preach the Gospel to every creature." '

Moffat arrived back at Kuruman in December 1843, something of an elder statesman among missionaries. Livingstone met him at the crossing of the Orange River. He had already been north. Kuruman was now the base for a number of missions among the Bechuana tribes, and for Moffat it might seem as though the pioneering days were over. Unhappily the world of missionary politics had also caught up with him and he had to contend with the jealousies of colleagues who resented the publicity he had received in England and the fortune they assumed he had made from his book. But Livingstone, a severe critic of missionaries, was impressed by Moffat's reception by his own people: 'Many of the Bechuanas met Mr and Mrs Moffat with tears of joy. One poor Bushman who has been brought up by him wept aloud when he approached him; and as I had gone to meet him I received many thanks for bringing him. They had believed he should never return. . . . He is truly a good man and will shine when all his enemies are forgotten.'

But the best news for Moffat was the knowledge that Mothibi had at last become a Christian, after resisting for twenty-five years. He was an old man now and losing his hold on his people. Like Moshesh, the outstanding chief of the Basuto, Mothibi felt compelled to make his confession of faith before it was too late. Stooping and grey-haired, he came with his ailing queen to pay his respects.

But instead of being left behind as the century advanced, Moffat found himself once more caught up in the forefront of events. On 2 January 1845 his eldest daughter Mary married Livingstone and so brought that restless spirit into the centre of his household. And it was largely because of Livingstone that he was called on to renew his acquaintance with the African king whose destiny, like Livingstone's, was bound up with the north. The history of missions in Africa could almost be written around dialogues between tribal rulers and their Christian mentors. Moffat's relationship with King Moselekatse of the Matabele is one of the most baffling, and fascinating, of all encounters between a monarch and a missionary.

CHAPTER THREE

MONARCH AND MISSIONARY

9 *Moselekatse and his warriors dancing*, by Charles Bell, 1835

I

Early travellers in South Africa often spoke of an exceedingly fierce people living in what is now north-eastern Natal. They called them Caffres, or Zulus. These people became a force in South Africa's history under the formidable Chaka, who seems to have been the first African king to organise young men in special regiments for war, disallowing them marital and other rights until they had completed their term of duty in this respect. His system of government gave the Zulus a near invincible superiority over all other tribes in southern Africa, its object being two-fold, to secure cattle, on which men grow fat, and to glorify the king. Indeed, the one fulfilled the other.

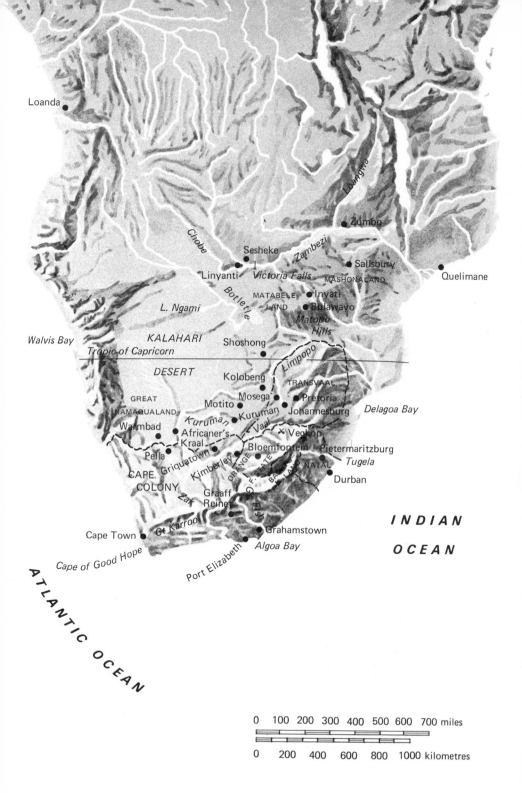

Loanda

Zambezi

Chobe

Sesheke

Linyanti   Victoria Falls   MASHONALAND   Quelimane

Zumbo

Salisbury

L. Ngami   MATABELE   Inyati
LAND   Bulawayo

Walvis Bay   KALAHARI   Matopo
Hills

Tropic of Capricorn   Shoshong

DESERT   Kolobeng   Limpopo

TRANSVAAL

GREAT   Mosega   Pretoria   Delagoa Bay
NAMAQUALAND   Motito   Kuruman   Johannesburg

Warmbad   Kuruman   Vaal   Vegkop

Africaner's   Bloemfontein   Pietermaritzburg
Kraal

Pella   Griquatown   ORANGE   Tugela
Kimberley   F. STATE   NATAL

CAPE   Durban
COLONY   Graaff   Gt Fish
Reinet

Cape Town   Gt Karroo   Grahamstown   INDIAN

Cape of Good Hope   Algoa Bay   OCEAN

Port Elizabeth

ATLANTIC OCEAN

0   100   200   300   400   500   600   700 miles

0   200   400   600   800   1000 kilometres

Little is known about Moselekatse's origin. His father, Machobane, was apparently an independent chief who was killed in a tribal affray, whereupon Moselekatse sought Chaka's protection. He became a kind of feudal war-lord in command of Chaka's frontier, until he incurred his patron's wrath by withholding some captured cattle. Chaka swore vengeance and Moselekatse fled westward with his own troops, now to be distinguished as Matabele. By boldness and deception, by affecting friendliness with gifts of cattle one minute and rounding savagely on his hosts when they were off their guard, he cut his way through the Bechuana tribes, setting up waves of migration of which the Mantatees were a notable manifestation. The Mantatees, it turned out, were mostly refugees from tribes destroyed by Moselekatse.

A similar process took two other Zulu hordes northwards from Natal, one into what was then Portuguese territory south of the Zambezi, the other to the lakes of Central Africa, two thousand miles from their starting point, where they finally settled as the Angoni people. The devastation caused by these bloody migrations goes some way towards justifying this description of Chaka by a Royal Navy officer at Port Natal, who knew him: 'Chaka is one of the most monstrous characters that ever existed; Attila himself was hardly his fellow.'

Shortly after initiating these movements, Chaka was murdered by his half-brother, Dingaan, an even crueller tyrant, who continued the feud against Moselekatse. But Moselekatse recovered the cattle and manpower he lost in his flight from Natal by imposing the Zulu system of military rule on subjugated Bechuanas. The scars on his body showed he had proved his manhood in battle, and he well deserved Moffat's description of him as an African Napoleon. When Moffat first heard of him he was based about 250 miles north-east of Kuruman, near the modern Pretoria, and his name was feared from the Drakensberg to the Kalahari.

For forty years Moselekatse dominated the African scene north of the Orange River, one of the most remarkable men in African history. During this period Moffat saw him on five separate occasions, living among his people for weeks at a time. His first two visits took place when Moselekatse was living in the Transvaal area, the last three when he had moved further north into the region of the modern Bulawayo. Nineteen years elapsed between the second and third visits, but there was a continuity in their relationship which stood above the currents of change in southern Africa. It brought Moffat no human glory such as the world accorded Livingstone; nor did he win converts from it. The Matabele remained indifferent to the gospel for many years after his last contact with them. Moffat came away finally with a foreboding that he had somehow failed, and with the strange record of their meetings which he wrote up in his journals. As he put it at the end of one visit, he could not help being astonished 'at the kindness of a savage tyrant of great power to a plain Christian missionary, which perhaps has never been surpassed'.

2

In 1829 an embassy of two Matabele notables arrived at Kuruman in the company of a trader and asked for Moshete, the white man whose fame had reached the ears of their king. Moffat described their arrival: 'They were astonished beyond measure with everything they saw, and as they, according to the custom of their nation, were in a state of nudity, their appearance very much shocked the comparatively delicate feelings of the Bechuanas, barbarians as they were.' The Matabele were impressed by the order of the mission station, especially by Moffat's workshop, but they feared they would be killed by vengeful tribes before they could report back. They persuaded Moffat to escort them over the journey and meet their king.

Before his meeting with Moffat Moselekatse had set eyes on only two white men – the traders who called on him briefly earlier in the year. From the first he regarded Moffat as someone special. A thousand armed warriors were waiting in a cattle-fold to receive him. Alternately they stamped out a wild war-song which scared Moffat's horses, and then stood perfectly motionless for minutes on end, fixing their eyes on him. Whether this was to honour or intimidate him Moffat was never sure. Moselekatse too was much impressed by the white man's skills. Nervously clinging to Moffat's arm, he inspected the wagon – his 'moving house' he called it. He had never seen anything like it before. 'My heart is all white as milk,' he said, looking intently at Moffat. 'You have loved me, you have fed me, you have protected me, you have carried me in your arms. I live today by a stranger of another nation.' When Moffat expressed astonishment at his words, the king pointed to the men he had sent to Kuruman: 'These are my principal men whom I greatly love. They are my eyes and ears, and what you did to them, you did it to me.'

The tyrant whose name was a byword for ferocity appeared a mild enough man. Moffat described him as short and stout, with a cheerful face and a voice that was soft and feminine. He was struck by the contrast between the affable king and the despotic nature of his rule. 'I had never before seen such savage and degraded minds, such an iron sceptre and such relentless cruelty.' Moselekatse was not really interested in spiritual matters; it was the white man's skills he wanted. 'Did God give the white people all that wisdom,' he asked Moffat, 'or were they made long before the black people?' But when Moffat said good-bye, Moselekatse made him promise to return. 'You are Machobane, my father,' he said. 'Your visit to me appears a dream. My heart will follow you. . . . Let the road to the Kuruman remain open.' And so it was during the next few years. Anyone coming to the Matabele under Moffat's auspices was certain of a safe return.

It was needed, for they were years of murderous commando raids by Griqua and Dutch freebooters outside the control of the government. Traders and missionaries caught up in these affrays were lucky to escape with their lives. On reaching the borders of Moselekatse's kingdom Moffat had found a Wesleyan missionary and his wife who had been held up for many days on the king's orders. They were glad to make a quick getaway once Moffat had cleared the way with Moselekatse. In October 1830 three members of the Paris Evangelical Missionary Society, a French Protestant organisation introduced to Africa by Philip, passed through Kuruman intending to settle at Mosega, close to Moselekatse's new headquarters, and near the modern Zeerust. But the lawlessness which had afflicted Kuruman in the previous decade had now shifted this far north, and the French-men were soon driven to retreat to Motito, a sub-station of Kuruman. Their most rewarding field of labour was to be among the Basuto people under their great king, Moshesh, founder of the modern Lesotho.

Moffat thought so little of his first visit to Moselekatse – he only stayed eight days – he did not even report it to his directors in London. 1829 was a time of spiritual awakening at Kuruman, the first fruits of Moffat's patience, and it was accompanied by much nervous excite-ment which required Moffat's close attention. There was a sudden demand for clothing, for advice on hygiene, for candles to read by, for trade with the colony. The runaway slave, Arend, having bought his freedom from his former master, was the first to be baptised. He paid for a new school house and early in 1830 the foundations of a church building were laid. To raise funds for the church and to collect type for a printing press Moffat had to go to the Cape, a six-month journey which ruled out any quick return to Moselekatse.

But the colonists were also interested in the north. They seized on information brought back from beyond the frontier, which was usually supplied by traders. In Cape Town Moffat found himself the centre of inquiry concerning Moselekatse and the Matabele. The upshot was the formation in 1833 of *The Cape of Good Hope Association for Exploring Central Africa,* which financed an expedition northwards under the auspices of the expansionist governor, Sir Benjamin D'Urban. It was led by the Army Surgeon at the Cape, Dr Andrew Smith, who in 1831 had been on a similar, though secret, mission to Dingaan in Natal.

Dr Smith's expedition had practical, fact-finding objectives; it was part military, part scientific, and part commercial. Thomas Maclear of the Royal Observatory at the Cape took a keen interest. Attached to it were two traders, those free-lances of all frontiers, called Hume and Scoon. They had visited the north before – it was Scoon who brought the original Matabele embassy to Kuruman in 1829 – and as soon as they could they made off on their own to collect ivory. But there were regular soldiers, too, seconded from the Cape garrison and supplied with 400 pounds of gunpowder from the magazine of the brig *Test* riding in Algoa Bay. A surveyor, two draughtsmen, an artist who doubled as chaplain and personal servants for the officers made up the rest of the party, in all a score of white men and ten wagons, with at least fifty Hottentot followers. It was an impressive show for those days.

Dr Smith came to Kuruman, having been warned by Moshesh of the Basuto not to cross the Vaal River without first contacting Moffat. He found him nursing a sick and pregnant wife. Only Dr Smith's timely arrival, Moffat believed, saved Mary's life and he felt obliged to repay the doctor's kindness by introducing him in person to Moselekatse. Also he was glad of the opportunity to prepare Moselekatse for another party of missionaries recently introduced to Africa by Philip. They were Americans, this time, one half of a two-pronged effort to reach the Zulus and Matabele, the Maritime Zoolahs and the Inland Zoolahs as they called them. Thanks to Moffat they were able to settle at Mosega, where the Frenchmen had first gone, and build onto their unfinished houses.

Thanks to Moffat, also, Dr Smith's cumbersome entourage was admitted without difficulty to the Matabele kingdom. As they neared Moselekatse's headquarters, in June 1835, Moffat rode ahead to greet the king.

Six years had passed since their first brief encounter, but the memory of it had not faded. 'Bayete! Bayete!' the messengers shouted.

'Hail Majesty! Moshete is here!' Moselekatse's warriors roared out his titles. He was the Great Lion, the Great He-Elephant, the King of Kings, and Moshete was his friend. He repeated Moffat's name softly, stroked his head and ran his fingers through his beard. The king's bodyguard watched motionless, their bodies glistening in the bright sunlight, and their lionskin shields and short stabbing spears laid nearby. At last Moselekatse collected himself. 'Now my eyes see you again and my heart is white as milk,' he murmured, motioning for beer and meat to be brought, whereupon his warriors took up their songs of praise and began beating down the grass again with their feet. Moselekatse's display of affection astonished Moffat.

Later that afternoon the long trail of oxen with their 'moving houses' rolled into Moselekatse's kraal, and Moffat introduced Dr Smith to the king. It was one of those encounters between white men and natives which in one form or other were taking place all over the globe. Charles Bell, the artist-chaplain, sketched the scene.

There sits the monarch on his wicker stool, quite naked and wearing the ringed head-piece of the Matabele elders, with the missionary at his feet (Moffat's black beard is easily recognisable); the expedition leader sits on his own stool, an elegant figure who does not let himself be intimated by this show of native power; the traders keep in the background, and the warriors squat in the grass, wide-eyed and expectant, ready to obey their master's command in an instant. In this fleeting moment of African history is a tableau of the different

10 *Moselekatse giving audience to Dr Smith in 1835*, drawn by Charles Bell

forces at work in the continent, the spiritual and the temporal, religion and commerce, black and white – and the contrast in styles is striking.

The organisers of Dr Smith's expedition had asked Moffat to become an official member of it, but he flatly refused, and he would have nothing to do with its political objectives. He made it clear he was not under the doctor's command, and he found the military atmosphere of the expedition distasteful. Dr Smith formed his wagons in laager every evening, reprimanded his men when they slept with their boots off, and set sentries with bells to ring the hours of the night watch, a precaution which irritated Moffat whose relationship with Africans was based entirely on trust. The coarse language of the soldiers disgusted him, and he preferred eating on his own. Where the missionary invariably showed courtesy to chiefs when he moved through their territory, the doctor was inclined to bully; where Moffat put himself in the hands of Moselekatse, Dr Smith brooded on what Moshesh had said about the Matabele, and forgot that Moselekatse would be suspicious of anyone who had spoken with Dingaan, his deadly enemy. But despite these differences Moffat and Dr Smith respected each other's qualities. They remained personal friends long after Smith had left Africa to become, in due course, Director General of the Medical Department of the British Army, in which capacity he bore the brunt of the scandals brought to light by Florence Nightingale and the British press during the Crimean War.

No fears for his own life ever entered Moffat's mind while he was with Moselekatse. He stood as straight as a church steeple in his presence, in striking contrast with the king's Matabele attendants who had to crouch on their hands and knees whenever they approached their master. Moffat did not hesitate to denounce the 'diabolical tyranny' of Moselekatse's rule. Matabele executions were everyday matters, and were normally carried out by impaling the criminal on a sharp stake which was thrust up the anus until it emerged beneath the chin. 'In this state they are left to writhe horribly, till they die, when they become a portion for vultures.' Women were tied to trees and strangled, having had their eyes torn out. They were left hanging there for the hyenas. More fortunate victims were drowned or speared on the whim of the moment and for trifling offences. Such scenes formed a constant background to life among the Matabele, and were often talked about by Dr Smith's men round their camp fires, lending a certain urgency to the 'All's well!' of the night watch. (It is perhaps worth bearing in mind that the last time a man was executed in Britain by being hanged, drawn and quartered was as late as 1839.)

Moffat saw at once that Moselekatse himself was the only door through which his people could be reached. From first to last he had nothing to do with his bloody meat-offerings and flattering speeches, but spoke to him of a world not ruled by human power in which war-mongers would receive their just deserts. 'Pray to your God to keep me from Dingaan,' was Moselekatse's immediate response, and he asked for Moffat's telescope to enable him to see what his enemy was doing on the other side of the mountains.

'Why should I abandon war?' asked the king.

'Look at the bones of all the men your armies have killed,' replied Moffat. 'To me they speak in awful language that he who lives by killing others shall himself be killed by others.' But the king's attention strayed to his cattle and his wives, and Moffat never pursued the subject of eternal fate for long.

'Shall Machobane, my father, rise from the dead?'

'Yes, and so will all who have lived and died, and all who ever shall live and die.'

'Shall all rise?'

'All. And every particle of human dust carried away by the wind, and every bone scattered on the hillsides and plains.' That long, bloody exodus from Natal haunted Moffat's imagination. 'They shall all come together at the last day to be judged by the ever-living Son of God.'

It was a technique Moffat often used on chiefs, never without effect. 'My ears hear today,' one of them said after a long silence. But they were words, words only, he reflected, to those who are perishing and who listen to the songs of warriors praising the majesty of a king who has white men eating from his hand. 'It excites a gloomy reflection to think that all these people are dancing headlong to everlasting torment,' he wrote in his journal. 'I feel very gloomy when I look at the dreadfully degraded state of this people. . . . Can these dry bones live?'

He was puzzled by the king's feelings for him. His own affections were so firmly planted at Kuruman it never occurred to him that Moselekatse may have been looking for a deeper human relationship than was possible in tribal life. But that was not enough for Moffat. The hateful surroundings in which he found himself, the wicked and disgusting morals of the Matabele way of life, were 'tremendous barriers which must be broken'. 'As a missionary I am bound to look to fields of labour beyond the one I occupy, and those who shall plant the cross here must again look beyond and beyond. . . . They will need to add to a strong faith, patience.'

Moffat tried to secure the release of a Griqua child, Gertrude or Troey, taken from a cattle-raiding party. But Moselekatse would not part with her, still less with the wagons he had captured, until he had some proof that the White King was his friend. It was a reasonable attitude, thought Moffat. Would Christian rulers give up prisoners and property in a similar position? But he gladly gave Moffat permission to collect timber for his new church, the nearest suitable trees being in his dominions. Moselekatse returned with Moffat as far as Mosega and there they parted on the friendliest of terms.

Dr Smith's brief was to put to all chiefs he met a series of questions, like a secular catechism. Whether they wanted traders and teachers of 'the "Great Word" ', and 'Would you ensure to them your countenance and support and zealously guard them against insult and injury?' He had medals and cloaks and treaty forms (the medals were similar to those distributed to Indian chiefs in England's North American colonies), and he had been ordered not to force his way through anyone's territory. Amongst other things he was to inquire into the fate of two English officers who had disappeared somewhere in the north in the first decade of the century.

After spending some weeks in Moselekatse's domains, closely watched by Matabele scouts, Smith returned to the Cape, his wagons loaded with 5,000 specimens of birds and quadrupeds, 500 drawings, and 1,800 assorted implements illustrating the domestic and military crafts of the natives. He had reached the Tropic of Capricorn where he climbed a tree, looked around, and turned back in accordance with his instructions. 'From the top of a tree elevated about forty feet I obtained a rather extensive view; the country nearly flat and everywhere covered with bush.' No wild surmise about that! Only one man's life was lost outside the colony, and he was a drunken ne'er-do-well who disobeyed orders, slept out in the bush and was chewed by a lion. Nowhere had Smith found it necessary to fight, and he even escorted back to Cape Town a Matabele embassy, Umnombate, the same nobleman who guided Moffat to Moselekatse in 1829. Umnombate duly fixed his thumb print to a treaty engaging 'the King of the Abaqua Zooloo or Qua Machoban, Umsiligas, to be a faithful friend and ally . . .'

That was how the world liked to make history – with treaty forms, an 'alliance' and an embassy secured for 'trifling considerations'; with travelling exhibits, dead or alive, which found their way into museums and anthropology books. In wordly terms Dr Smith's expedition was highly successful, while he himself was a fine example of British rectitude – temperate, interested in religious matters (no trekking on Sundays unless in an emergency), ready to take note of any scrap of information that came his way. But his diary has no soul; and he leaves behind a sense of something incomplete, something missed, an account only half rendered.

Or is there something there after all? Item five of Sir Benjamin D'Urban's report on the expedition to Lord Glenelg, the Colonial Secretary, reads: 'It has made us aware of the existence of an infinity of misery in the interior, with which we were previously unacquainted, a circumstance which in all probability, will lead eventually to the benefit of thousands, who, without some such opportunity of making known their sufferings, might have lived and died even without commiseration.'

They were strange words, not the kind Lord Charles Somerset would have used. *An infinity of misery* was the language of the Clapham Sect, with whom Lord Glenelg was connected. Were they put in solely for his benefit? Or did they reflect a growing conviction that the colonial state had its own mission in the world?

That perhaps, after all, Dr Smith had something else in mind is suggested by a single entry in his enigmatic diary. On 26 June, describing the countryside he is passing through (not far from the modern Johannesburg), he adds, almost as an afterthought, 'the whole of the tract . . . might be thickly colonised . . .'

Had Dr Smith a secret mission, like the one he undertook to Dingaan in 1831? Did he, as on that earlier occasion, make a verbal report to the Governor in private? Were Moselekatse's suspicions that he had come to spy out the land correct? Or was this really the best the British Enlightenment could produce for Africa – a military expedition to count the number of quagga and measure the length of a rhinoceros's penis?

At all events, Dr Smith's expedition bore no worldly fruit. Two years later the Dutch Voortrekkers began crossing the Orange and Vaal Rivers and rolled towards the north to decide for themselves the future of southern Africa.

3

The exodus of Dutch farmers from what had become an English colony governed by English laws is rightly remembered as an epic adventure of the human spirit. With their long teams of oxen and loaded wagons, their wives and children and dogs, their flocks, cattle, farmyard animals and 'servants', the farmers simply de-camped, hundreds at a time, along routes they had secretly scouted out months, perhaps years, before. Men-folk out on horses in advance, muskets across knees, hide-whips and bull-voices reverberating through mountain passes 'trek! trek! pull! pull!', they overcame every obstacle such as only men could do who had no other home-land. If we could follow them by day, travelling in a cloudy pillar of dust, or picture them as they gathered at night for a psalm beside their camp fires, their faces as perhaps Brueghel might have painted them, the comparison with another exodus would be irresistible.

Undeniably they had 'a zeal of God', to use the words St Paul applied to the Jews of his day; and though Moffat did not draw the parallel, it is surely the right one to make in distinguishing the religion of the Voortrekkers from that of the English missionaries they so mistrusted. For more than anything else the Dutch farmers were offended by the idea that Africans might also become the people of God. 'They were provoked to jealousy by them that are no people,' Moffat could have followed St Paul in quoting the history of Moses's people. 'To my mind,' wrote Moffat's eldest son Robert, who lived among the Voortrekkers, 'they are the most peculiar people under heaven.' The farmers wished to preserve their peculiarity with a religious intensity incomprehensible to most Englishmen.

The Americans who had newly arrived in South Africa under-stood it better, as they were reminded vividly of recent experiences in their own expanding states. The settlers of Georgia, for example, had not hesitated to manipulate laws in order to dispossess the Cherokee Indians, well on the way to becoming a progressive Christian community. Now they were called on to witness similar upheavals in both the Zulu kingdoms where they had started work.

The party at Mosega felt the first shock. Moselekatse's orders to stop white men (other than those coming from Moffat) from entering his territory led to a memorable clash at Vegkop, the 'Hill of the Fight', in October 1836, when a handful of Boers withstood a massive onslaught by Moselekatse's bravest *impis*, or regiments. The battle began with a three-hour running fight on horseback, in which the Boers had the advantage of mobility but failed to deter the Matabele warriors. The horsemen then fell back on their laager in which their women and children were placed in the centre of a square formed by drawing up wagons one upon the other, with sharp thorn bushes, rocks and other obstacles packed between the wheels. Prayers were said, the women helped load the muskets, and in this way thirty-

five white men beat off a hundred times their number, using their
heavy elephant guns loaded with buckshot to devastating effect.
Two of the defenders were killed against two or three hundred of the
Matabele. When it was over, more than a thousand assegais were
counted as having been thrown into the laager.

Moselekatse had attacked without warning, and contented himself with 50,000 sheep and goats and 5,000 head of cattle which his
men took from the Boers. They also killed a number of families who
had not made it to the laager in time, and their captured wagons
were brought in triumph to his headquarters, where they passed
before the eyes of the American missionaries at Mosega.

Under the command of one of their sternest leaders, Hendrik
Potgieter, the Boers retaliated in January the following year with a
whirlwind commando raid on Moselekatse's villages, choosing
Mosega as their main target. Most of the Matabele forces were away
at the time, and the Americans were down with fever which may
have affected their judgement. With the thunder of the commando
raid in their ears, and knowing the Boers were systematically destroying the surrounding villages, the Americans decided their usefulness to the Matabele was at an end. Then and there they made up
their minds to quit Moselekatse's dominions, without even waiting to
offer him an explanation of why they were doing so. They left the
same day with the Boers on a hair-raising fifteen-day trek, expecting
to be attacked any minute and travelling for up to twenty hours a
day with barely time for meals or rest. No one felt safe until the
entire party was over the Vaal River. The experience left Daniel
Lindley, the leader of the Americans, deeply impressed by the
qualities of the Boers.

The effect on Moselekatse, however, of the missionaries' sudden
departure was to strengthen his suspicion of white men, apart from
Moffat. Harassed now by Boers and Griquas from the south and
pressed by Dingaan's *impis* from the east, the Matabele king took his
people on towards the north, his 'alliance' with the White King
forgotten. The Americans decided to join their colleagues in Dingaan's
territory in Natal.

But the writing was on the wall for Dingaan too. With his American experiences in mind, Lindley wrote: 'We cannot think of the
American Indians and the natives of this country, without fearing
that years of missionary labour among Dingaan's people may yet be
sacrificed to what is called the enterprise of civilised men. The
emigration of the Boers, now going on from the Colony, will make,
we doubt not, an important èra in the history of the aborigines of

11 *Zulus attacking Boers after Piet Retief's murder in 1838*
(*Battle of Blaauwkrantz*). Painting by Thomas Baines

South Africa.' The only hope for rulers like Dingaan, thought
Lindley, was for British protection.

In February 1838, however, Dingaan clubbed to death Piet
Retief and sixty or so companions in a memorable act of treachery,
witnessed, as it happened, by an English missionary who was not
harmed. The Boers were unarmed in Dingaan's kraal at the time,
having approached him for a grant to settle in his land. The Zulu
impis then went out in the night and killed every Boer family within
reach, in all over 500 men, women, children and infants, and their
servants. Killings continued and the survivors, including the unfortunate Americans, fled to Port Natal where they just managed to
escape by sea. Retribution was certain, though not without savage

fighting. Many of Dingaan's chief men deserted him and his brother, the father of the future Cetewayo, threw in his lot with the Boers. Dingaan was driven from his capital to an unknown death. The Boers renamed his bloody Hill of Execution Pietermaritzberg, and after some hesitation the British in 1843 annexed Natal to make it, in due course, their second colony in South Africa.

More realistic than many of their English colleagues, the Americans recognised that you could not stop those brave, tough, pioneers from crossing frontiers, with or without the sanction of the colonial government. 'All England's power on land and water will not prevent the emigration of her subjects from her territories,' wrote Daniel Lindley. 'What can prevent the emigration of Americans to the West? A strong barrier raised sky-high would be pulled so low that every little child that should come to it would step over it and not stumble.' Discouraged by his experiences with Africans Lindley decided to take up work with the Boers themselves, since he enjoyed their confidence, admired them, and reckoned they too had souls which needed saving for the long-term benefit of the Africans.

From the time of the Great Trek the term Boer is therefore used, usually in disapprobation, to distinguish the emigrant farmers from the 'good' men who remained in the colony. The colonial government at the Cape, in the person of Sir Henry Smith, a veteran of the Napoleonic and Indian wars, tried to bring them under British rule again, but they merely pushed on further north, and the attempt was abandoned, for the time being. 'Where will this trekking end?' asked the younger Robert Moffat when for a short time he was officially responsible for them at Bloemfontein. By the Sand River Convention in 1852 the British recognised the authority of the Boers north of the Vaal River and two years later of those north of the Orange River, territories which respectively became the independent republics of the Transvaal and Orange Free State. The British agreed to abstain from entering into alliances with 'the coloured nations to the north' and to provide the Boers with an open gunpowder market; on their part the Boers agreed to abstain from slavery.

In political terms it was a sensible arrangement. 'Law and order', the prime consideration of civilisation, was safeguarded as far as the colony was concerned, with the Boers replacing the Griquas as frontier police. The two English colonies controlled the ports and trade routes, and their commercial development ('free trade') could go forward unimpeded by costly entanglements with native tribes. This development was expedited by new immigrants from Britain and coolie labour from India. Meanwhile within the constitutional framework of the growing British empire progress towards liberal institutions seemed assured, even for Africans. Like Pilate a colonial governor could wash his hands of matters outside his province. Britain in effect said to the Boers, See ye to it.

Though Kuruman was too far to the west and too close to the Kalahari to interest the Boer farmers, the outward movement of missions which Moffat had spoken about when he was in England seemed doomed. 'It is a time of ebb with us,' was the note of many of his letters in the decade after his return to Bechuanaland. One of the oaths which bound the Voortrekkers together was to disown English missionaries. With independence, they did not hesitate to eject men who stood in their way. The Frenchman, Jean Frédoux, who was married to Moffat's second daughter Ann, was forcibly prevented from preaching to a tribe under Boer influence. Bechuana chiefs who disobeyed Boer commandants were summarily executed. Many had their villages destroyed, their cattle removed and their children enslaved. At Kolobeng, 250 miles north of Kuruman, where he now lived with his convert Sechele, Livingstone ran up against Potgieter, the most uncompromising of Boer leaders. 'In his blood-thirstiness he has poured out drink offerings to the Devil,' was how Livingstone summed him up. At the end of August 1852 the Boers rode into Kolobeng, shot down Sechele's men and carried off two of his children. Accusing Livingstone of supplying Sechele with guns, they sacked the mission station and destroyed Livingstone's laboratory equipment, books and papers. Livingstone believed they would have killed him had they found him at home.

'What an idea these natives must form of the character of the white man,' Moffat reflected, 'always aggressive, always unjust, always cruel.' The Bechuana were bitterly resentful of England's withdrawal of interest and the veto on their supply of guns. Livingstone believed guns were a deterrent to tribal wars, giving weaker people equality with the strong. 'The tribe would never have enjoyed the gospel but for the firearms,' he once wrote. Moselekatse had taken his Matabele army to the north only to leave the Bechuana a prey to the Boers. They preferred the rule of the African king, they told Moffat, to the depredations of the 'white Bushmen' as they called the Boers. Sechele's brother Khosilintse spoke for them all:

'We have been told that the English is a wise nation. Ashu! Bah! What is wisdom? We have been told that the English is a strong nation. They have driven their white Bushmen [Boers] into our country to kill us. Is this strength? Have the English no cattle and slaves of their own that they send their Bushmen to take our cattle and children to sell? We are told that the English love all men. They give or sell ammunition, horses and guns to the Boers, who have red teeth [with blood], to destroy us, and if we ask to buy powder, we can get none. No, no, no! Black man must have no ammunition: they must serve the white man. Is this their love?'

At the time of the Boer raid on Kolobeng – 'a gallant brigade of Satan's own, reeking red from Pandemonium' he called them – Livingstone as it happened was at Kuruman preparing for his do-or-die effort to break through the encircling Boer commandos in the north and establish a new route into the interior of Africa from the Indian or the Atlantic Ocean. He had just seen his wife and children off to England on a boat from Cape Town in order to be free to travel quickly along the waterways connected with the Zambezi, where the tsetse fly and the mosquito were lords of nature (no one at that time knew the mosquito carried malaria). Famous now as the discoverer of Lake Ngami, Moffat's 'Lake of Stars', he had also met the great Sebetwane just before he died. After the Battle of Lattakoo this famous African had led his section of the Mantatees through a hundred adventures to the Zambezi valley, where they settled as the Makololo with their headquarters at Linyanti. The loss of his possessions at Kolobeng left Livingstone unencumbered for his great adventure.

He left Kuruman in December 1852, having spent eleven years as a conventional missionary with the Bechuana. He had now finished with the south; finished with the overstaffing of colonial missions, with the bickerings of missionaries and the weakness of the government beyond the frontier; above all he had finished with the Boers, those old-fashioned men whose stubborn pride and strength of purpose matched his own. He never set foot in southern Africa again, except briefly at Cape Town in 1858.

At Kuruman, right at the end of organised communications, where news from the south took as long to arrive as from the Zambezi, the Moffats waited anxiously. For more than a year they remained in the dark as to Livingstone's whereabouts and then in February 1854 they received a letter, several months old, in which Livingstone confirmed his plan to open a pathway to the coast in order to start up a new mission himself with the Makololo. Suddenly Moffat realised that the key to the situation now threatening southern Africa – and the key perhaps to his own life's work – lay with the Matabele and the enigmatic hold he exercised over their king, Moselekatse.

4

In the middle of May 1854 two traders called at Kuruman, making for the north. One of them, Chapman, had already been on the Zambezi and his contacts there were one of Livingstone's links with the outside world. The other, Sam Edwards, was the son of a Bechuana missionary. He later became an important link with the Matabele, when he was known as 'Far Interior Sam' and was the trusted adviser of Lobengula. On the spur of the moment Moffat decided to go with them. They were both young men in their twenties, not uncongenial companions, though he disapproved of their vagabond way of life and told them plainly his business had nothing in common with theirs.

Nineteen years had passed since he had last seen Moselekatse, a long interval for Europeans but not so for Africans unused to counting the passage of time in years. Moselekatse was based in what is now Rhodesia, almost as far to the north of Kuruman as Cape Town was to the south. But distance was no drawback to Moffat; travel stimulated him as a change from translating; and like Livingstone he felt that in the far north there was hope of new things.

Sweeping through the Bechuana tribes like an Old Testament prophet, picking up goods destined for Livingstone from Sekhomi, the one-eyed and weak-minded chief of the Bamangwato, whose capital Shoshong was at the cross-roads of the north, Moffat entered the unknown regions behind which Moselekatse had hidden himself. For ten days his party felt their way forward without seeing any sign of human life. Then, on the morning of 22 July, he at last approached the royal kraal of Matlokotloko, near today's Bulawayo.

All that morning messengers were on the move reporting his latest position to Moselekatse and returning with urgent messages of welcome. Once again, his name Moshete was on everyone's lips, and he heard the salute for the Matabele king: 'Bayete! Bayete! Majesty! Majesty!' Unconcerned, Moffat walked at the head of his party into an immense cattle-fold where the Matabele notables were standing by the far wall. A hush fell the moment he entered. One of the nobles led him to an enclosure and retired, leaving Moffat uncertain of what was to happen next. Suddenly he found Moselekatse at his side, just inside the fence, and was shaken by what he saw:

'There he sat – how changed! – the vigorous active and nimble monarch of the Matabele, now aged, sitting on a skin, with feet lame, unable to walk or even to stand. I entered, when he grasped my hand, gave one earnest look, drew his mantle over his face. It would have been an awful sight to see the hero of a hundred battles wipe from his eye the falling tear.'

Moffat was deeply moved by the impression his arrival made on Moselekatse. 'My heart yearned with compassion for his soul. Withdrawing his head, he looked at me again, his hand still in mine, and again covered his face.' There was no one else present to witness this extraordinary scene, except a few of Moselekatse's women. The king kept repeating 'Moshete!' 'Moshete!' like a child.

'I have come to see you once more before I die,' Moffat began. 'God has preserved us both over a long period for this meeting.'

Moselekatse found it hard to speak for emotion. 'Your God has sent you to help me and heal me,' he muttered softly. 'It was your medicines which helped me long since.'

No one had warned Moffat of the king's condition; it was sacrilege even to mention his illness, which must be dropsy, Moffat thought, brought on by too much beer. He wondered what he could produce from his medicine chest to help him.

They spent the rest of the day unpacking their things, Moselekatse sitting contentedly in the sun watching them. In the evening, under cover of darkness, he came over to the wagons supported by his wives and seated himself in one of Moffat's armchairs. It was a cold night and Moffat gave him an old pair of socks for his swollen, gouty feet. They talked of what had happened to them both over the years. Moffat's beard was white now, and shorter, and most of his teeth had gone, but Moselekatse would not hear of age or death. Despite his power and possessions, he seemed very unhappy. Master of all his eye took in, he could not face death.

Moselekatse, it turned out, had never doubted that one day he would see Moffat again, though his messengers had returned many times without news of him. They went first to the Zulus of Natal, hearing he was there, only to be told he was still at Kuruman. Then came a report that he was dead, which Moselekatse refused to believe. He sent other messengers to fetch him from Kuruman. But these Sekhomi murdered. Even so he refrained from avenging their deaths out of respect for what Moffat had told him about bloodshed. As the years passed, he refused to give up hope of Moffat's return, and began sacrificing oxen to the spirits of his ancestors, to Machobane his father, to bring his white father to him. Now that he was proved right, his hold over his people was greater than ever. With his hand on Moffat's shoulder, he turned to his nobles and said: 'This is

Moshete, this is my father whom you all thought I should never see again.'

There were few faces that Moffat recognised, but among them was his old friend Umnombate, the guide who had first led him to Moselekatse and the king's ambassador to Cape Town. He was much aged but highly regarded by Moselekatse, and must rank with the king as one of the most outstanding African leaders of his generation. The wagon he had brought back from Governor D'Urban was there too, though rotting away and crammed with useless bric-à-brac like a magpie's nest, mostly gifts from traders.

At Moselekatse's court Moffat also met William the Griqua and his cousin Troey. Since their capture as children twenty years before from a Griqua hunting party they had been brought up in Matabele fashion. William was now in charge of several villages and acted as interpreter between Moffat and the king. Moffat determined to plead for Troey's release.

Moffat was to spend eleven weeks on this visit to the Matabele, much of the time with Moselekatse himself, whose infatuation for him seemed boundless. Sundays only excepted, Moffat attended daily to small jobs to please the king, supervised purgatives for his overloaded bowels, rubbed home-made ointment onto his sore feet, and bled his wives whose fatness was their glory. But he spoke his mind when called on with a freedom which left the interpreter speechless with terror and which, in Moffat's unique phrase, 'oblongated' Moselekatse's normally round and benign expression.

Nothing in the Matabele way of life had changed. Every day he had to witness cattle being slaughtered before his eyes by a spearthrust in the lungs, which brought them down frothing in blood. It was enough to make him a vegetarian: 'Animals – oxen and cows – are alive and apparently happy, like most fat things, at 5 p.m.; the whole, except skin, bones, horns and dung, deposited in stomachs by 10 p.m.' Every night as he retired behind the flap of his wagon to write up his journal, he was serenaded by scores of naked men and women dancing round the pot. 'I must enquire if they have got "shame" in their language' – 'The Matabele is a very wicked tribe' – 'The Matabele are a nation of warriors . . . and until that system, which may be said to constitute their very existence as a people, is broken, the barriers to the introduction of knowledge are of fearful magnitude' – 'Such a government needs the axe putting to its root.'

It was the wildness that oppressed him, in nature as in man. 'Everything tame is lovely,' he wrote once, thinking of Kuruman, and on another occasion the death of a pet kitten which was savaged by dogs when his back was turned brought forth an outburst of feeling. The din, the blood, the shamelessness and, above all, the ignorance – these were marks of the spiritual as well as the physical degradation of natural man. 'They see the stars as they see stones, and the sun shining in his glory is to them nothing more than a thing that gives light and is sometimes very hot.'

The Zambezi, Moffat reckoned, could not be more than 150 miles further north and he pressed Moselekatse for permission to make contact with Livingstone. For a month the king prevaricated, fearing to lose him to the Makololo. Then to Moffat's astonishment he announced that he was going with him.

'How far?'

'As far as you go.'

'I thought in my mind that he was getting cracked in the head as well as in the feet,' noted Moffat.

So began the strangest expedition ever seen in those parts of Africa. Monarch and missionary sat side by side on the forechest of Moffat's wagon while they rolled slowly through the bush, with Matabele warriors trotting along beside them, preparing the route, throwing up shelters at night, executing the business of government. For much of the time Moselekatse would lie in Moffat's bed and invite him to sleep beside him. Or he would rifle through Moffat's things with the innocence of a child. There were long periods of silence when the interpreter was absent. If their wagons stuck in the sand, Moselekatse gave orders and the oxen were unyoked, the warriors seized the shafts themselves and heaved them through at a run. Wherever they stopped, cattle were ready for slaughtering and women appeared from nearby with beer for the men and 'white beer' (milk) for Moffat. Only his canvas wagon-flap separated him from the king's living quarters; every night he could hear men gossiping at one end of his bed and the king's harem quarrelling at the other.

They were brought to a stop by the tsetse fly, whose bite was fatal to ox or horse, and which may therefore be accounted one of the most important factors in Africa's past. It had caused Moselekatse to halt this side of the Zambezi on his long trek north. But the king agreed to send Livingstone's goods forward with Matabele runners and, before he and Moselekatse parted, Moffat had the satisfaction of hearing they had discharged their duty. Though the Makololo were too frightened to meet the Matabele party, they collected the goods from the spot where the Matabele left them. On his return from Angola a year later Livingstone found them safely stored away on an island just above the Victoria Falls.

Had Moffat a desire for worldly acclaim and the triumphs with which explorers were rewarded, this was his chance. He could easily have beaten Livingstone to the discovery of the Victoria Falls and the 'open path' down the Zambezi to the ocean. He was half-minded to attempt it for the sake of the Matabele, when he learned from them of white men who traded guns for ivory with the Mashona in the north-east of Moselekatse's kingdom. These traders were apparently Englishmen and not tobacco-eaters (Portuguese), and the guns were genuine Tower muskets of English manufacture. Coarse cotton cloth and beads had also made their way inland. For Moselekatse it offered an opportunity of new trade outlets by means of which he could consolidate his position in the north and keep at bay the 'civilisation' that was creeping forward from the south under the guns of the Boers. Sound arguments in a world of reason; Exeter Hall type arguments, even.

But with Moffat to preach the gospel came before everything else; he had no interest in the survival of the Matabele as a pagan culture. Were they to reject the word of God, he viewed with equanimity their likely disappearance from history as a just reward for their crimes, though it pained him to see professing Christians like the Boers becoming 'the sword of Jehovah'.

But the Matabele had not yet been given the chance of hearing the gospel, as permission to preach depended on the whim of one man, whose own conversion seemed impossible. Moffat found the company of 'his greasy majesty' disagreeable, but at least their physical proximity gave him an opportunity of introducing what was on his mind. But Moselekatse knew what was coming and slipped away whenever he saw Moffat reach for his Bible. On Sundays he kept out of sight altogether. 'Moselekatse is just as afraid of religious instruction as a condemned criminal of the gallows.'

The moment had now come when Moffat decided he had to force the issue. He had a prophetic sense that he had a duty to perform, and this was the time. With a trembling interpreter between them, Moffat faced the king and told him bluntly that if he denied him the opportunity of preaching to his people before he went back to Kuruman, he would leave him with a heavy heart, never to return. They should not meet again, he added, until they stood together before God. Moselekatse could resist no longer.

Sunday, 24 September 1854, saw the climax to this extraordinary duel of wills between the man of God and the man who embodied all earthly power in that remote fastness of Africa. Moffat stood up, Bible in hand, in front of his wagon; he was white-haired now, but as

12 *Moffat towards the end of his time in Africa*, from an original
crayon drawing

erect as on the day he first set foot in Africa thirty-seven years ago.
Beside him sat the king, naked, obese, a cruel tyrant for all his outward geniality. In rows on the ground squatted his warriors, old men
and young, all professional killers, all quite naked. The temperature
rose into the nineties, but no one stirred, and as Moffat began to
speak a profound silence fell as though all creation had paused to
listen.

Moffat wrote later:

'I felt perhaps as much difficulty to know how to address a congregation as I ever
did in my life – a congregation of people no one of whom had ever heard the
gospel in their lives and had no other impression in their minds than that Moselekatse was God and whom they address and honour as such. A man who has four
hundred wives, . . . his principal men a number of wives each, and all his soldiers
an army of whoremongers, a people taught from childhood to fear no one, to love

no one, to offer thanks to no one but to Moselekatse, a nation of murderers whose hand is against every man. I earnestly sought divine direction, and believe it was granted.'

Moffat often declared himself willing to suffer any kind of hardship, die any kind of death, if he could only touch the moral consciousness of the Matabele. 'Know, King, these things, the preaching of the gospel to you and your people are dearer to me than life,' he once told Moselekatse. One sermon, he well knew, would not result in their immediate conversion, but until men were made aware of the gospel, he believed, real progress in human affairs was impossible. 'My word shall not return unto me void,' was a text he often quoted.

For him history was made the moment the word of God was preached where it had never been preached before. Moffat never knew a Matabele Christian; but on the day when he stood up before Moselekatse and addressed his people he fulfilled his mission. As did St Paul when he stood before Caesar's judgement seat, and Augustine when he met Ethelbert of Kent at Canterbury.

For a week Moffat preached freely. Moselekatse had halted a few miles from Matlokotloko hoping to keep Moffat with him for as long as possible – perhaps for ever. It was the hottest time of the year, so hot they held the services in the evening. Large crowds attended, and Moffat insisted that the women should be free to hear him. As the week went by the weather grew more sultry than ever, and the smoke from countless small fires hung in the air, hiding the sun. Each day the people listened to the word of God 'with the stillness of death'; and each day Moselekatse took up his position at Moffat's side. What was going on in his mind?

Moffat could only guess. But he did not mince matters out of deference to the king: 'My subject was the happiness of the people whose God was Jehovah. . . . It must have been like caustic applied to raw flesh to hear that he, and such like with all their power – the terror of their names, their riches and their hundreds of wives and their thousands of servants and subjects who worshipped them as gods – were sinful guilty worms like the meanest of the thousands whose blood they had shed and with whom they would stand in equality in the judgement day, differing only in the greatness of their crimes.'

At the end of the week Moselekatse reluctantly gave the order to move back to Matlokotloko where they were greeted once again with war dances and pagan hallelujahs. While Moffat prepared for the long trek south to Kuruman Moselekatse loaded him with gifts of ivory and cattle, even agreeing to the release of Troey, the Griqua captive. He did everything possible to put off the moment of his white friend's departure and on the appointed day was shame-facedly discovered trying to stampede Moffat's oxen in a final attempt to delay him another twenty-four hours.

Moffat spent these last hours with the Matabele urging the king to change his way of life before it was too late. He again suggested that he should open a trading depot on the Zambezi where he could deal with white men without involving the Boers. But when he spoke of the punishment that would follow a king who lived by the sword, Moselekatse laid his hand on his friend's arm. 'Enough,' he said gently, 'enough. I have not forgotten the fulfilment of the warnings you gave me at Mosega.'

Moselekatse, it seemed, never doubted for an instant the truth of Moffat's words, and perhaps Moffat did not see that his gifts and his longing for Moffat to remain were more than mere worldly affection; they were, rather, a sacrifice to Moffat's God for the moral courage which he saw in the missionary but knew he lacked in himself.

5

Moffat's last two visits to Moselekatse were closely connected with Livingstone's affairs, and he never achieved the same intense relationship with the king as during those eleven weeks in 1854. When they next met, in the autumn of 1857, both men were feeling their age, though Moselekatse refused to admit it, and Moffat, now over sixty, was brooding on death and the destiny of man. In the background were wider issues of missionary policy which distracted him; while building up off-stage were bitter controversies, of which he was unaware at the time, but which have since attracted much attention.

As far as Moffat was concerned, the circumstances were these. In July 1857 he received a letter from the London Missionary Society announcing that after discussions with Livingstone, who had arrived in England in December 1856, they planned to open two new missions, one each for the Makololo and the Matabele. Res-ponsibility for organising supplies and travel arrangements would devolve on him, which meant he would have to visit the Cape. Moffat had not recommended a mission to the Matabele and doubted its wisdom. But he felt that he should be the first to communicate so momentous a decision to Moselekatse.

He left for the north at once. Moselekatse had shifted his capital again sixty miles to the north-east, largely at Moffat's suggestion, though he still called it Matlokotloko, but traders, concession hunters and Boer officials were all waiting to follow Moffat's trail into his territory. Some of the white men were of poor character, like Swartz, an illiterate Boer peddling firearms, and Collins, an ex-slaver from the east coast; they and, more audaciously, the northern Bechuana tribes were exploiting Moffat's name to gain access to the Matabele, caring little for the consequences. More than ever Moffat felt the pressures of the outside world closing in on Moselekatse, especially as Bechuana chiefs like Sechele seemed to be throwing in their lot with the Boers.

Moselekatse was in a deplorable physical condition. His legs and feet were more swollen with beer-drinking than ever, making it impossible for him to move unaided, and his hands were so shaky he required the constant attention of his wives to raise a vessel to his lips. Moffat found him in his hut, the entrance to which was a semi-circular aperture no more than a foot and a half high through which all visitors had to crawl on hands and knees. It was a wonder to Moffat that Moselekatse's wives ever managed to push or pull him through it. The king sat in a corner all day, ministered to by women with huge distended bellies and ponderous breasts who implored Moffat to bleed them as they found it gave them relief. The king asked for treatment too and once again Moffat had to apply his pills and ointments and exhortations to stop drinking. Moselekatse had his head shaved while Moffat was with him which in Moffat's eyes put a final touch to his bizarre appearance.

The king was rarely seen in public, it seemed. He took a keener interest in fleecing visiting traders and keeping the ivory business to himself than in developing new outlets via the Zambezi as Moffat had suggested. When Moffat asked about his vassal tribes like the Mashona, Moselekatse was excessively cautious over giving away information about what lay in the north-east of his dominions. But he welcomed his old friend warmly enough and agreed with a click of his fingers to the idea of a permanent mission in his country. 'By all means let me have teachers. . . . You know what is good for us and the country better than I do. The land is yours.'

This was how Moffat recorded the conversation, which answered the immediate object of his visit. But he delayed leaving for ten weeks in the hope that he might hear from Livingstone. Moffat, of course, knew about Livingstone's successful break through to the Indian Ocean at Quelimane which showed that interior tribes like the Makololo and Matabele could reach the civilised world without passing through Boer territory. Two months for the return trip from Linyanti, the Makololo headquarters, was Livingstone's estimate. From his son-in-law's most recent letters Moffat understood that he fully intended to start work himself among the Makololo after a few months' rest in England. Livingstone had asked him to send up his plough, mill, books and seeds at the first opportunity. It was now October 1857, and from what Livingstone had said in these letters (the latest had been written in January of that year), Moffat calculated that Livingstone was already back on the Zambezi and within reach of Matabele messengers. Accordingly, he wrote him a long letter from Matlokotloko describing Moselekatse's situation and his own hopes for the future.

With its racy phrases and unsentimental approach to Africa and Africans the letter shows how well Moffat understood his son-in-law, and respected him. The Moffats were often in the dark as to Livingstone's actual movements and, with the natural concern of a mother and grandmother, Mary Moffat had not hesitated to scold him for taking his wife and children on those arduous trips across the Kalahari to Lake Ngami and the north. But they were both humbled by Livingstone's faith that he was carrying out God's purpose, and his courage and single-mindedness saved them from the temptation to become stay-at-homes themselves. Moffat assumed that husband and wife were now together again, and he commiserated with Livingstone's having to leave his children behind in England: 'This is forsaking for a glorious purpose and not as thousands do for sordid dust. . . . How does Mary the sweaty tropical sun?' Give her a father's warmest love, he added.

At Matlokotloko, then, Moffat waited to hear from the Zambezi. 'Shall we meet again on earth?' He looked forward to it and to a new intercourse between missions and tribes along the Zambezi, and even to coming one day 'on shanks noggy' to meet Livingstone on the banks of that great highway of central Africa.

The idea of the two new missions was a grand one, worthy of the Britain of Palmerston – one to the Makololo north of the Zambezi inspired by Livingstone and the other to the Matabele south of it inspired by Moffat, two great African states brought into civilisation by a navigable river open to the world and protected by the Royal Navy. At the time it seemed to be the culmination of Moffat's hopes for the 'beyond', the vision he and Livingstone shared of Christianity leaping, like a forest fire, across every barrier of race, tribe and geography into the heart of the continent.

Livingstone, however, was still in England, chagrined at what he felt was a restrictive attitude towards missionary work expressed by his society. He was now campaigning for full-scale colonial development of central Africa, what he called 'commerce and Christianity'. Receiving no reply from the Zambezi, Moffat left Moselekatse in December and came straight on south to the colony from Kuruman to organise the three years of supplies which each of the two new missions would need. Father and son-in-law met not in a grand Victorian manner on the banks of the Zambezi, but in Cape Town where Livingstone called in April 1858. Now Her Majesty's Consul in command of a government expedition he sailed on to the mouth of the Zambezi, leaving Mary, who was pregnant again, with her parents. He would not arrive at Linyanti until August 1860, too late as it turned out, to meet up with the Makololo mission. He and Moffat never saw each other again.

At Cape Town Moffat also met the recruits from England for the new missions, among them his second son, John Smith Moffat and his bride. The younger Moffat had fallen under Livingstone's influence and like him severed his connection with the London Missionary Society, preferring to work independently. Livingstone was, in fact, financing him out of the proceeds of his book.

By the end of 1858 the two missionary parties, with wives and children, had assembled at Kuruman when suddenly the Boers intervened, threatening to block their passage northwards and expel them from Kuruman altogether. Moffat appealed at once to the colonial government. The Governor, Sir George Grey, was hoping to unite all southern Africa in one system of law and order and he was interested in keeping communications open overland with Livingstone on the Zambezi. He wrote a blunt warning to Pretorius, the Boer leader, stating that Kuruman was a British interest and the missionaries British subjects entitled to 'protection'.

There was no knowing whether the Boers would take notice of the threat implied in this letter. They accused Moffat of fomenting trouble among the Bechuana tribes and replied to Grey that 'the missionary station at Kuruman will be warmly supported and protected, in the same manner as all other missionaries in the State, when we have the conviction that the seeds of discord are not sown there, nor the heathens are instigated to wage war with Christians, but that the true Gospel of Christ is preached.' With this grim communication, it seemed, the Boers were set on destroying Kuruman as they had destroyed Kolobeng. Once again Moffat found himself preparing to escape across the Orange River as he had done when he was a young man. He took his books and papers to safety in the colony and sent Mary Livingstone and her new-born infant back to the Cape and England.

The attack, however, did not materialise and in July 1859 the two mission parties set off for the north, separating at Shoshong. In October Moffat arrived with his group in Moselekatse's kingdom for what was his fifth and last visit. But he was a preoccupied man, and one feels that the opportunity for saving the king's soul was now past. Moselekatse's infirmities seemed worse than ever and there was no let-up in his beer-drinking and self-indulgence. He put in an occasional appearance, slumped in Moffat's wooden chair, so fat a sparrow might nest in his navel, and wearing Moffat's old duffel coat and highland cap, which he had put on back to front. The century was moving forward to an era when white men would make fun of such sights, an era which belonged to Moselekatse's son Lobengula and Moffat's son, John Smith Moffat. Lobengula was not in evidence, as Moselekatse treated his offspring as ordinary Matabele warriors, and the succession was uncertain. But John Smith Moffat was present when Moselekatse's nobles finally led them down to the river at Inyati and announced: 'The king says "if the valley you see pleases you, it is, with the fountain, at your service. Choose where you wish to build and occupy as much land as you please."'

But six weeks had passed before Moselekatse brought himself to give this permission, a period which strained his friendship with Moffat as never before. Word had finally reached the king of all that the Boers had done in the south and how the English had withdrawn their interest in the tribes beyond the colony. It strengthened his suspicion that Boers would move in behind these missionaries too, as they had done when the Americans came to Mosega. He could not bear to refuse his old friend to his face, so he removed himself to a distance and left his nobles to prevaricate. The uncertainty left the younger missionaries irritated with Moffat too. They felt he had misled them, and it took all his patience to prevent the party breaking up in despair.

Later generations would sometimes measure missionary activity by results, in numbers of converts and visible return on effort expended. Not so pioneers like Moffat. 'O that I were young again!' he wrote, feeling the criticism of his juniors. 'Difficulties, hardships, disappointments and more must be looked for at the commencement of every mission of importance. I should not like it if it were not so.' As his dialogue with Moselekatse drew to a close, Moffat allowed his eyes to dwell on the beauty of the countryside they were in, on its trees spangled with flowers and its rich soil, so healthy and green. It was, indeed, a desirable country. But what prospects were there for its present inhabitants, he asked himself, so long as they remained in 'mental darkness'? It would not be long before other pioneers would arrive carrying the British flag and their own ideals. There would be bloodshed and they would then write the word Rhodesia, after the name of a white man, across the land where the missionary went down on his knees to rub the feet of the Matabele king.

6

The Matabele mission was now established. Moffat stayed with them until June 1860 and then took his last farewell of Moselekatse. He reached Kuruman safely in August unaware that tragedy had over-taken the sister mission to the Makololo. By then fever had killed Holloway Helmore, his wife and two of his children, and Mrs Price

13 *Onset of Matabele warriors*, by Charles Bell

and her infant daughter. Roger Price was left alone with two surviving Helmore children, barely able to extract himself from the clutches of Sebetwane's successor, Sekeletu, at Linyanti. The Makololo chief's abrupt change of feeling towards the white men in their terrible plight was inexplicable to those who had read Livingstone's high opinions of him. Too late to be of help, Livingstone characteristically blamed the disaster on the missionaries themselves, spreading uncharitable insinuations about Roger Price, whose own feelings for Africa were only deepened by the experience.

When the news of the disaster eventually reached him in November Moffat at once went north again to escort the survivors back to Kuruman, which they reached in February 1861. Later the same year Roger Price married Elizabeth Lees Moffat, the daughter born on board ship during their harrowing voyage to England in 1839. He gave the rest of his life to Africa, dying at Kuruman in 1900 with the sound of Boer artillery in his ears in what the British called the Boer War, by which time the Makololo had disappeared from history.

Personal tragedies now multiplied for the Moffats. In August 1862 their eldest son Robert died. He had pained them considerably by taking to trade and even setting up shop at Kuruman; but honest Christian traders, after all, would logically be needed to meet Livingstone's ideas for opening up the interior. In September the same year came news that their daughter Mary had died on the Zambezi on 27 April. She had suffered in body and mind in the years she was separated from Livingstone and when they heard she was joining him on that fever-ridden river the Moffats knew they would lose her. She succumbed in Livingstone's arms at Shupanga, leaving him desolate. Then in March 1866 their French son-in-law Jean Frédoux was killed when a wagon filled with gunpowder belonging to a careless trader exploded. The Moffats were left to look after his widow and their seven grandchildren.

Moffat had warned the LMS against starting the Makololo mission without Livingstone's personal supervision, while he only agreed to undertake the Matabele mission out of loyalty to his society. His forebodings were justified, but he felt his own usefulness was ending. Early in 1869 seven of his colleagues came to Kuruman to discuss future policy. Before them lay questions relating to native education, church services and salaries. The mission had become institutionalised. Moffat's own position at Kuruman was partly responsible. He had been there fifty years, and had set on it the stamp of his own theological outlook, more suited to a prophetic role among the savage Matabele than to organising a church in a growing empire. Before the meeting broke up, he announced that he would shortly retire to England, though Kuruman was his home and he had nowhere in England to go. In March the following year he preached his last sermon and made his last, long, trek southwards to the sea.

With his departure an era came to an end. South of the Orange River the Anglicans had established colonial bishoprics and had even nominated dioceses for the Boer Republics. The South African colonies, as Moffat and Livingstone never ceased to point out, were better served with missionaries than anywhere else in the unconverted world, with almost every European society represented there, while the opportunity to make a Christian civilisation of Africa beyond the colonial frontier was lost.

Perhaps the opportunity never existed. The discovery of diamonds in 1867 and the annexation of the Basutos in 1868 pointed the way forward to a new kind of South Africa.

Before he left Kuruman Moffat learned that Moselekatse was dead. The old warrior king breathed his last in September 1868, having gone into a sad decline. One of the missionaries went to see him in his final illness and found him painfully enfeebled. He only brightened up at the mention of Moffat, and the knowledge that he was still praying for him and his people. His nobles could not bear to witness his death. They buried him in a cave in the Matopo Hills, surrounded by granite boulders. For a time Umnombate held the tribe together. In a last service to his dead master, he installed Lobengula as king in March 1870, whose fate it would be to deal with Cecil Rhodes and preside over the collapse of Matabele power.

In his book, published in 1842, Moffat had written prophetically of the need to find new routes into Africa instead of the long and tedious journeys from the Cape. 'It is now quite time to look to the eastern and western coasts of the continent, and form a chain of stations, from either, or both, towards the centre; and establish Missionary Colonies on lakes, or at the sources of those rivers which fall into the ocean.'

This was before Livingstone had set out on his travels, before Moffat was fully aware even of the Boer factor, before his own journeys to Matabeleland which extended communications a thousand miles north of the colony, and before he knew of the existence of other missionaries with the same vision, but with no more than a foot-hold on the mainland of East Africa.

But in 1857, as he journeyed north, he met three Lutherans who had just arrived in Bechuanaland from Natal, on the invitation of the

Boers who hoped they would displace English missionary influence with the subtle Sechele. They had sailed down the East Coast of Africa, they told Moffat, intending to work among the Galla. But the Sultan of Zanzibar had forbidden it, and all they had been able to do was call in at Mombasa where they found a solitary Christian grave and a Mr and Mrs 'Rotman' who 'could do nothing but study the language. They both looked weak, thin and sallow with the climate.' 'These valuable men', Moffat wrote in his journal, 'had had hard uphill work with, humanly speaking, no prospect of success.'

He could not know what precisely had taken place on that East African coast. But in those regions, he predicted, Christianity would 'ere long enter the tropics, and advance towards nations which will require another mode of warfare, to oppose pioneers of Islam delusion.'

Other faiths and other flags, a Sultan and British interests in the Indian Ocean, and another chapter of African history.

CHAPTER FOUR

MUSCAT AT ZANZIBAR

14 *Arab of Zanzibar*, from the portfolio accompanying *Documents sur l'Histoire, la Géographie et le Commerce de l'Afrique Orientale*, by M. Guillain, Paris 1857

I

One morning in February 1824 the British frigate *Leven*, twenty-four, under the command of a Captain Owen, appeared off the East African coast making for Mombasa. Through his telescope the captain espied a remarkable scene. A cannonade was in progress between a fleet of Arab vessels lying off shore and the guns of Fort

Jesus, an old Portuguese stronghold situated above the harbour. Neither party seemed to be inflicting much damage on the other, but what caught the captain's attention was a makeshift British flag fluttering over the citadel. As the British man-of-war approached, the bombardment ceased and both parties prepared to honour the newcomer.

British ships were not often seen in those waters. They were known in previous centuries as the haunts of pirates, and recent reports were no more encouraging. In 1798 Commodore Blankett led a small squadron round the Cape to forestall Napoleon's intrigues in Arabia and found himself struggling for weeks against the monsoon off the mouth of Rogues River, as the English called the Juba. A party he sent ashore for supplies was chased by natives for ten miles along the beach, the long-boats keeping pace with them, but being unable to put in because of the breakers. The seamen only escaped by shedding their clothes as they ran to distract their pursuers until, stark naked and terribly sunburnt, they were able to get aboard their boats again.

In 1811 the Bombay government commissioned a voyage of research in the same area in the belief that Rogues River was connected with the Nile and might yield information as to the fate of Mungo Park, the explorer of the Niger, who had disappeared several years before. Admiralty charts were clearly imprecise, and Captain Owen was charged with making a proper survey of the coast from the Gulf of Oman to Natal.

The defenders of the fort, it turned out, were Mazrui Arabs. Of Persian origin, they had been established at Mombasa for generations and were ill-disposed to recognise the claim to sovereignty in East Africa which was then being canvassed by the Imam of Muscat. In 1807 they offered the overlordship of their territory to the Bombay government, and in 1823 they repeated the offer, throwing in the promise of a rich trade in ivory, gum and cattle. The British flag flying at Fort Jesus did not belong to a British establishment, nor was it sanctioned by British authority. The Mazrui had run it up on their own, so anxious were they for British protection. Owen, indeed, was not altogether surprised to see it there. He had met Mazrui envoys at Bombay, and called in a no-nonsense sailor's manner upon their titular suzerain at Muscat.

Like many seamen of his time Owen believed that the ending of slavery was the divinely appointed task of the Royal Navy, now that France was beaten and Britain ruled the waves. Working his way northwards from Cape Colony, he had witnessed with mounting indignation the lucrative trade in slaves which was still in full swing. From Mozambique and Madagascar French and Portuguese vessels carried them westwards to Rio and the Caribbean; from the mouth of the Rovuma northwards Arab dhows brought still more to Zanzibar and Arabia. The horror of this sea-borne trade was imprinted on every naval officer's mind, reinforced by accounts of remorseful slave-captains of the previous century, like John Newton, whose pamphlet *Thoughts upon the African Slave Trade* was a powerful weapon in the abolitionists' armoury. At Muscat Owen exchanged gifts with the Imam, an Arabic Bible for a sword of Damascus steel, and bluntly informed him that if the people of Mombasa asked for British protection, 'I should feel it my duty to my King to grant it to them, in which my principal motive would be the suppression of that hellish traffic.'

Which is precisely what Owen did on that February day in 1824. On behalf of King George IV he accepted the Mazrui offer, which extended to some 300 miles of coast, from Lamu to the mouth of the Pangani river, including the island of Pemba. The Mazrui, of course, were pushing their own claims to the territory, but Owen knew that only British intervention could effectively stop the slave trade. 'It is to me', he reported to the Admiralty, 'as clear as the sun that God has prepared the dominion of East Africa for the only nation on the earth which has public virtue enough to govern it for its own benefit . . . I have taken my own line to the honour of God and my King and to the benefit of my country and of all mankind.'

No one thought Owen's views odd, nor his action outrageous. It was an age which expected bold if unorthodox decisions by commanders on the spot, since communication between London and the colonies took so long. Only a few years earlier, in 1819, Stamford Raffles had taken Singapore in arbitrary fashion to make it the lynch-pin of British power in the Far East. Besides, added Owen, 'perhaps there is not a more perfect harbour in the world than Mombasa'.

But Owen's annexation of Mombasa was not to be confirmed, though two years passed before the order to disengage worked its way out to the Indian Ocean. His superiors at Cape Town and Mauritius prevaricated and during those two years the British establishment at Mombasa operated. It consisted of a 21-year-old lieutenant, a midshipman, a corporal of marines and three seamen, and that was enough to assert sovereignty. When an Arab slave-dhow appeared in the harbour, the youthful governor promptly seized it, freed its cargo and settled them in a small colony on what is now English Point. Contact was made with natives along the coast and an expedition planned to the interior, where due west of Mombasa a great lake was known to be situated, its banks thickly populated with Africans. Under British protection trade with India flourished.

The protectorate came to an end as suddenly as it began, also by the action of a visiting British sea-captain. On 25 July 1826 Captain Arland of the *Helicon* called at Mombasa with dispatches for Lieutenant Emery, the Governor. The captain found the Mazrui had grown restless under British rule and were plotting to take over again. The British establishment itself seemed in need of protecting, which Arland was unwilling to do. He ordered the British flag to be hauled down, and took on board the *Helicon* the garrison (one officer, one sergeant, one private of marines and four seamen) together with twenty-seven survivors of the 'free black' colony, the remainder having disappeared.

For a further eleven years the sovereignty of Mombasa remained in dispute between the Mazrui faction and the Imam of Muscat. But in 1837 the latter finally gained control of Fort Jesus. Once that key fortress was in his possession, the Imam was ready to extend his operations in East Africa.

Seyyid Said was a man of blood who mellowed with age and success into an exemplary oriental ruler. In 1806 when he was fifteen, he invited his cousin and rival to a 'friendly' discussion and stabbed him to death to secure for himself the title of Imam of Muscat, the seaport on the Omani peninsula which has the Indian Ocean on two sides and desert on the third. Having entered on his long rule by murder, he lived by intrigue and violence. Threatened always by pirates at sea and puritanical militants from the desert at his back, Said owed his survival to troops from British India, whose governors sought to promote orderly clients along the Persian and Arabian seaboard; but he owed much also to his own skill in detecting and playing upon the fears and ambitions of greater powers, and by boldly accepting for himself a wider role than could ever be found in his uninviting triangle of Arabia.

The records of East Africa's distant past show that for centuries Persian and Arabian mariners had sailed with the monsoon winds across the Indian Ocean to found among the coral reefs and islands of its coastline the rich colonies which the Portuguese discovered and took over in the fifteenth and sixteenth centuries. As Portuguese power declined in the Indian Ocean, so these oriental free-booters moved back southwards down the coast – to Mogadishu, Lamu, Malindi,

Mombasa, Pemba, Zanzibar and Kilwa, though these settlements were but shadows of their former glory. By Said's day their attachment to their nominal overlord, the Imam of Muscat, was also shadowy. But it was this shadow that Said grasped.

In the Napoleonic wars France lost all her possessions in the Indian Ocean. At one time they were considerable, but only the island of Bourbon – or Réunion as it was renamed in 1848 – and Tamatave in Madagascar were restored to her in the Peace Treaties, from which bases Frenchmen were soon looking for new openings in the East. The British, victors in war and secure in India, were concerned only with restricting French activities and in suppressing the slave-trade. Said used the French interest to bait the British; and by pretending to an enlightenment over slavery his subjects would never share, he approached Britain in the guise of an ally rather than an obstacle. It was a time when empires were being remodelled and the only certain claims along the East African coast were those of the Portuguese, whose decaying settlements stretched from the mouth of the Rovuma River (Cape Delgado) to Delagoa Bay. In 1822 Said was quick to agree to a British proposal that he should prohibit his subjects from selling slaves south of Cape Delgado, for it implied recognition of his claim to sovereignty north of that point. Hence his dismay at Captain Owen's descent on Mombasa and the diplomatic uncertainty that made it possible; hence too the government of India's insistence that the protectorate be given up and Said's friendship cultivated instead.

Yet it was neither the British nor the French who first revealed to Said the commercial possibilities of an East African empire. Surprisingly, this role fell to Americans. In the half century since the Boston Tea-Party and the breaking of English trading monopolies Americans had moved quickly into the rich markets of the East, undercutting the East India Company in tea and silk from China, and exploring the by-ways of Africa and Arabia. It took 106 days from Salem in Massachussetts to reach Mocha, the coffee emporium at the mouth of the Red Sea, and enterprising American masters found they could also make a profit from exchanging cotton, nails and wire, muskets and powder, glass mirrors, and many other small items of western manufacture for the products of Africa – skins, ivory, gum, dates, ostrich feathers, turtle shells and beeswax. At Lamu there was grain, at Zanzibar salted beef which could be sold to feed the slave plantations of Havanna. At Mombasa or Malindi, perhaps, ivory, while Delagoa Bay had long been frequented by whalers from Nantucket.

No doubt these expanding commercial horizons helped stimulate American interest in overseas missions. The American Colonisation Society, founded in 1816 to deport free blacks back to Africa, made its first settlement on the west coast, which became the Republic of Liberia. Although the Salem merchants kept the knowledge of the East African trade to themselves so far as they could, rumours got around that Americans were also planning colonies along that coast, perhaps at Natal, perhaps further north. When the American missionaries actually arrived in South Africa, feelings against them ran high among English colonists. 'Political pioneers' Governor D'Urban called them. In 1833 President Jackson sent a sloop with an official representative to Muscat to negotiate a commercial treaty with the Arab power. Said was delighted. Here was another opportunity to strengthen his claim to overlordship north of the Portuguese territory. The terms were quickly agreed and a flowery reply returned to 'the most high and mighty Andrew Jackson, whose name shines with so much splendour throughout the world'. In 1837 an American consul took up residence in Zanzibar, the first western official to do so, and tried to persuade the American Board of Commissioners for Foreign Missions to start work on the East African coast. Two years later, a party of American missionaries on their way to India called to see him, but nothing came of their visit. So popular, however, did American cotton cloth become that the word *merikani* was quickly adopted along the coast as the new currency for labour, porterage, or barter. Other nations hastened to make similar treaties.

Zanzibar was clearly becoming a new focus of political and diplomatic interest. In 1838, at the suggestion of the British, Said adopted the secular title of Sultan to emphasise his new status; and in 1840 he felt ready to move from his troublesome fly-blown state on the Arabian peninsula to the tropical calm of the Indian Ocean where his monopoly of cloves brought him rising profits, and he could more easily watch the activities of all these newcomers. The following year he was joined by Captain Hamerton, an officer of the East India Company, who was to act as British consul for the next sixteen years.

This was the stage onto which stepped Ludwig Krapf, a short-sighted, self-effacing German pastor from Würtemberg, in the service of the Anglican Church Missionary Society, the first Protestant missionary to set foot on those shores. Without his glasses Krapf could barely distinguish a white man from a black at ten yards, but alone among all the men of power drawn to East Africa, he had the vision to see it not as an appendage to Arab or European or British Indian empires, but as the homeland of Africans.

2

At the end of the year 1843 Krapf found himself at Aden, having been
expelled from Abyssinia after five years of vain attempts to reach the
Galla in the southern Ethiopian highlands. Apparently they were
five years of failure. In worldly terms he had achieved little except the
distribution of some 8,000 copies of Amharic and Ethiopian Bibles.
But Krapf was not discouraged. Of his Bibles, he wrote: 'These will
not be lost, nor remain without a blessing; but we must *believe*, and not
expect to *see*. If a man cannot believe in the hidden and wonderful
works of God, he cannot understand spiritual or missionary work.'

While he was in Abyssinia Krapf had often asked himself why no
one had tried to reach the Galla from the East African coast, where
European consuls were now stationed, and the Sultan was spoken of
as an enlightened ruler who would do for his dominions what
Mahomet Ali was doing for Egypt.

15 *Ludwig Krapf*, frontispiece to his book *Travels,
Researches, and Missionary Labours*

Aden was, in Krapf's words, no more than 'an expensive depository of coals', recently acquired by Britain. There were no regular services down the East African coast, and to reach Zanzibar Krapf and his wife had to take their chance with such Arab vessels as might be bringing back pilgrims from Mecca, or returning for further cargoes of slaves, cloves and other East African produce. It was a slow and uncomfortable journey. The passengers lived in crowded confusion on the deck, with rats, mice, cockroaches and other vermin running all over the place. It was also dangerous, as Arab sea-captains navigated by landmarks along the shore and often ran aground in waters where the Somalis lay in wait to plunder the owners and sell the crews into slavery.

Krapf seems to have been the first European to have made the voyage in this fashion. He succeeded in picking up for himself those precious items of information which every pioneer needs, about the coastal people, about the caravans that made their way on camels and donkeys to mysterious centres far inland, about a lake or sea somewhere deep in the interior. It was a hazy geography, with tantalising references to the Christian remnant he was set on reaching, and with strange reports of a vast river system, supposedly the Nile, to which the rivers of the coast were in some way connected. At Mombasa he learnt about the English connection, how welcome their protectorate had been and how much their departure was regretted. After eight weeks of wearisome travel, he arrived at last, on 7 January 1844, in Zanzibar 'sole and single to attack the old bulwarks of darkness'.

Hamerton, the British consul, took him to see Said. The Sultan's palace was a featureless, rectangular building, like a barracks, with dingy green-red tiles and peeling white-wash. In everything he did, everything he said, Seyyid Said was the epitome of discretion. No jewel flashed in his turban, no gold on his sandal. He lived frugally, dressed plainly, and kept his seventy-five wives well hidden away behind the walls of his harem. Krapf was not unimpressed:

'He conducted us into the audience-chamber, which is pretty large and paved with marble slabs; American chairs lined the walls, and a stately chandelier hung in the middle of the room. The Sultan bade us be seated, and I described to him in Arabic my Abessinian adventures, and plans for converting the Gallas. He listened with attention and promised every assistance, at the same time pointing out the dangers to which I might be exposed. Although advanced in years he looked very well, and was most friendly and communicative.'

This was how most visitors found Said, now that he was established in his new dominion. Gracious and fatherly, always ready to help, ready to please. Without hesitation he gave Krapf the permission he wanted and a letter to his governors on the coast, recommending 'Dr Krapf, the German, a good man who wishes to convert the world to God. Behave well to him and be everywhere serviceable to him.'

Hamerton was 'a man of the old school' as history books like to put it, not very keen on missionaries and not very keen either on natives or foreigners. But he had an Irishman's taste for conviviality which all visitors were welcome to share. 'A tall, broad-shouldered, and powerful figure, with square features,' was Burton's description, but that was in 1857 when the consul's complexion was 'bleached ghastly pale by ennui and sickness'. He was frequently ill, and was several times on the point of death, when the Sultan showed a genuine concern for him. Hamerton was touched by his consideration, and the relationship between the two men grew closer than official duties alone required. So much so, it aroused suspicion and resentment among other expatriate officials in Zanzibar. Perhaps it was because Hamerton and Said both knew how precarious was the East African empire their joint diplomacy was creating. There was an unreal comic-opera side to the Zanzibar regime which showed itself in a series of inept gifts bestowed by British sovereigns on the Sultan. First there was a steam yacht from William IV which the Arabs had no idea how to sail and which Said passed on to the Governor-General of India; then, a state carriage from the young Queen Victoria (there were no roads in Zanzibar) which he passed on to the Nizam of Hyderabad; finally, in 1845, what seemed ideal, a china tea-service. Hamerton was there to see the crate ceremoniously unpacked in the presence of the Sultan. Inexplicably, in place of those delicate English cups and saucers, out came a tombstone!

Krapf and Hamerton were hardly made for each other. The missionary gave the consul credit for his professional abilities, and he was grateful for his kindnesses, but Hamerton's drinking habits and violent language took him aback. They seem to have been 'cultivated in the military expressions of the old and rough school', as Krapf quaintly put it, and 'must offend even the people who are not very punctilious in point of vital religion'. Krapf described a New Year's evening party which lasted till three in the morning and at which Hamerton sat up drinking with his guests so hard that 'when I saluted him, he could hardly stand on his legs, and his language was quite confused, thundering on his stunned servants who, when he did not see them, laughed and mocked at the intoxicated master'.

It was hardly surprising, then, that Krapf preferred the company of Waters, the American consul, who was the only other man on the island interested in promoting Christianity. While he was in Zanzibar Krapf and his wife lodged with him.

Krapf was often pictured wearing a kind of skull cap like a medieval scholar, which may account for the impression he leaves of being a somewhat impractical figure in that very worldly scene. Scholar indeed he was. His quick grasp of vernacular languages and ability to reduce them to simple forms amounted to genius, and his contribution in this field alone was of great value for the future of Africa. But for all its meekness, his was a strong face, with steady eyes and a firm purpose behind them. However improbable his plans might seem to the men of the world, Krapf was not ignorant of that world. 'Be ye harmless as doves and wise as serpents,' was the rule he best exemplified. His years in Ethiopia, caught between local rulers and rival French and British political missions, taught him not to place any hopes in secular powers. 'Expect nothing, or very little, from political changes in Eastern Africa,' he wrote later. 'As soon as you begin to anticipate much good for missionary labour from politics, you will be in danger in mixing yourself up in them.'

On one issue, however, he could not remain silent, at least so far as his private letters to his society in England were concerned. On his voyage from Aden he had seen for himself what Arab rule meant in East Africa. Wherever there were cultivated plantations, rich in millet, rice and beans, and groves of fruit trees so delightful to the eye and to the taste, there were also many thousands of slaves. They were a distinct community, with large families, business interests (which they shared with their masters) and slaves of their own. They manned the Sultan's ships, formed the bulk of his armies and caravans, and worked his vast plantations of cloves, which brought him huge profits and sent a whiff of spices out to sea, telling visitors they were approaching the island. And at all those decaying towns and harbours, at many a small creek, there were also slaves in chains waiting to be shipped to the markets of Arabia, Persia and India.

So Krapf came to Zanzibar with no illusions about its Sultanate. Though the prince was gracious, his people were cruel beyond belief to Africans; though the consuls were hospitable, the trade they promoted in East Africa was the product of a slave economy and well they knew it; and though Britain had abolished slavery in her own colonies, Arab slaving enterprises were financed and organised largely by subjects of the British Crown. These were the Indians, both Moslems and Hindus (who were called banyans). They were to be found in every port down the coast; they farmed the local customs, regulated the price of slaves, and sat at the right hand of local Arab rulers.

To his patrons in London Krapf was quick to point out the reality behind the facade of Britain's Indian Ocean diplomacy: 'Any secular business, which an European may undertake in the Imam's territory, must be conducted by slaves, either purchased by the European or hired from an Arab Master. There is absolutely no other expedient; he must openly or in secret deal in the slave-trade, or he must withdraw his mercantile establishment altogether from this coast.'

The treaties and slaving regulations which looked so good in English parliamentary reports, and even now read so convincingly in the historical record, were nothing but a sham to any disinterested observer on the spot. 'In other words,' Krapf concluded:

'European governments must either stop slavery in this quarter or they must allow their subjects to be hypocrites and secret transgressors of their laws enacted at home. . . . It is therefore the world turned upside-down, if some of our distinguished statesmen endeavour to work the Mohammedan power, especially that of this coast, up to a flourishing state, without having first abolished the slavery system. The result will be, that slavery increases, and God in His just punishment which He inflicts at this time upon political sins as well as private ones, will turn that power against those who have supported it from wrong motives.'

Later writers were to complete the picture with gruesome accounts of the manner in which the slave-trade was conducted: coarse inspections and parades through the market, public floggings, attacks on unsuspecting villages, the sickening trail of a slave caravan through the bush, when the loiterers would be stabbed or hung up on a wayside tree or simply left to starve to death, the fate of those who were thrown overboard in mid-ocean when a British cruiser appeared on the horizon. Krapf added his own description of a party of Galla who had just purchased three little slave-boys from the Sultan's men. They would keep them, he said, as an insurance against marriage. When a young Galla male wished to take a bride, he had to present her family with the trophies of manhood. To save having to find a victim in the bush, the slave-boys would be roughly castrated instead.

Despite this, despite all that he knew about slavery and the slave-trade (the two could not be distinguished in East Africa), Krapf did not allow it to distract him from his central purpose. 'I consider the abolition cause as a secondary object of the missionary,' he wrote, for the missionary 'must carefully discern whether his primary object, the preaching of the Gospel which makes men free indeed, is not endangered by pressing the abolition cause upon the natives.'

Zanzibar was unhealthy and uncongenial. Three out of every four persons on the island were slaves, while their Arab masters spent their lives 'in merry talk, in prayer, in the debaucheries of the harem and in playing cards', the last, apparently, an innovation from India. Arabs and their families, together with assorted ruffians of the bazaar and slaves, all lived together in the most insanitary conditions imaginable. Morally, a later visitor wrote, Zanzibar was 'scarcely superior to Sodom'. White society was little better. 'I have at no place observed so much strife, jealousy and slandering conduct, as among American, German, French and other foreign residents,' Krapf was to write when he found to his cost just how treacherous these white-skinned outsiders could be. The consuls apart, they were the vagabonds of civilisation attracted by the noxious transplant from Arabia. Hamerton enumerated them in disgust as 'miners, sugar-makers, men skilled in finding long-concealed treasures, French and English writers'. How familiar the list sounds!

This is how Zanzibar remained for the rest of the century. A kind of observation post where the watchers spent their time watching each other; in sight of the coast of Africa, but as remote from its interior as London or Paris, Boston or Bombay. Much later, the Anglicans would erect a cathedral on the island, choosing the site of the slave market; but in Krapf's day Englishmen could not be found for missionary service in East Africa. Once his reconnaissance was done and his permit obtained, he lost no time in making for the mainland.

3

Despite its fine harbour Mombasa was unimpressive. On his visits to his protectorate Owen was struck by the contrast between the imposing citadel built by the Portuguese and the poor shacks inside its walls where the Arab notables lived. 'There are houses of stone, but the majority are wooden huts. A tolerably large fortress commands the harbour and the town,' was all Krapf could find to say about it. The island was only partially cultivated, with a few groves of mangoes and coconuts, oranges and limes, in an otherwise uncared-for tangle of luxuriant vegetation criss-crossed by narrow tracks, where wild cinnamon might be found and wild swine introduced originally by the Portuguese rooted about. A few hundred Arabs and a score of Indian merchants lived in the old town, while Fort Jesus itself was garrisoned by 400 of Said's Baluchi mercenaries. The Governor, Ali-ben-

16 *Mombasa in 1848*, from Guillain's portfolio

Nasser, was one of the Sultan's most trusted lieutenants. He had twice been on diplomatic errands to London, had met Queen Victoria, slept at Windsor and negotiated with the British government. He was also, Krapf knew, a slave-dealer whose ships traded in French and Portuguese waters, contrary to the treaty he had signed in London on behalf of the Sultan.

North and south along the coast stretched sandy beaches fringed with palm trees and broken here and there by narrow creeks. Some fifteen miles from the sea, the land rises a few hundred feet, as though cutting off the coast itself from the continent behind, and giving the impression that it does not really belong to it.

In Krapf's day natives of the Wanika tribe lived among the palm trees along that first line of elevation, and the coastal strip itself belonged to the Swahili (a word of Arabic derivation meaning 'those who live on the East African coast'). The Swahili were not strictly a tribe but a people of mixed race who spoke a common Bantu language. Confined to that narrow, fertile strip, with the ocean on one side and the continent on the other, they had grown into hard, self-reliant men in whose faces, it seemed, a cruel Semitic streak predominated. Krapf thought there must be half a million of them scattered along the whole length of the coast, from the Rovuma to Mogadishu, and they had mostly taken the Moslem faith. Like the Griquas on the South African frontier, they were the go-betweens of East Africa, the henchmen of Arab governors and Indian merchants and European explorers, indispensable as guides and interpreters, the armed guards of caravans and dealers themselves in slaves and ivory. They formed a curtain through which everyone had to pass to reach the tribes of the interior.

As yet not many Swahili had ventured inland, and then for no great distance. It was rather the Kamba and Wanika who came down to trade at the coast. With the help of these tribes, Krapf hoped to be able to bring the word of God for the first time ever to the centres of population which he knew must lie somewhere in that great hinterland.

In May 1844 he brought his wife to Mombasa from Zanzibar. He had married Rosine Dietrich in Cairo in the autumn of 1842. She came from a good family in Basel and had at one time been betrothed to a fellow missionary who had died in Krapf's arms in Marseilles, on the eve of his own departure for Africa. She and Krapf had never met, but she was strongly recommended to him by friends as a suitable missionary wife. Without hesitation she accompanied him to the Red Sea and on the galling march into Abyssinia, where away from all medical help she gave birth to their first child. The baby lived a few hours only, and they christened her Eneba, 'a tear', before burying her beneath a tree on the wayside. Hustled along by the natives who had turned against all Protestants, the mother had no time for rest or remorse. Now she was pregnant again, and she and Krapf looked forward to a new beginning in East Africa, with the blessing of another child. In June he began to translate the Bible into Swahili with the aid of the Cadi, the Islamic magistrate of Mombasa. He noted the date, 8 June 1844, as being one of the most important in his life.

Then came tragedy. The rains that year were unusually severe and in the unhealthy conditions of Mombasa's old town, fever quickly spread. Krapf succumbed first, Rosine soon after. They lay helpless side by side as the time for her confinement drew near, and although Krapf rallied a little, he was too weak to do much for his wife. On 6 July she gave birth to a healthy girl, but three days later became delirious, regaining her senses only as death approached. In agony himself, and hardly aware of what was happening, Krapf staggered to her burial. Within a week the baby was dead too. This time he was too crushed to think of giving her a name.

Rosine's dying wish was that her grave might be on the mainland of Africa. Waters, the American consul at Zanzibar with whom she had stayed, kindly arranged for a stone monument to be erected beside it, just across the water from the old harbour of Mombasa in sight of the mellow walls of Fort Jesus, where the track began that led to the interior. There it caught the eye of those Lutherans who spoke about it to Moffat in Bechuanaland. Over the years passing sailors would sometimes use it as a target for revolver practice, and it can still be made out, the bullet holes plugged with cement, a poignant reminder of the brave soul who died as a new history began for East Africa. As a later memorial puts it in Swahili: 'Thus was the living Church of Christ discovered in this country.' Let her death speak for the many hundreds of missionary wives who made the same sacrifice.

Years later Krapf wrote to console one of his successors on that coast who had suffered a similar loss. At first, said Krapf, his grief was overwhelming, but afterwards he felt as if more had been given to him than had been taken away. Suffering purged him of human desires and gave him a clearer sense of mission. Death, he came to see, was not to be feared by the missionary, provided his vocation came from the heart and was truly rooted in love for others. But if he chose to be a missionary out of pride in himself – Krapf called it the *Ego* before Freud was born – then, said Krapf, to risk death in order to gratify his self would, morally speaking, be suicide. Death, of course, was always a risk, if not from native spears then from disease. Krapf was to be seldom free from ill-health, but whenever people advised him to take a rest-cure at the Cape, he retorted:

'A natural man judges naturally, but a spiritual man considers things in a godly light. He knows that all his hairs are numbered, and that no malignity of the climate can destroy him without his Heavenly Father's will . . . Therefore I will not abandon the field committed to me by human and divine will. Where I am to labour, there I also will die, if God be so willing.'

Like Moffat Krapf took the Bible as the textbook of his faith; but in his letters to his friends in Europe he revealed a mystical side based on suffering and self-analysis which perhaps had more in common with German tradition:

'I believe nothing to be as precious as to be able to weep for oneself and the world, only then does one look into the heart of Jesus. The enemy enters into the highest happiness and the serpent penetrates into the garden of knowledge, but where the heart weeps for Jesus the devil cannot go.'

Alone again in Mombasa Krapf threw himself into his language studies and an even more intense longing for the redemption of Africa. Like Moffat, whose book he was reading at the time, he had a

vision of a chain of mission stations spanning the continent from
East to West. They would join hands, he liked to think, on the great
lake of Uniamesi (Tanganyika) which by all accounts lay in the
centre. Ultimately, he prophesied, there would be black clergy and a
black bishop as true representatives of African civilisation.

4

With the help of a Swahili trader named Abdalla, whom he had
rescued from prison by paying his debts, Krapf made his first contact
with the Wanika tribesmen. Abdalla had bought a plot of land from
them on which he maintained a depot where he exchanged goods
from the bazaar with whatever the Wanika and Kamba brought
down to the coast. His plantation lay at the head of one of the many
creeks in the lagoon which embraced the island of Mombasa. Beyond,
the ground rose abruptly to a ridge from which there was a fine view
eastwards over the town and ocean, while inland the plains stretched
away as far as the eye could see. This was Rabai, the scene of the
first Christian mission on the mainland of East Africa. It happened
to rain when Krapf first entered their village, which auspicious event
led the Wanika elders to agree at once to his request to live among
them. In June 1846 he was joined by his fellow Würtemberger,
Johannes Rebmann, and together they prepared to move to Rabai.

But on 25 August, the day appointed for their formal start at
Rabai, Krapf and Rebmann were both down with fever at their
lodgings in Mombasa. 'Whether the result be life or death,' wrote
Krapf, 'I said to myself, the mission must be begun.' They tottered
up the hill together, Krapf the weaker of the two on their only
donkey, Rebmann obliged to stop every few yards, until at last they
reached their destination, where Krapf collapsed onto a cow-hide and
slept for several hours. 'Scarcely ever was a mission begun in such
weakness.'

So began a period of great activity, familiar to all missionary
pioneers, in which with their own hands Krapf and Rebmann built
their mission settlement of African style huts among the palm trees at
Rabai. 'If any one had seen us then and there in dirty and tattered
clothes, bleeding from wounds caused by the thorns and stones,
flinging mud on the walls in the native fashion and plastering it with
the palm of our hands, he would scarcely have looked upon us as
clergymen.' It was what Krapf described as the human phase of
missionary labour.

17 *Rabai in 1848*, from Guillain's portfolio

Travel in East Africa was not, as in the south, by horse and ox-wagon in which a man could live for months at a time with his tools, guns, cooking utensils, repair kit, medicines and all the necessities of life packed into his 'moving house' as Moselekatse well described it. In East Africa, in Krapf's day, you could only go on foot, or perhaps on the back of a donkey, and you had to have porters. Inland from Mombasa there was a wilderness of thorn trees, without water or tracks, through which no one dared travel alone. It was the terrain of the Masai, Nilo-Hamitic people, as brave as the Matabele, who lived off the blood of cattle mixed with milk. All cattle on earth they considered theirs, and to prove their manhood the young Masai would spear anyone who crossed their path without a second thought.

Through this inhospitable land, where no white man had set foot before, Krapf and Rebmann made several journeys in the quest of missionary openings inland. While one of them stayed at base, the other ventured out with a few Wanika carriers and a Swahili headman. In a little over two years they traversed between them the principal lines of communication which would eventually link East

Africa with the outside world. Incidentally, they made two startling discoveries. On 11 May 1848, in the course of a trip to the Chagga country, Rebmann set eyes for the first time on the snow-capped dome of Mount Kilimanjaro, a magnificent sight to the traveller in the dry plains beneath. At the end of the following year, Krapf was visiting the chief of those Kamba traders whom he met at Abdalla's plantation and at Rabai, and who occasionally came as far as Mombasa. Kivoi posed as a powerful chief who sensibly thought of developing a trade route from the Kenya highlands down the River Tana to the coast. Krapf hoped the Kamba might prove effective transmitters of the new religious ideas they encountered in white men. On 3 December 1849, as clouds in the north-west cleared, he saw the huge mass of Mount Kenya rising to its two jagged peaks – and they too were covered with snow. We may imagine the excitement with which the missionaries discussed these great signposts of nature and fitted them into all the other items of information they had collected. They seemed to confirm, in its essentials, Ptolemy's description of East Africa.

No one in Europe or America had heard of the existence of the mountains, and the world's experts at once ridiculed what the missionaries said about them. The scientific mind of the day was not ready to accept the word of two German clergymen (nor the evidence of frost-bitten fingers and verbal descriptions of the snow provided by natives), and said they must have suffered from hallucinations. 'They have so little of shape, or substance,' wrote one of England's most respected geographers, 'and appear so severed from realities, that they take a quite spectral character.' Livingstone, whose discovery of Lake Ngami the same year earned him a special award from the Royal Geographical Society, was also sceptical.

In 1850, with another German named Erhardt, who had recently joined them at Rabai, Krapf hired an Arab ship and sailed down the coast to the mouth of the Rovuma to complete his survey of missionary prospects. In his book, *Travels, Researches, and Missionary Labours*, published in 1860, Krapf unwittingly volunteers many delightful vignettes of himself as an explorer. On this occasion, we see him out at sea clutching his Bible and hunched up on his back in the bottom of a native canoe, which is no more than a hollowed out tree trunk. In heavy surf the frail craft capsizes, fortunately close enough for Krapf to wade ashore, as we now learn that he cannot swim. Wind and rain make rescue impossible, and darkness falls with Krapf shivering on the open beach and preaching to the natives who have surrounded him. By such means, he found out the essential facts about East African geography and looked forward one day to visiting Lake Nyasa, as well as Lake Tanganyika.

The prospects looked good for missionary work. Krapf left Erhardt and Rebmann at Rabai and returned to Europe for more men. It was his first sight of his homeland for thirteen years. Like Moffat ten years before, he was paraded in the cities of Europe and introduced to the great men of the day, especially in Germany. Like Moffat, too, the experience alarmed him. He was glad to return to Africa with his recruits, which included three artisans, an agriculturalist, a smith and a mechanic. All were Germans. They were commonly called industrial missionaries. It was hoped that they would make the mission self-supporting and give an example of Christian family life. In effect, an embryonic Christian colony; what in later years was to be promoted under Livingstone's slogan of 'commerce and Christianity'.

But Krapf returned to Africa to a multiplication of trials.

First there was trouble with the ordained men. One dropped out before he even left Europe, one quit on the voyage, ostensibly for liturgical reasons, and the third died soon after arrival, like an earlier reinforcement, from fever. Then the three who had been chosen for their practical skills became so ill they had to be invalided straight back. They were again only three men, Krapf, Rebmann and Erhardt, and a start had still to be made with a new station beyond Rabai.

On top of this whirlwind of disaster, Krapf suffered another kind of test. He had only been away from Rabai a year, but when he rejoined his colleagues it was to find that Rebmann and Erhardt had lost faith in the idea of making an immediate beginning inland. They had left their humble Wanika-style huts and were building new and grander mission houses a mile or so distant. At this new site, Kisulutini, they had acquired thirty acres of land from the Wanika chiefs. When Krapf expostulated, they retorted that the time was not ripe for moving inland, and they must first have a firm base at the coast.

Krapf was distraught. What of their instructions from the CMS to branch out far and wide? Erhardt agreed to move inland, and then put it off again. Krapf threatened to resign if Erhardt were not removed from the mission, and then withdrew his threat 'lest I should appear a runaway missionary like Jonah'. 'As to Mr Rebmann, I know he will be the old humble and beloved brother, with whom I should be able to co-operate heartily, as soon as Mr Erhardt be removed.' As in all such disputes, there was good sense on both sides of the argument. But frequent attacks of malaria, the torrid climate, the lack of any other civilised Christian society, made their life together oppressive. In such conditions all men suffer nervous strain and the quarrels of the three Germans at Rabai, otherwise so unedifying, help us to understand the break between Barnabas and Paul at Antioch.

After his last journey inland, however, poor Rebmann had no heart to make another attempt. What happened was this. He was hoping to penetrate to the great lake, Uniamesi (Tanganyika), further than either of them had yet gone and the goal of all their plans. It was the rainy season, which dampened the spirits of everyone in the party, and when he reached the chief through whose territory he had to pass, Rebmann found that one by one all the articles with which he hoped to pay his way beyond were taken from him. This simple system of blackmail, called *hongo*, was to bedevil every traveller in Africa. Only unusual strength of personality or superior physical force could break it down.

The extortions of the chief reduced Rebmann to tears. 'Why are you crying?' asked the chief. 'Because of the loss of his goods,' replied one of Rebmann's men. But no, it was because of the loss of his missionary purpose. In Rebmann's own words: 'Other persecutions were added to robbery, and my health as well as my spirits gave way under the influence of the cold and wet weather, and the smoke with which my miserable hut was filled.' They lost the very clothing from their backs before being allowed to leave. Rebmann was thankful to escape with his life. He never ventured again into the interior.

That left Krapf the only one prepared to return inland. Kivoi, the Kamba chief, had said he would welcome white teachers, and his people seemed to be effective middle-men between the coast and the Kikuyu and allied tribes in the Kenya highlands. Doggedly, Krapf decided to make a start by settling himself on the Yatta plateau, a little over a hundred miles inland. With an undisciplined crowd of thirty Wanika porters, he passed by way of Voi, Tsavo and the Athi River, and found the people ready to let him stay with them. Somewhat casually, they put up a hut for him – six feet high and as many feet wide, with no roof or door. The villagers crowded in on him, curious, begging, suspicious. He grew moody, and at one moment was so low in spirits, so lonely, he wished he were dead.

Krapf was restless; the people were restless; there was famine in the area and many villages were deserted; Galla and Masai warriors were said to be in the neighbourhood. Despite this, ivory caravans, several hundred strong, were making for the coast and other parties were on the move inland trading in tobacco or slaves. Krapf decided to join one of these parties to meet Kivoi at his headquarters at

Kitui, in the heart of the Kamba country, and explore inland up the Tana River.

Kivoi was glad to see him again and promised him his protection and ivory. They set off towards the Kikuyu forests and then, all of a sudden, they were set upon by unidentified robbers. The Kamba dispersed, Kivoi was killed, and Krapf had to run for his life, hiding by day and moving cautiously by night.

Once again, it is a very human and very unheroic picture that Krapf draws of himself. The wonder of it is that he ever lived to tell the tale.

At the moment of the ambush, he fires his gun in the air to scare off the intruders (he never turned it on a fellow human), but in his excitement he leaves the ramrod in the barrel. Next he loses his powder horn, so he turns his gun into a makeshift water-bottle by filling the barrels with water and stopping up their ends with grass. Desperate for food, he reveals himself to a party of Kamba villagers and overhears them planning to kill him to purge Kivoi's death. On the run again, he loses his gun altogether, comes face to face with a rhinoceros, and is stuck in a large tree as a group of women collect brushwood beneath him. After two weeks of this nightmare existence, he finds himself back at his ramshackle hut at Yatta. But there is no heart left in him for a mission there, and he staggers back to Rabai with his clothes in tatters from the sharp-thorned acacia bushes, 'those relentless tyrants of the wilderness', to find that word has already got around that he is dead.

Krapf's insistence on moving inland was spurred by the knowledge that Christianity was competing with a rival faith with no inhibitions about the way it propagated its doctrines. For everywhere they went, as merchants and as slave-traders, the Arabs were missionaries of the Koran. In the bazaars along the coast Krapf encountered men who cursed Christianity with a fanaticism that recalled the Middle Ages. 'God has no son; neither is He begotten nor begets,' they would argue when they discovered who he was. Islam was on the march inland and Christian missionaries were in danger of being outflanked by huge caravans organised from Pangani or Bagamoyo, which prepared to move, a thousand armed Swahili at a time, to the ivory and slave-gathering centres of the interior. There they put about stories that white men were cannibals and worse than heathen. There was no time to be lost, Krapf felt, if Christianity was to forestall the blight of Islam settling over the whole country. Despite his rough experience with the Kamba, he turned at once to what was the most promising of all his missionary openings.

5

When Krapf first arrived off the coast of East Africa in 1844, one of the sights that caught his eye opposite the island of Pemba was a range of mountains inland which seemed to pose an obscure kind of challenge. They were the mountains of Usambara; 'those ramparts of East African heathenism', he called them. Four years later he succeeded in penetrating to them after a long overland journey from Rabai, something the Swahili said was impossible because of the Masai, and he found they belonged to an African king called Kimeri. Krapf was impressed by the order and fertility of his kingdom, and the warmth of his reception of him. Two of Kimeri's sons were Moslems and apparently could read and write; he had Swahili advisers at his court acting as secretaries and medicine men, but when these tried to frustrate the object of Krapf's visit, the king silenced them at once. 'I see what his words are; they are words of the Book.' He pressed Krapf to return with skilled men, writing paper and other aids to development, and showed him an easier way in and out of his dominions by the River Pangani and the sea.

On his voyage down the coast with Erhardt in 1850 Krapf found emissaries from Kimeri on the shore who repeated the king's desire for the white man's return; and one of the purposes of his visit to Europe was to obtain the men to meet Kimeri's request. With other routes inland apparently closed, Usambara was 'the key to the countries of the interior'. If missionaries were to move easily to the great lake of Uniamesi, where all central Africa could be served by water, there must be a station en route, Krapf argued, and Usambara was ideal. It was healthy, strongly governed, safe from robbers, and within easy reach of the sea. In 1852, therefore, his new recruits having died or been sent home, Krapf decided to return to Kimeri alone to fulfil his earlier promise.

Hiring a boat at Mombasa, he set sail for the mouth of the Pangani which took him by the town of Tanga, where he landed to inform the Arab governor of his movements. The governor, however, refused to sanction his journey, unless he had the Sultan's written authority, which obliged Krapf to sail on to Zanzibar. He found that Hamerton was away, and the Sultan apparently also absent. Krapf returned to the mouth of the Pangani to spend a restless night, oppressed by obscure forebodings. Should he proceed or not? Would he have to fly for his life again as on his recent trip to Kivoi? He could only describe his feelings in Biblical imagery, as though he were a Jacob wrestling with the angel of God, or an Abraham overcome in sleep by horrors too dark for words.

He awoke next morning determined to plunge inland. There were no obvious obstacles. Kimeri's men were waiting to escort him to the capital, and a few days later the king himself arrived, preceded by a bodyguard shooting off their muskets into the air. Krapf positioned himself beside the track so as to greet the king as he passed. Kimeri stopped abruptly. Though he knew Krapf from his visit four years earlier, a white man was still an apparition from another world. At a loss to know what to say, the king said nothing, and disappeared into the hut of his chief medicine man, a Swahili named Osman.

The black king's court was little different from his white counter-part's, Krapf drily noted – or, for that matter, from that of his modern equivalent. In this ageing, stout, African potentate walking barefoot with a cloak over his shoulder is the prototype of all Presidents of the Republic with their noisy motor-bike escorts. Kimeri sat on his bedstead smoking his pipe 'with great gravity, which in savage life is unmistakable evidence of monarchical dig-nity'; the courtiers waited for his nod, applauded when he coughed and intoned his praises: 'Oh Lion! Oh Lion of Heaven!' A humming sound, 'Mmmmmmm' was the invariable answer from the royal lips.

If this were Speke or Stanley or a later Victorian hero, the white visitor would impose his will on the scene. But Krapf sat quietly at the king's feet waiting his turn to speak. The business of state, which consisted of gossip and the examination of presents, made serious talk impossible. Krapf was not in Africa to prosecute scientific enquiries, but as a witness to the drama of life and death being enacted then and there: 'During the moments which I passed at Kimeri's feet he might have received what is of more value than his whole kingdom; he might have listened to words of everlasting life, which would have laid the foundation of his true temporal and spiritual happiness. And, besides, he might have been instrumental in procuring the salvation of millions of souls in his own kingdom and in Eastern Africa.'

Like Moselekatse, Kimeri had been a brave fighter in his youth; now, in his old age, he was seeking ways to keep up with the new world which had appeared on his horizon. Tribes living nearer to Zanzibar who were formerly his subjects were able to defy his soldiers with muskets procured from European and American business houses in the island. In Krapf, the first white man he met, he saw his chance of making direct contact with Europeans and obtaining their skills.

His relationship with Sultan Said was ambiguous. The Swahili at the mouth of the River Pangani acknowledged Kimeri as their ruler and paid him tribute. Kimeri appointed one of them to act as his representative, or headman, but this official also took presents from the Sultan to look after Arab interests. No doubt Kimeri's Swahili advisers played the same double role. As on his previous visit, Kimeri's Moslem magicians opposed Krapf's mission, until he threatened to lodge complaints against them in Zanzibar.

Kimeri quickly granted his visitor's request for a Christian mission in his realm. Assigning one of his chief men to look after the matter, he asked Krapf to introduce him to the white men in Zanzibar, so that he might deal directly with the outside world and not through Swahili middlemen. In practical terms Krapf's visit was as successful as he dared to hope.

Within a month he was back at the mouth of the Pangani. On the return voyage to Rabai, he stopped at Zanzibar to introduce Kimeri's ambassador to the European and American merchants. Hamerton and Said were still away and he was entertained on the island, as he had been in the past, by the French consul, a Creole called de Belligny, whose secretary shared Krapf's interest in East African topography. It made his visit to that otherwise disagreeable island a pleasant interlude in his life. They got out their maps and discussed Krapf's latest journey. Did the African ruler's authority really extend to the coast? asked the Frenchman. Of course, it must do, replied Krapf. How else would he be able to levy tribute and appoint governors there?

That was in April 1852. The Sultan returned to Zanzibar later the same year. Meanwhile gossip in the slave-market made much of the appearance in the island of the 'infidel' ambassador of Kimeri. The Swahili resented the African king's attempt to sell ivory direct to dealers from Europe and America, and played upon the religious factor. Other white men – Germans and Americans – had been at dinner that night when Krapf spoke of his experiences in Usambara, with the result that a rumour soon spread that the French were planning to make a treaty with the African king and plant a colony on his part of the coast. Perhaps Krapf was unwise to say anything at all in that poisonous vortex of intrigue, where the white expatriates were for ever quarrelling with each other. But, Krapf would protest, why should he, a missionary, be a party to these intrigues, and how could he be ungrateful to a kind host? Why not tell the truth?

But his kind of truth counted for little in Zanzibar, or in the world of international diplomacy for that matter. No one, apart from the missionary, thought of the future of East Africa in terms of the Africans themselves. Certainly not the French and British consuls. The French thought the British were hypocritical over slavery, and the British thought the French were cynics, their trans-shipment of so-called 'free labourers' being the slave-trade under another name. When these rumours came to his ears Hamerton jumped to the conclusion that the French were intriguing, as there was a pro-French party among the Arabs at Zanzibar, and he blamed the German parson for showing them the way. The boozy, genial Irishman who was Queen Victoria's representative in East Africa had only one professional interest, and that was to keep the French out; his private interests lay in his wine and his cigars and his after-dinner company. One French merchant was already working out of Lamu, and a French naval squadron was known to be on its way to Zanzibar – a courtesy visit, of course, but enough to set Said and Hamerton whispering in each other's ears. When Hamerton learned that other missionaries were heading his way – they were the Lutherans who eventually turned up in Bechuanaland – he decided they must all be firmly discouraged. He set the diplomatic machinery working, so that in dispatches between Zanzibar, Bombay and London, Krapf was cast as a meddler in politics. 'Mischievous meddling in secular affairs' was how the Indian government put it.

Unaware of all this, the three Germans had passed an unhappy year. Erhardt's refusal to move to Usambara reduced Krapf to despair. 'I have infinitely suffered in my mind,' he wrote to CMS headquarters. 'I shall commence the Usambara mission with or without Mr Erhardt . . . for we dare not deceive King Kimeri . . . I cannot go home until that mission is commenced.' All his hopes for a chain of stations across Africa, all his labours and sacrifices, were concentrated in making that new beginning. But they patched up their differences, so that when an order came from the CMS re-calling Erhardt from East Africa, Krapf agreed to give him one more chance to take up the opening in Usambara. He himself would return to Europe, once he knew that Erhardt had arrived safely with King Kimeri.

Erhardt reached Kimeri in August 1853 and stayed at his capital for three months. The king was friendly, though he complained when he received Erhardt's gifts, 'Krafu brought me more.' He showed more interest in reviving his fleshly appetites with an aphrodisiac he hoped Erhardt would give him than in any religious talk, leaving it to his magicians to interrupt whenever Erhardt introduced the sub-ject of an after-life. The king would never die, they said. Surrounded by sorcerers and executioners Erhardt now experienced at first hand what it was like to live in the shadow of an African ruler. 'At no place in Eastern Africa,' he wrote, 'have my feelings been more grieved and shocked than by those wanton outrages of depraved human nature which have been perpetrated here.' Sensibly, he decided to move away from the capital to a site where he could begin work on his own.

But then a strange thing happened. Just as he was about to take leave of Kimeri, a message arrived from Zanzibar. The Sultan threatened the king with war if he allowed the missionary to stay. A curious message, as Erhardt had already obtained the Sultan's blessing for his mission. Was it the work of those Moslem advisers acting secretly on Said's behalf? Or was it the outcome of some new intrigue in Zanzibar? Whichever it was, it was enough to bring Erhardt hurrying back to see the Sultan personally. He presented him with a letter from Kimeri: 'In the name of God. Thou Said Ben Sultan hast sent to me a Musungu (white man) with a letter from thine hand. Thou hast told me to treat him with honour and civility as thou wouldst do me. I have shown him honour. But this Musungu wants a place for to sit in my country; shall I give him permission to sit down or not? Tell me. This I have to say. Kimeri.'

It was now December 1853. Erhardt listened as Said repeated the charge of political intrigue against Krapf, who had left for Europe in October. As usual Zanzibar was full of rumours. Word had apparently got around the expatriate white community that the missionaries disapproved of the British consul's way of life, so Hamerton was ice-cold to the wretched Erhardt. 'I cannot give you permission to go to Usambara,' the Sultan told him as he read Kimeri's letter, 'if I give you permission I must give it to the French and Americans also and this I will not do.'

No indeed! That was the reality behind all the gossip and intrigue which made a scapegoat of Krapf now that he was no longer there. Assured of British support, Said took possession of that stretch of coast which Krapf said did not belong to him; and where Kimeri had given permission for a Christian mission, the Sultan quietly built a fort and garrisoned it with his Baluchis. He allowed Erhardt to remove himself to Tanga, where he remained a short while in ineffectual suspense until the CMS redirected him to India. Thanks to Britain, a Moslem power now controlled all the entry and exit points on the eastern coast of Africa.

A vast extension of the inland slave-trade was to be the next development. Deprived of alternatives, Kimeri, like many another powerful chief, joined in it himself in alliance with the Arabs who soon established regular colonies inland, notably at Tabora on the caravan route and at Ujiji on Lake Tanganyika. From these bases they made slaving expeditions further west into the Manyuema country, northwards to Uganda and south-west to Cazembe's. 'It is not a trade, but a system of consecutive murders,' was to be the judgement of David Livingstone, the man destined to uncover this cancerous growth and confirm Krapf's worst fears for the future of East Africa.

6

'God forbid,' Krapf once wrote before setting off into the unknown, 'God forbid that I have any scientific scheme of African discoveries or that we act from any love of fame.' Even so, honours and awards came his way from international societies. But when the row broke out over his innocent conversation with a fellow geographer (unfortunately French) Krapf returned them all, rendering back to Caesar the things that are his: 'Let Science fall and geography perish, if but the cause of Christ and of immortal souls be sustained.'

How ironic it is, then, that history books record the names of Krapf and Rebmann chiefly because of their geographical discoveries. Even more ironic that the famous 'missionary map', which appeared in Europe early in 1856 and prompted Burton and Speke to explore East Africa, was canvassed by Erhardt and not by Krapf. Krapf would not have combined the great central African lakes in one grotesque 'monster slug of an inland sea', as Speke called it. Yet even in this respect Krapf began something which eventually led to Christianity breaking through the barriers which he was the first to encounter.

The interior, the interior, the interior – the word rings out like a bugle call in all his writings to warn against plausible voices which advise caution, delay, waiting for the world to change.

First it was the American Waters, the only man in Zanzibar interested in what Krapf was doing. He had tried to persuade Krapf to stay in the island, preaching to the Europeans, founding schools, preparing vernacular literature, making a base for the future. How sensible it sounded in worldly terms. That was to be the way of both Anglicans and Roman Catholics in the future.

Then it was Rebmann and Erhardt, Krapf's own colleagues, who thought they should dig themselves in at Rabai and wait on a better turn of events. Their defection pained Krapf more than anything else. 'When a general sees that there is an access to a fortress he attacks it at once by leading his forces to it . . . and now that the Christians of England are aware of their duty, their own soldiers advise them to protract the attack to a more convenient time.'

Even when the blow fell in Usambara and Hamerton betrayed him, Krapf urged the missionaries not to retreat. 'We must go beyond the territory of the Imam,' he wrote, 'we must be out of the reach of the Muhammedans as well as of the Europeans.'

He never gave up this vision. When he heard that Rebmann had left Rabai for a time because of Masai threats and the CMS were thinking of giving up East Africa altogether, he protested vigorously that at all costs the door should at least be kept open. He intended returning to Rabai himself after his mission to Ethiopia for Theodore in 1855, but ill-health prevented it. For health reasons too and perhaps because he no longer felt called to serve an Anglican missionary society, Krapf then left the CMS after twenty years service to promote a new Swiss missionary venture on the Nile.

Said and Hamerton did not long survive his departure. In 1854 the old Sultan returned for the last time to Muscat to deal with another outbreak of trouble in his Arabian state, leaving Zanzibar virtually in Hamerton's care. He died in October 1856 on the voyage back and through Hamerton's vigorous action the succession passed peacefully, as Said had wished, to two of his sons. Thereafter the Zanzibari half of the empire was a separate entity from Muscat.

Hamerton died in July 1857. Almost his last act was to cross with Burton and Speke to Bagamoyo on the mainland, now the principal starting point for expeditions to the Arab colonies inland, to set them on their way on what was to be the first of a new series of adventures leading eventually to the destruction of Arab power altogether.

But Krapf had not yet finished with East Africa. In January 1862 he returned for what was to be his last act of missionary service in that region. The Methodists in England had been impressed by his recently published book, in which he appealed for volunteers for Africa. They asked him to meet them in Manchester late in 1860, when a number of volunteers offered themselves, with the Galla particularly in mind. The upshot was the formation of a joint mission consisting of two Methodists and two Swiss Protestants trained at Krapf's Chrischona Institute near Basel. Krapf proposed leading the party out himself and settling them in suitable locations. Once again, however, the old terrors of East Africa held sway. Caught in a fight between an English warship and Arab slavers in Mombasa harbour, the two Swiss decided East Africa was not for them. Meanwhile, one of the Methodists was taken so badly with fever he had to withdraw and Krapf himself was unable to stay out in that climate as long as he originally hoped.

But he was able to get the surviving Methodist started. Krapf negotiated on his behalf for a site a few miles beyond Rabai called Ribe which, it turned out afterwards, was thought by the Wanika to be haunted. Here they erected a prefabricated iron house which the Methodists had brought out from England. Krapf was apprehensive of his reception in Zanzibar, but the new British consul laughed away his fears. The French had just moved in and were building a large barrack-like religious establishment on the island, more suited to a military garrison (which the Sultan was afraid it was) than a mission. The consul had insisted that Britain should have equal rights and Krapf's gaffe, if gaffe it really had been, was a thing of the past.

Eight years had passed since Krapf and Rebmann had last seen each other, and there was a moment of tension between them when Rebmann accused the new mission of trespassing on his area. He was doing little effective missionary work himself, but periodically took refuge in Zanzibar when he heard of Masai war parties approaching Rabai. He had been authorised to accompany Burton's expedition in 1857, but declined. 'An honest and conscientious man, he had all the qualities which secure unsuccess,' was Burton's off-hand dismissal of him. Krapf left him to his solitary life among the palm trees at Rabai and caught a ship with the autumn monsoon to be back in Europe by the end of the year. At Ribe the Methodists were to come up against the same obstacles in the years ahead – Masai astride the routes inland, malaria at the coast, and Arab slavers making peaceful commerce impossible. Here Thomas Wakefield, the survivor of the original party, gave twenty-five years' service before finally retiring to England in 1887.

So Krapf disappears from the East African scene. He was defeated after all not by the climate and the terrain, tough obstacles though they were, nor by native rain-makers or magicians. He preferred these primitive signs of a belief in the supernatural, which could be found in most tribal customs, to western man's idea of progress. Even such things as the killing of twins in infancy and ordeal by poison were an advance on the godless materialism of European liberals: 'A civilised man, who has no fear of God, is indeed ten times worse than a savage of Africa who fears his charm and leaves his neighbour's property alone. Hence I firmly believe that these savage nations can and will be saved in process of time, whilst the anti-Christian nations of Europe, which worship merely outward civilisation as their idol, must utterly perish.'

What defeated Krapf was Britain's policy of building up a tin-pot oriental ruler on an island in the Indian Ocean in order to safeguard British interests in India. The fact is, Said's move to Zanzibar in 1840 was the signal for a fatal exploitation of East Africa, the beginnings of which Krapf saw with his own eyes during the ten years he was there. When, in Europe, he heard of what had taken place in Usambara after he had left and his alleged responsibility for it, he could only apologise and abase himself to protect other missionaries. But he did not hide his feelings about Hamerton from the CMS nor fail to point out the real damage he was doing to Britain by not giving her missionaries greater support. When he published his book in 1860, though he felt it prudent not to antagonise the authorities by too open an attack on the Zanzibar regime, just as Livingstone soft-pedalled on the Portuguese part in the slave-trade, Krapf wrote of the Sultan's 'nominal' claims on the mainland with a meaning that was clear to discerning readers. Things would never improve on that coast, he concluded, so long as Arab rule is maintained 'in its present state'.

The world, of course, could always argue that the Arabs succeeded in effectively 'opening up' Africa, where Christendom failed or had not bothered; that Livingstone and others were following up trails blazed for them by Arabs and Swahili, and used them as their contacts, postmen, guides, warrant-officers, shopkeepers; that not all Arabs were slave-traders and that, in any case, they treated their slaves well.

At what cost in human terms? Livingstone thought that for every slave brought to the markets on the coast, ten would have lost their lives either in the capture or in the journey down. Others suggested that the ratio of live to dead should be one to five. There are, of course, no records of the numbers shipped from all those creeks along the coast or sold in the slave markets of the principal towns. At one time they were said to be passing through Zanzibar at the rate of 10,000 a year, which would have meant an annual death toll of either 100,000 or 50,000 depending on the ratio chosen. So that in the half-century in question, on the most conservative estimate, the loss of African lives must be reckoned in many millions.

But Krapf was a missionary and a German, and his words counted for little in Britain. All the glory for exploration went instead to David Livingstone, whose fame was at its height when Krapf retired to Europe. It was translating Livingstone's *Missionary Travels* into German that prompted Krapf to write his own book, in which he quoted with approval a slightly different version of the notable phrase with which Livingstone summarised his own achievement: 'I view the end of the geographical feat as the beginning of the missionary enterprise.' That was Krapf's legacy also to East Africa. How it was to be realised belongs to the next episode in the story.

CHAPTER FIVE

ELIJAH AND ELISHA

18 *David Livingstone*, frontispiece to *Last Journals*

I

The conversion of one soul to Christianity, wrote David Livingstone, is like a piece of wood thrown onto the surface of a river; it shows the direction of the current. Just as the whole of nature's law can be found in the tiniest rivulet in the most out-of-the-way place, so the whole truth of the Christian mission may be judged in one soul saved. The current is destined to become a mighty flood which will overflow the world. 'We work', he wrote,

'for a glorious future which we are not destined to see, the golden age which has not been but will yet be. We are only morning stars shining in the dark, but the glorious morn will break – the good time coming yet. The present mission stations

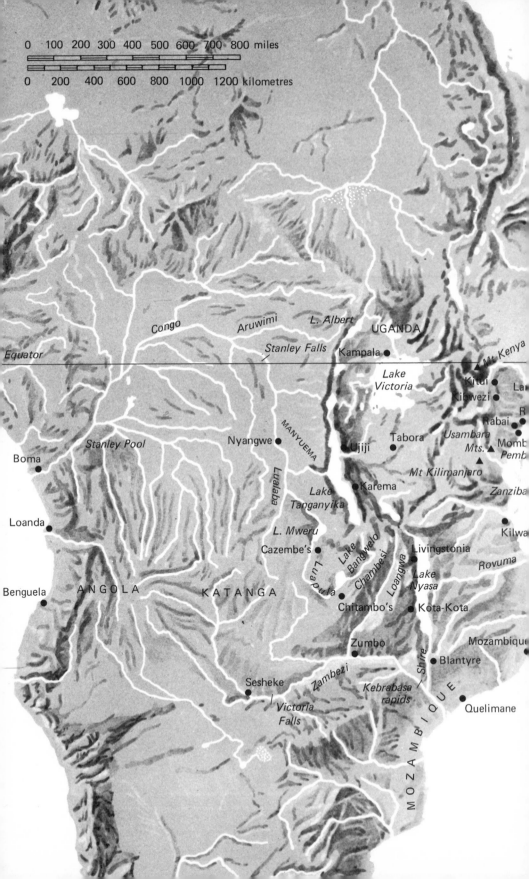

will all be broken up. No matter how great the outcry against the instrumentality which God employs for his purposes, whether French soldiery as in Tahiti or tawny Boers as in South Africa, our duty is onward, onward, proclaiming God's word whether men will hear or whether they will forbear. A few conversions shew whether God's spirit is in a mission or not. No mission which has his approbation is entirely unsuccessful. His purposes have been fulfilled if we have been faithful. "That nation or kingdom that will not serve me shall entirely be destroyed." This has often been preceded by free offers of friendship and mercy. And many missions which he has sent in the olden time seem bad failures. Noah's preaching was a failure. Isaiah thought his so too. His fellow priests and prophets such a set of tippling bardies, how could the cause prosper? These drunken billies, every place smelling like the forecastle of a passenger steamer the first rough night by the vomiting of these greedy dogs. Poor Jeremiah sitting weeping salt tears over his people, everybody cursing the honest man, and he ill pleased with his mother for having borne him among such a set of ne'er-do-wells as could one day thrust him into a filthy muddy dungeon and the next ask him to prophesy to them, though they fully intended to do the opposite of what he should say. And Ezekiel's stiff-necked rebellious crew were no better. Paul said, All seek their own, not the things of Jesus Christ; and he knew that after his departure grievous wolves would spring up, not sparing the flock. Yet the cause of God is still carried on and on to more enlightened developments of his will and character, and the dominion is being given by the power of commerce and population unto the people of the saints of the most high. And this is an everlasting kingdom, a little stone cut [out] of a mountain without hands which shall cover the whole earth. For this time we work. May God accept our humble imperfect service.'

Livingstone wrote these words in his private journal one Sunday in January 1854, reflecting, as he often did on Sundays, on mankind's destiny and his own part in it. He was forty years old, and at the height of his powers. All his experience, his emotions, his will, all his spiritual life, were concentrated into a single objective. It carried him to the Atlantic from the heart of Africa, and then right back across the continent to the Indian Ocean and the pinnacle of fame.

He was never to achieve such success again. Livingstone's Zambezi expedition, which occupied him from 1858 to 1863, did not realise the great hopes placed on it. Its ostensible purpose was to see whether ships could navigate the Zambezi into the region which he reported to be fertile, healthy and rich in natural resources. But navigation was soon shown to be impossible because of the Kebrabasa rapids which Livingstone had bypassed when he descended the river to Quelimane on his transcontinental journey; while on closer inspection the country looked less promising. The expedition then concentrated on exploring the Shire River, a tributary of the Zambezi, which led them to Lake Nyasa (now Lake Malawi). In 1863, to everyone's relief, the government recalled the expedition which by then had turned into a bitter experience for all concerned, and from which

CENTRAL AFRICA IN ABOUT 1880

much recrimination resulted. What was worse, it was accompanied by yet another missionary disaster.

In 1861 a party of High Church Anglicans, hurriedly organised after Livingstone's visit to Cambridge and known as the Universities Mission to Central Africa (UMCA), joined Livingstone on the Zambezi. In charge was a bishop, Charles Mackenzie, recently appointed for the purpose. The members were zealous and brave, but disorganised, and like a clerical light brigade they charged into the interior of Africa to confusion and death. Fever claimed the bishop and three of his companions, and the slave-trade, active in their area, disrupted the plans of the survivors whom Bishop Tozer, Mackenzie's successor, then withdrew to the island of Zanzibar, much to Livingstone's disgust.

In 1864 Livingstone returned to England with a sense of failure, less of a missionary than ever, in the conventional sense of the word, and now an unsuccessful colonial pioneer. He had lost his wife on the Zambezi, and with her his hopes for his own future in Africa. The missionary establishment cold-shouldered him, and it looked as though he was on the shelf for good.

Then in 1865 the President of the Royal Geographical Society, Sir Roderick Murchison, invited him to return to Africa as a geographer. Livingstone jumped at the offer which brought him, via Egypt and India, to the tropical island which Krapf had found so disagreeable.

Livingstone found it no better. Stinkibar, he called it. Like Krapf he was presented to the Sultan, Said's son Majid. For Livingstone, a British grandee who came with expensive gifts from the government of India, there was coffee and sherbet and an excruciating brass band which played 'God save the Queen'. But, said Livingstone, 'it is the old, old way of living – eating, drinking, sleeping; sleeping, drinking, eating. Getting fat; slaving-dhows coming and slaving-dhows going away; bad smells; and kindly looks from English folks to each other.'

All the same Zanzibar was coming up in the world. The arrival of the French missionary establishment, followed by the High Anglicans, gave it additional status. Increased trade came its way in the 1860s, the greater part of it British and German, while the ports along the coast saw greater activity too, thanks to huge caravans moving between the growing Arab colonies inland. Mombasa was now starting to be used for parties making for the Kenya highlands, and the Sultan had built himself a new town, Dar-es-Salaam, on the mainland coast in case he was expelled from his island.

The opening of the Suez Canal was shortly to bring a new communications system into the Indian Ocean, with Zanzibar an important link in it marked by its connection in 1872 to a monthly steamer service with Aden and Natal. Instead of seeming a pestilential appendage to Arabia, Zanzibar acquired standing as the focus of interest for East Africa. Nevertheless there was a fatal lethargy about the place, which Livingstone immediately detected. The Anglican mission, still something of a private matter between the bishop and his friends, seemed as far from the heart of Africa in Zanzibar as in Lambeth Palace, while inland, Islam and the slave-trade were striding ahead.

Glad to see the backs of his own countrymen as much as of the pariah Arabs, as he called them, Livingstone sailed from Zanzibar on his birthday, 19 March 1866. 'We start this morning at 10 a.m.' he wrote in his journal. 'I trust that the Most High may prosper me in this work, granting me influence in the eyes of the heathen, and helping me to make my intercourse beneficial to them.' So began his last, longest and most bizarre journey, which was to end with his death seven years later. It took him up the River Rovuma to the southern shore of Lake Nyasa, northwards to Lake Tanganyika, westwards to Lake Mweru, southwards again to Lake Bangwelo, back to Lake Tanganyika, westwards through Manyuema territory to the River Lualaba, back to Ujiji, where Stanley met him, and finally southwards again to Lake Bangwelo, near which he died. The world only knows about this extraordinary odyssey from what it cares to read into his journals and letters, and from the evidence provided by Stanley, the only white man he saw in those seven years.

2

At the end of 1866 Livingstone wrote in his journal: 'Will try to do better in 1867, and be better – more gentle and loving. . . . May He who was full of grace and truth impress His character on mine.' He had been given a vaguely worded consular commission which could be disowned by the British government if necessary, but was a precaution in case any 'real' discoveries such as gold or diamonds came to light. He had entered Africa with a motley crowd of Indians, Africans, freed slaves and pack-animals; but gradually they fell away. His experimental use of pack-animals proved disappointing, the greater number of his followers deserted or had to be sent back, and he moved steadily further and further away from civilisation. On 1 January 1868 he wrote: 'Almighty Father, forgive the sins of the

19 *Section from Livingstone's journal, 14 January 1856*

past year for Thy Son's sake. Help me to be more profitable during this year. If I am to die this year prepare me for it.'

By November 1869, when the Suez Canal at last brought East Africa into closer contact with Europe, Livingstone had already been gone three and a half years. From time to time vague rumours of his activities had filtered down to the coast. He could have been dead for all the world cared, and one false report of his death led to somewhat off-hand obituary notices appearing in the London papers. An expedition under a naval officer, Young, was hurriedly organised to investigate what had happened. Although Young failed to make contact with Livingstone, he was satisfied that he was still alive. Little else could be done to help him.

Still Livingstone plodded on. On 1 January 1870 he wrote in his journal: 'May the Almighty help me to finish the work in hand, and retire through the Basango before the year is out. Thanks for all last year's loving kindness.'

He was then in the country of the Manyuema tribes west of the great lakes, where he remained for the whole of that year. It proved more frustrating and crippling to his health than any he had yet lived through. Attacks of pneumonia, cholera, ulcers and malaria warned him 'to retire while life lasts'. 'O Father!' he wrote on the next New Year's day, 'help me to finish this work to Thy honour.'

A year later again, 1 January 1872, almost the same words appeared in his journal: 'May the Almighty help me to finish my work this year for Christ's sake! We slept in Mosehezi Bay . . .'

He was with Stanley by now, exploring Lake Tanganyika, refreshed in body and mind by the timely appearance of the young American reporter. On his birthday that year, 19 March 1872, a few days after Stanley had left him, he noted 'Birthday. My Jesus, my king, my life, my all; I again dedicate my whole self to Thee. Accept me, and grant, O Gracious Father, that ere this year is gone I may finish my task. In Jesus' name I ask it. Amen, so let it be.'

Little more than another year of life was then left him. 'Can I hope for ultimate success?' he wrote on 19 March 1873. 'So many obstacles have arisen. Let not Satan prevail over me, Oh! my good Lord Jesus.' This was his sixtieth and last birthday. 'Thanks to the Almighty Preserver of men for sparing me thus far on the journey of life,' he added. He was then floundering in the swamps of central Africa, around Lake Bangwelo, losing pints of blood, in constant pain and making no more than a mile or two in a day. He still had with him a few faithful servants, but they had to carry his tortured body almost all the way. The entry for 25 March 1873 reads: 'Nothing earthly will make me give up my work in despair. I encourage myself in the Lord my God, and go forward.' The end was near. On 10 April he wrote: 'I am pale, bloodless, and weak from bleeding profusely ever since the 31st March last: an artery gives off a copious stream, and takes away my strength. Oh, how I long to be permitted by the Over Power to finish my work.'

After a few more days of struggle his prayer was answered. In the darkness of early morning, 1 May 1873, in a rough mud hut his servants had put up for him in the village of a chief called Chitambo, death intervened.

What was Livingstone's 'work'? Why did he use this word whenever he reflected deeply about his life, notably on his birthdays and at the beginning of each new year? What did his life, seen as a whole, add up to?

The world's answer, of course, was, and still is, to find the source of the Nile. For much of the time Livingstone gave this impression himself. It was indeed the ostensible object of his return to Africa in 1866 under the auspices of the Royal Geographical Society.

If this were really so, what more pitiful, what more absurd figure could be imagined? The quest was hopeless. The time he was taking, the distances involved, his physical condition which was exacerbated by his refusal to be operated on for piles when he was in England, to say nothing of his geographical delusion (that he was tracing the Nile system, when he was already at the same altitude as the Nile, though the river was hundreds of miles away), all this made his journey a farce. A farce, that is, if we ignore his religious inspiration and think of it only in secular terms. He would just be another in that list of men, all more or less contemporaries of his, who climbed mountains, sailed up rivers and went to the lakes of Africa 'to further science'. Men who were famous in their day, but have little to say to posterity: The Germans, Albrecht Roscher (murdered near Lake Nyasa) and Baron von der Decken (murdered on the Juba); Charles New, the first man to reach the snow-line of Mount Kilimanjaro; Samuel White Baker, rich sportsman married for the second time to a vivacious Hungarian fifteen years younger than himself, an exotic pair at the court of King Kamrasi of Bunyoro, reached via the Nile; Petherick on the White Nile, ruined by Speke's calumnies; Grant always tagging along in the rear; and of course Burton and Speke. Is there a more ludicrous spectacle than this pair, the one delirious with fever, the other so afflicted in the eyes he could barely make out a lake when he saw one, and both of them bickering wildly then and afterwards about what they had or had not found?

Similarly with Livingstone's Zambezi expedition of 1858–63, and its quarrels and intrigues, its involvement with High Anglicans, Greek texts and liturgies, its dreadful boats and missed rendezvous, its officials half-crazed with fever trying to deal with ladies turning up unexpectedly, its deaths, disappointments and bitter aftermath – leave Livingstone's Christian commitment out of it, and what material there is here for a Voltaire!

Livingstone, however, never thought of himself as a mere explorer, though he counted these men as his competitors and was always jealous they might upstage him; still less did he think of himself as a mere traveller – the very idea of it, he said, contained a lie coiled like a viper in its bosom. Like Moffat and Krapf, he despised traders with their 'brandy and water twaddle'. His 'work' was, as he once put it, a 'venture for Christ'. 'Thy work shall be rewarded. . . . And there is hope in thine end,' says the Old Testament prophet. Livingstone, who knew his Bible backwards – he read it four times through while in the Manyuema country – undoubtedly saw his own life, his mission, in the same prophetic terms. His faith rested on a single point, this hope that God would redeem his life with all its faults and turn it to an eternal purpose. Obscure though this purpose might be, and it must have seemed very obscure that May night at Chitambo's village, Livingstone never betrayed in his journals or letters or conduct any doubt as to its ultimate justification.

But just as prophetic language may be read at two levels of meaning, like a cypher, so a religious man may live at two levels of reality. Whereas with Moffat or Krapf the spiritual realities were always in the foreground of their lives, with Livingstone, a child of the industrial revolution and the Scottish Enlightenment, a believer in material progress through self-help and technology, they were often confused with the conventional wisdom of his time. Moffat and Krapf put conversion before civilisation; so did Livingstone sometimes. 'Civilisation, the lower end of our missions, ought perhaps to sink lower still. If the love of Christ enters the heart, civilisation follows in due course.' 'I appreciate the effects of commerce much, but those of Christianity much more.' More often, especially after he had given up being a conventional missionary, he put first what he called the indirect results of missions: the 'other than saving influences of Christianity', or 'the wide diffusion of better principles', and 'every effort made for the amelioration of our race'.

His was one of the most complex characters of his time, as though he had stepped from the pages of one of the masterpieces of fiction which were then appearing in Russia. At times vain and ambitious, he could be cantankerous, blind to the suffering of others and intolerant of their weaknesses. Yet as his journals show, throughout his life he was seldom without a prayer on his lips and a consciousness of the need for grace in his heart: 'I will place no value on anything I have or may possess, exept in relation to the kingdom of Christ' – 'It is difficult to say from the heart, "Thy will be done"; but I shall try' (this was after his medicine chest was stolen) – 'May the Lord clothe me with humility' – 'Ezekiel says that the Most High put His comeliness upon Jerusalem. If He does not impart of His goodness to me I shall never be good: if He does not put of His comeliness on me I shall never be comely in soul' – 'I have nothing to do but wait till He who is over all decides where I have to lay me down and die'.

No one used stronger language about Africans: 'Their mind is darkness itself' – 'Nothing can exceed the grovelling earthliness of their minds. They seem to have fallen as low in the scale of humanity as human nature can' – 'The more intimately I become acquainted with barbarians the more disgusting does heathenism become. It is inconceivably vile' – 'The Manyuema are the most bloody, callous savages I know. . . . I am heartsore, and sick of human blood'. Yet no one was as successful in communicating to Africans, by his presence alone, his message of love: 'Don't shed human blood, my friends; it has guilt not to be wiped off by water' – 'I exercise no authority but that of love and kindness'. Well did Stanley sum Livingstone up by saying that his life itself was 'a sermon acted'.

Like Moffat in Matabeleland, Livingstone witnessed much cruelty; he often came across men with ears and hands cut off, noses slit, eyes put out. At Cazembe's he had to live in the company of the chief's executioner, a dwarf who carried around swords and scissor-like instruments for cropping limbs. Yet spiritually he was always able to rise above his surroundings, either in the wonder of nature, or, as in this passage from his private journals, in an apocalyptic vision of the future:

'The obstacles to the coming of the Kingdom are mighty, but come it will for all that.
     "Then let us pray that come it may and come it will for a'that,
     That man and man the world o'er, shall brothers be for a'that."
The hard and cold unbelief which distinguished the last century, and which is still aped by would-be philosophers in the present, would sneer at our faith and call it superstition, enthusiasm etc; but were we believers in human progress and no more, there must be a glorious future for our world. Our dreams must come true, even though they are no more than dreams. The world is rolling on to the golden age. The inmates of our workhouses have more comforts than rich chieftains in Africa have; they have soap, clean linen, glass windows, and chimneys.'

In these and many similar passages, which seemingly owed more to Robert Burns and Robert Owen than to the Biblical prophets, to Joseph Wright of Derby than to William Blake, Livingstone found himself gripped by the conviction that man has a historical as well as a spiritual destiny. In other words, science and technology, if used for the glory of God, would help further the Kingdom of Heaven. But how could he personally bring that destiny nearer? He was like the Ancient Mariner, knowing in his heart that God had a purpose for him, but not knowing how it would be revealed. He inscribed a verse of Coleridge's poem on the cover of one of his notebooks.

This feeling that whatever he did was under divine control, even the most minute actions, is what gave him his spiritual strength. Any other kind of interpretation of his life and actions he dismissed as 'all gammon'. 'But for the belief that the Holy Spirit works and will work for us I should give up in despair,' he once wrote.

So he was led from being a missionary in the conventional sense to become an explorer, then a government official in command of an expedition, like Dr Andrew Smith in South Africa thirty years before, and when that ended in failure, to refuse an ordinary career in the world, such as the consulship that Frere, the governor of Bombay, offered him – where he might, after all, have done a great deal to improve the lot of others. It led him to end his life as he had really lived it all along, as a great propagandist for Africa. This was his 'work', his mission.

To us, it may seem a strange pilgrimage, but it is what gives unity and meaning to a career which otherwise might be judged erratic, wilful and wasted.

One of the most dramatic moments of his life occurred on 14 January 1856, as he was on his return journey from Loanda to the Indian Ocean. He had arrived at the confluence of the Loangwa and the Zambezi, two mighty rivers, when he found himself surrounded by a belligerent tribe who easily outnumbered his Makololo escort. It was the most dangerous situation he had ever faced, but he still found a moment to scribble down what he thought might be his last words:

'How soon I may be called to stand before him my righteous Judge I know not. All hearts are in his hands, and merciful and gracious is the Lord our God. O Jesus, grant me resignation to thy will, and entire reliance on thy powerful hand. On thy work alone I lean. But wilt thou permit me to plead for Africa? The cause is thine. What an impulse will be given to the idea that Africa is not open if I perish now. See, O Lord, how the Heathen rise up against me as they did to thy Son. I commit my way unto thee. I trust also in thee that thou wilt direct my steps. Thou givest wisdom liberally to all who ask thee. Give it to me, My Father. My family is thine; they are in the best hands. O be gracious, and all our sins do thou blot out. A guilty, weak, and helpless worm on thy kind arms I fall. Leave me not, forsake me not. I cast myself and all my cares down at thy feet. Thou knowest all I need, for time and for eternity.'

Evening came without an attack. Feeling calmer, he abandoned the idea of a secret escape by night. That had not been Nehemiah's way when the walls of Jerusalem needed building up, 'and should such a man as I flee? Nay, verily. I shall take observations for latitude and longitude tonight, though they may be the last. I feel quite calm now, thank God.'

In the morning the armed mob reappeared, still threatening. Livingstone quietly distracted them with his equipment, while his party made repeated crossings in the one canoe available, until all were on the far bank except Livingstone himself and the boat's crew. The moment came when he too must leave. 'I thanked them all for their kindness and wished them peace.' Not one spear was raised against him.

Such a baring of the soul is rare in Victorian heroes, and when he

described this incident in his book Livingstone cut out his prayer.
But wilt Thou permit me to plead for Africa? Plead not in heaven in a
sacrificial sense, but on earth and among men, plead with latitudes
and longitudes, with scientific observations and comments on native
life, with brilliant asides and insights, with all that makes his *Missionary Travels* a classic of Victorian literature.

On that occasion he was approaching his triumph. Eight years
later, his Zambezi expedition had ended in failure and recrimination,
so that he could hardly bring himself to return to England. Before
doing so, he took his boat, the *Nyassa*, on an extraordinary 2,500 mile
voyage across the Indian Ocean, an epic feat of navigation in itself. It
gave him time to think about his life and prospects, and in the course
of it he made this entry:

'Have I not laboured in vain? Am I to be cut off before I do any
thing to effect permanent improvement in Africa? I have been un-
profitable enough, but may do something yet, in giving information,
if spared. God grant that I may be more faithful than I have been,
and may He open up the way for me!'

In giving information to effect permanent improvement in Africa – these
words could stand as his epitaph. Accordingly, it was in the belief
that he would be led to reveal something to the world that Livingstone returned to Africa in 1866, exhilarated by a new adventure, but
gentler now, and still seeking the Wedding Guest to whom he could
tell his tale. And as we watch him struggling along, the months
becoming years and the years becoming a way of life, we can but
marvel at his courage and persistence that his work of propaganda
would bear fruit.

What, then, can his feelings have been when after five years of
inconclusive labour, he found that the white man who entered Ujiji
on 10 November 1871 was not a competitor, but the brash, school-
boyish correspondent of one of America's most popular newspapers?

3

Stanley is the herald of today's world of mass communications. He
travels in style, puts up at the best hotels, and in Africa takes with
him his own bath tub and silver. He has put his trust in technology
rather than psychology, in fire-power rather than moral persuasive-
ness. A whip clears his way through the crowd and a slave-chain
enforces obedience among his followers. He is not an intellectual
man, nor is he a writer in the sense of one who communicates ideas;

he is a man to whom writing is a means of earning a living. Activity is an end in itself – 'Joy's Soul lies in the doing' was his motto – and it is the activity of watching other men's activities.

It is a somewhat unlovable face which Stanley himself presents to the world, with his self-centred manner, his sneers, innuendoes and bragging, his affectations – a cigar in the corner of the mouth, a black servant boy in attendance, an assumed accent; in short, with all that the reporter finds necessary to assert his ego. But there is a directness to him, an earnest attempt at actuality, which sets him apart from other observers of the African scene.

Stanley wrote for his public, and that public was also himself; his writing was an extension of his own personality, that strange combination of precocious maturity and perpetual school-boy, of experience and innocence, which was the product of a Victorian workhouse. How many of his readers must have clawed their way along much the same path as Stanley took in the America of the mid-nineteenth century! He was an authentic frontiers-man, hot-tempered, up to all the tricks, trying to shed a disreputable past. Stanley had to make an impression, was keen to please and be praised, was technically highly competent; but he longed also to be a name in his own right,

20 *Henry M. Stanley, Discoverer of Livingstone,* from a popular contemporary print

to be the equal of those he had to write about. American Indian wars, Spanish insurgents, Persia, Turkey, the Crimea – it was all much the same to him. Here he was in Africa, but he did not know how to introduce himself to the man he had come to meet.

Actually, it was not until the following day, 11 November 1871, that Stanley made clear who he was and why he had come.

'You have heard of the *New York Herald*?' he said by way of introduction.

'Who has not heard of that despicable newspaper!' retorted Livingstone. But there was a twinkle in his eye, for he and Stanley understood each other at once. The journalist's scoop would do them each a good turn. Expressing himself deeply grateful for the American interest in his material welfare, he jumped at the opportunity for propaganda suddenly presented by Stanley's unexpected appearance there in the heart of Africa. Was it not the answer to his prayers?

For his part, Stanley realised that his achievement did not lie in reporting geographical sensations, but simply in the fact that he – and through him, that fast-growing American newspaper public – had found Livingstone when the professional fuddy-duddies of the old world had not. That in itself was his story.

Far from resenting the presence of an outsider, as the Europeans in Zanzibar had hinted, Livingstone invited Stanley to come with him back to Manyuema territory. From his point of view, what better witness to his 'discoveries' about slavery?

'Had he knocked me down he could not have more astonished me,' Stanley wrote in his diary, adding, what was very revealing in view of his subsequent career: 'I do not think I was made for an African explorer, for I detest the land most heartily.' It was all too nerve-racking, too unhealthy, too difficult! 'The blacks give an immense amount of trouble; they are too ungrateful to suit my fancy.'

He declined the offer of going to Manyuema, but suggested instead that they should explore the northern shores of Lake Tanganyika. 'Everybody', he told Livingstone, 'expects it of you,' and by everybody, of course, he meant his newspaper public. It was not serious exploration, but more like a picnic for Livingstone who soon recovered his strength and good spirits. Although Stanley suffered frequently from fever, he too enjoyed the carefree atmosphere. They raced each other on the waters of the lake, the Stars and Stripes and the Union Jack fluttering from the mastheads of their boats, and they went after the big game which abounded, Stanley delighting in Livingstone's heavy sporting gun – though Livingstone had to teach him how to harden his bullets by adding zinc to them.

From what John Kirk had told him Stanley expected to find an elusive and bad-tempered old man, who might even have gone native. Kirk had been a loyal subordinate of Livingstone on his Zambezi expedition, and Livingstone had got him his present job as British vice-consul in Zanzibar. Stanley was astonished to find how wide of the mark was his judgement of his former chief. Livingstone proved to be a man full of fun, with an astonishingly retentive memory. He was dignified, open and humble. Withal, a man with such personal integrity as Stanley had not found in six years of journalism. In effect Livingstone told him everything that mattered about his travels, throwing out stories and ideas so fast Stanley was not able to note them all down.

The explanation Livingstone gave for his movements over the last five years was plausible enough. The men Kirk had sent up from Zanzibar, he told Stanley, were the worst sort of Indian-owned slaves who mutinied when he was within a hundred miles of his goal, making it impossible for him to continue without risking certain death. Having already explored 600 miles of the watershed of central Africa, 'the central line of drainage', he was forced to return 700 miles to his supply base at Ujiji only to find his stores plundered by these worthless men from Zanzibar. 'If I had only gone one month further, I could have said "the work is done".'

Livingstone also gave a plausible explanation of his future intentions, at least it was plausible enough for Stanley, who, to tell the truth, did not greatly care once he realised that Livingstone would not return with him to the coast. Copper mines in Katanga and weird underground houses now featured in Livingstone's programme, along with the mysterious fountains of the Nile and their two hills, Mophi and Crophi, known to the ancients. With supplies which Stanley promised to send up for him, Livingstone proposed to traverse once again the rivers and lakes of his grand system, and connect them all up from their source to their junction with the Nile – or was it the Niger or the Congo? It would take him, he thought, a year and a half. He would do it alone; and he would not return to Europe until the work was finished. Duty compelled him.

Stanley took all this at its face value; only later when he retraced Livingstone's footsteps west of Lake Tanganyika did he come to understand 'the dream-life', as he put it, 'in which Livingstone passed almost all his leisure hours'. Stanley then also came to share in Livingstone's mystical idea of progress for Africa; but at the time what impressed him was the older man's sense of being under an obligation to the President of the Royal Geographical Society. In the presence of other white men, and even at the thought of them, Livingstone often showed a very worldly side to his character, as worldly as Stanley's. Plain vanity was part of it: 'No one will cut me out after this exploration is accomplished'; he 'cannot conceive' how his opinions about the Nile can be mistaken. Another motive was the possibility of financial reward to provide for his family. Stanley also discovered in Livingstone, what the public never saw, a man still brooding over past grievances.

The two men lived continuously in each other's company for four months, travelling in complete harmony. No doubt the difference in their ages contributed to this happy atmosphere. Stanley was thirty, Livingstone fifty-eight, old enough to be his father; nor is it altogether fanciful to imagine that Livingstone saw in Stanley something of his own eldest son, Robert, who to his parents' great sorrow had taken a false name and disappeared in America to enlist in the Union armies in the American Civil War, where he died of wounds. Stanley's eye-witness account of the fighting in America, of the fever-ridden hospitals and prison camps where he nearly died himself, must have made Livingstone's heart yearn for the son he had lost. Stanley promised to arrange for Robert's remains to be transferred to the cemetery at Gettysburg. 'It will be a small comfort to remember that he lies among brave men who fought and died in a noble cause,' Livingstone wrote to his daughter, Agnes. He had named one of his lakes after Abraham Lincoln.

Perhaps, too, Stanley spoke a little of his own upbringing, finding in Livingstone a sympathetic listener, and allowing himself to be gently reproached by the older man when his temper flared against his African cook.

As most people would see it, the drama of those four months lay in Livingstone's influence on Stanley. From Livingstone's point of view, however, the effect of Stanley's arrival was equally momentous. Elijah has been very jealous for God, and feels himself abandoned in the wilderness; and God sends Elisha to minister to him, 'that good brave fellow Stanley who has acted as a son to me'. The Nile sources, after all, were only a means to an end, to give their discoverer power to speak out among men about Africa. At Nyangwe on the Lualaba, the most westerly colony to date established by the Arabs, Livingstone had witnessed a frightful massacre by slave dealers of Manyuema villagers attending the busy market. He had been a helpless bystander, warned not to interfere by the leading Arab present. The incident had scorched itself on to his mind, colouring all his thoughts about Africa. And almost at once God had placed in his hands an instrument to bring the evil to light, in the person of the American reporter. Like Krapf before him, Livingstone despaired of Britain's official policy in Africa: first, for not checking the Boers in the south, then over the Portuguese and the Zambezi, now with the Arabs and the Zanzibari Sultanate. Gladly he wrote a letter to Stanley's employer for publication in the *New York Herald*: 'If my disclosures regarding the terrible Ujijian slavery should lead to the suppression of the East Coast slave trade, I shall regard that as a greater matter by far than the discovery of all the Nile sources together.'

One Sunday shortly before they parted the two men discussed the prospects for Christianity in Africa. It was after their small morning service, and Stanley expressed the scepticism of a man of the world. There were too few men, he said; the continent was too vast and the people too backward.

'How would you go about it?' Livingstone asked.

By sending in men by their hundreds, Stanley replied, and organising them properly in large centres of population among the larger tribes where their influence would gradually spread outwards – essentially the reverse of the strategy then followed by missionary societies of working inwards from the coast, and essentially the reverse of the policy of those sensible men of power, Frere, Kirk and Co., who advocated settlements of freed slaves as nuclei of civilisation.

Livingstone agreed. But someone had to make a beginning, he said; he believed he was only doing for Africa what Christ had done for Christianity in the world; that meant, sowing the seed, sacrificing himself that others might live. Dark and dreary though the night was, the day would dawn even if he did not live to see it.

He went on to speak of his loneliness, his exile from family and friends, his wanderings to and fro across Africa. 'Why was it but to be a witness of the full horror of this slave-trade?' he said. 'My business is to publish what I see, to rouse up those who have the power to stop it, once and for all. That is the beginning; but, in the end, they will also send proper teachers of the gospel, some here, and some there, and what you think ought to be done will be done in the Lord's good time.'

By this time Livingstone had accompanied Stanley to Tabora, Stanley's own supply base which was within easy reach of the coast and clear of the bandits who periodically blocked the route to Ujiji and Uganda. Livingstone agreed to wait at Tabora for his new supplies, and he gratefully took over Stanley's surplus. Perhaps they came to a financial understanding whereby the *New York Herald* would pay for any further letters Livingstone might care to write for the benefit of American readers. At Ujiji Stanley had found Living-stone a physical wreck, haggard, toothless and grey bearded, with patched-up clothes and tattered belongings; in Livingstone's own words, 'a mere ruckle of bones'. At Tabora he left him, he told his paper, looking but forty-five or fifty, 'quite hale and hearty'. 'I have not the slightest fears about his health or of any danger coming to him from the natives.'

On 14 March 1872 they parted. Eager to capitalise on his scoop, Stanley hurried away from the African countryside, with its (to him) poisonous smells and hidden dangers. Ahead lay popular fame, lecture tours, financial success with his first book, *How I Found Livingstone*, and, inevitably, bitter controversy when Stanley, as Livingstone's mouthpiece, attacked John Kirk for negligence in the matter of Livingstone's supplies. Stanley used the word 'traitor' and the British establishment reacted furiously to uphold their man in Zanzibar. Ahead, too, lay an unavoidable involvement in the tricks of his trade. At Aden on his way back to civilisation he was handed a telegram: 'You are now famous as Livingstone,' he read in the make-believe language of Fleet Street. 'More splendid achievement', he read on, 'not in history of human endeavour'. His scoop was worth a lot of advertising revenue to his paper. 'We want to make as much as can be made of it,' he was told. Not to be outdone, rival New York papers began running stories about his disreputable past, and, scandal being also very much to the *Herald's* readers' taste, his own paper exploited the allegations with exaggerated denials. It all seemed shabby compared with the welcome Stanley had looked for-ward to when he said good-bye to Livingstone at Tabora. But no one could take the memory of those months away from him. 'Fare thee well Oh Livingstone true Hero and christian,' he wrote in his journal, 'be thou healthy and prosperous wheresoever thou goest. Thy work is holy – thy mission sacred.'

As to Livingstone, ahead lay a five-month wait for his supplies, a time he spent in musing about Christian missions and Africa's history. Ever present was the thought of the slave-trade. 'To over-draw its evils is a simple impossibility.' He wrote his last letters, among them one to the *New York Herald* 'trying to enlist American zeal to stop the East Coast slave-trade: I pray for a blessing on it from the All-Gracious.' That was on 1 May. At the end of June he received a letter from his youngest son, Oswell, who was down at the coast, six weeks' marching away. Oswell had joined the Livingstone Search and Relief Expedition, organised belatedly by the Royal Geographical Society largely as a result of hearing from Stanley's

21 *Stanley (right), photographed with a companion after his return from finding Livingstone*

paper that the Americans were already in the field. But the expedition broke up in pique when they met Stanley returning in triumph, and Oswell was advised on health grounds, by Kirk, not to accompany the porters carrying his father's fresh goods. Livingstone was stricken with conflicting emotions of 'thankfulness, anxiety, and deep sorrow' at this unexpected news which brought him so near to, and yet finally separated him from, all that bound his heart to the world.

In August his reinforcements arrived at last and he set off once more for the bush and the jungle and the swamps of his rivers. There was not much more he could do to publicise Africa. He had written to Stanley's paper, as he had promised, and entrusted Stanley himself with his journals, which he knew would provide posthumous propaganda material. He had even given Stanley his famous consular cap. He had no wish to be carried off to retirement a physical wreck by another man's expedition, yet he knew better than anyone how vulnerable his constitution had become. He was risking death by continuing in Africa, and perhaps he sought it. Just as Jesus knew 'his time had come' when he heard that Greeks were asking after him, so Livingstone may have concluded that he would have to die for Africa now that the new world of mass communications was interested in him. Having cast his mantle on its young representative who had thrust his way so unexpectedly into his solitude, he had only to trust in the promise of his faith. Shortly before he left Tabora, he wrote in his journal:

'What is the atonement of Christ? It is Himself: it is the inherent and everlasting mercy of God made apparent to human eyes and ears. The everlasting love was disclosed by our Lord's life and death. It showed that God forgives, because He loves to forgive. He works by smiles if possible, if not by frowns; pain is only a means of enforcing love. If we speak of strength, lo! He is strong. The Almighty: the Over Power; the Mind of the Universe. The heart thrills at the idea of His greatness.'

4

'What is the news?'

'There is no news, I heard a few lies only!' So men used to greet each other in some African villages where everyone lived within five minutes walk of his family and neighbours. Livingstone made a point of noting the words down.

His Africa was a land of footpaths, for the most part less than a yard wide, which led from village to village, from mountain range to mountain range, through bush and forest and elephant grass higher than a man, criss-crossing in a myriad different directions like tunnels in a gigantic ants' nest. Endlessly trodden down by human feet, they seemed timeless, part of nature; they led everywhere – and nowhere. Nowhere, that is, in terms of history. For history, as the rest of the world understood it, had not entered Africa. Destiny, for most Africans, lay only in the past, from which the present was constantly receding and to which the future was linked through the spirits of the ancestors, those that were dead and those that were unborn. Bechuana chiefs, Moffat noted, were buried in their cattle kraals facing north, the direction from which their ancestors had come, and then the cattle were driven over the spot to obliterate all traces of it, the spirit of the chief joining his fellows in an invisible world of long ago.

In this Africa there was no writing, little art and generally speaking

no stone architecture or other visible record to transmit one generation's experience of earthly existence to another. In the interior of
Africa when Livingstone knew it, the wheel, the plough and the sail
were all unknown. The Manyuema people, he wrote, had come to a
'permanent halt', 'they are stationary, and improvement is unknown'. Before the coming of outsiders to Africa, the only news that
travelled along the footpaths were fables, 'lies', passed on by word of
mouth.

Suddenly, along these paths came greater lies than anyone had
ever heard before. Men who could drink boiling water (fruit salts),
who possessed two pairs of feet, a white pair for washing and a black
pair for walking, and countless other pieces of magic. Stanley put it
into words: 'The white people know everything and are very strong,'
he told an extortionate chief who tried to bar his way, remembering
something he had heard General Sherman say to a gathering of
American Indians. 'White men are different from the black. White
men do not leave their country to fight the black people, neither do
they come here to buy ivory or slaves.' They come, continued
Stanley, to explore and measure and climb mountains, to make
friends and hear good stories, and then they return to tell their own
people what they have seen.

'How is the world getting along?' Livingstone had asked Stanley.
The 'news' Stanley had to tell was about wars and revolutions,
elections, assassinations and dethronements; much as the world always
has been getting along, and always will. To Stanley's paper, to
Stanley himself, it was the 'dazzling light of civilisation . . . one of the
most exciting pages of history ever repeated'. 'I never wearied with
the strange news of Europe and America he told,' was Livingstone's
comment. 'The tumbledown of the French empire was like a dream.'

Stanley had also been able to tell Livingstone about the new canal
at Suez and a new railroad across America, both evidence of progress.
Livingstone and Stanley belonged to an age which believed in
improved communications as in civilisation itself. Letters meant
everything – hence Stanley's nervousness that he had not forewarned
Livingstone of his arrival at Ujiji, and hence too that famous line of
dialogue – mail runners were special people and the world was shaped
by a postal service however erratic and mail boats calling however
infrequently. This was what Livingstone meant by 'commerce':
something more abstract than exchange and barter in the market,
which the Arabs, after all, brought about very effectively, as could be
seen in the exotic and thriving market at Ujiji, well described by
Stanley. It was something more fundamental than trade routes and

people moving about (the Arabs were pioneers here too, and tribes like the Kamba and the Nyamwesi proved great travellers). 'Opening up' the country was another way Livingstone put it, which really meant colonies of white men protected by their own flags ensuring 'legitimate trade', which meant 'free trade', which meant western trade. 'Development' is our modern equivalent, and expatriate specialists working on contract. 'Railroads, steamships, telegraphs' wrote Livingstone, 'make the world one, and capital, like water, tends to a common level.'

All these things, of course, newspapers, notebooks, pens, paper and ink, were a white man's magic to the Africans. They were objects of superstitious awe, new idols replacing time-honoured fetishes. 'His words are words of the Book,' Kimeri had said to Krapf; and Livingstone was not always happy about using his prayer book because of the impression it gave of mumbo-jumbo to the watching Africans.

Yet the white man did, after all, possess good news – the truth – and that was why Livingstone was there. 'We cannot conceive their state of isolation and helplessness, with nothing to trust to but their charms and idols,' he wrote of the Manyuema. But why had the white man taken so long in coming? Why, Sechele asked Livingstone, had not the white man brought this good news to his ancestors? 'I thought immediately of the guilt of the church, but did not confess,' was Livingstone's response. 'My face has burned with shame while I have answered them, the Church has not cared for your souls,' was the reply of the American, Daniel Lindley. Why did not the English, who said they loved the black man, knew everything and were very strong, stop the Boers, the Portuguese, the Arabs? The only real answer was for the white man to give his life for Africans.

Meanwhile there was a cause to be won which necessitated reaching for the dubious instrument which Stanley wielded so expertly. It meant entering that world of faked date-lines, re-written copy and showy headlines; an equivocal world of polemics and advertisement. There was no denying that books of travel played an important part in stimulating the missionary movement, and there are countless testimonies to the impact the writings of Livingstone and Stanley made on others. Livingstone's *Missionary Travels*, for instance, went through fourteen editions, totalling 70,000 copies. Yet, there is always the danger that publicising a cause may lead to publicising a self, that power sought as a means – even the power of communication technique – will destroy the user. Moffat and Krapf hated publicity. Livingstone knew its value. Though he shunned it for himself, his use of language and his conspicuous wearing of his consular cap wherever he went in Britain showed he had a flair for exploiting it. But publicity was Stanley's metier and it often left him with bitter feelings.

In retrospect Stanley came to believe that his historic journey to find Livingstone had been the decisive religious experience of his life. Not, as most people have thought, the encounter with Livingstone himself so much as the experience of actually being in Africa. He was travelling, he explained, with the Bible and a quantity of old numbers of the *New York Herald* in which his goods were packed. Reading the two in alternating states of fever and *ennui*, he began to see how shallow was the world's view of reality as expressed in newspaper stories, obituaries, crime-reports, 'mere gutter-matter', profiles of fashionable personalities – everything, in fact, by which a journalist lives in the metropolis. In contrast, the Bible induced 'a charm peculiarly appropriate to the deep melancholy of African scenery'. He seems to have meant by this – and he singled out the book of Job and the Psalms – that he was brought to surrender himself to the Creator of all things in contemplating the immensity of the continent and the huge difference in cultural achievement between its people and the civilisation of Europe and America. It was as though he were stepping back into the world of the Old Testament.

'I flung myself on my knees', he recorded, 'and poured out my soul utterly in secret prayer to Him from whom I had been so long estranged, to Him who had led me here mysteriously into Africa, there to reveal Himself, and His will.'

Stanley kept it to himself at the time. *How I Found Livingstone* is a very egotistical work, as Stanley was the first to admit, and there is no trace in it of a deep religious experience. The impression Stanley leaves in his later writings, and especially in his unfinished autobiography, is of a man doggedly holding on to a truth he knows he is born with, but is in danger of losing in the rackety business of making his way in the world. Though he remained as reticent about his spiritual feelings as about his human origins, nevertheless the conviction that there was a God who answered prayer and that this God had a purpose for him grew steadily thoughout his life. And when at last he came to write his account of the Emin Relief Expedition, *In Darkest Africa*, he felt bound to confess that conviction in public.

What Stanley seems to have found in Livingstone was confirmation that 'with religious conviction we can make real and substantial progress ... without it, so-called progress is empty and impermanent.'

That, and his reception in England in 1872, turned him from a mere observer of events into a man of action. Although he continued to be a successful writer, it was not only with his pen that he strove to work out his destiny, but with his whole self.

In February 1874 he was returning from covering the Ashanti campaign in West Africa when he was handed a telegram. Livingstone was dead. It had taken nine months for the news to reach the outside world. To Stanley, it was the call to action. He would close the gap in the ranks himself. 'May I be selected to succeed him in opening up Africa to the shining light of Christianity!' he wrote in his diary. 'My methods, however, will not be Livingstone's. Each man has his own way. . . . May Livingstone's God be with me as He was with him in all his loneliness, and direct me as He wills. I can only vow to be obedient, and not to slacken.'

5

On 18 April 1874, in a moving service, Livingstone's remains were buried in the nave of Westminster Abbey. He was treated as a national hero and the missionary establishment of Britain turned out to honour his memory, even though it had effectively disowned him for the last ten years of his life. The story of how his servants had eviscerated the corpse of its vital organs and then carried the dried up remains a thousand miles through the bush, hidden in a bale of cotton, became overnight a favourite theme of missionary propaganda. It did not occur to the public to blame Livingstone for leaving his followers in the lurch in a country where they had no friends, nor was it generally realised that they had to resort to this dangerous expedient in order to be able to regain their homes with proof that they had not murdered, robbed or deserted their master. Perhaps the most moving sight at the graveside was the tall, patriarchal figure of Robert Moffat, who had recently lost his own grandson on the final expedition to find Livingstone.

The world which sneered at Stanley hailed Livingstone's effigy with equal extravagance. 'One of the greatest men of the human race,' wrote the surgeon who examined the mummified relics in London and identified them as Livingstone's from the bad setting of the arm-bone, the result of being mauled by a lion shortly after his first arrival in Africa. 'The greatest man of his generation,' wrote Florence Nightingale to Livingstone's daughter Agnes. Eulogies from *Punch*, from colonial governors and business men, and from many

people who had never known him, all went into the manufacture of a
Victorian saint. By his death Livingstone won greater publicity than
he could ever have hoped for during his life.

Many facts contributed to this outcome. In Livingstone's day
national heroes were all the rage in Britain, following the Indian
Mutiny and the Crimean War, as indeed were villains, especially if
they were black, brown or yellow, Roman Catholic, Slav or French.
Then again, political and educational reforms had introduced a new
populism into British life, which was soon to be reflected in the rise of
cheap daily papers. The idea of self-help, which Livingstone per-
sonified and in which he strongly believed, was also fashionable.
Samuel Smiles' famous work, *Self Help*, was published two years
after Livingstone's *Missionary Travels*, and Smiles cited Livingstone's
energy and courage with admiration. To many, Livingstone was a
shining example of social advancement, a meritorious achievement
in that age.

Stanley provided another explanation. In 1876, when he was back
in Africa and musing on Livingstone's fate, he wrote to an American
friend that he felt the English public had never understood Livingstone and had thought him even a bit of a humbug who did not write
as he really felt, 'in plain English . . . that he was something of an old
hypocrite'. It was a perceptive comment – and Stanley was sensitive
to these things – which does much to explain his own determination
to set the record straight.

The fact is that the news of Livingstone's death produced an
unprecedented emotional response in Britain. Whether or not because
they felt guilty, as Stanley suggested, men and societies who had held
aloof from his ideas were shamed into renewing their efforts. Money
and offers of service suddenly showed an upturn, though these were
years of economic depression in Britain. So much so that in 1875 the
UMCA ventured back onto the mainland with a base at Bagamoyo
centred on a nucleus of freed slaves, Tozer having finally left Zanzibar a broken man. In due course they made contact with Kimeri's
successor, some twenty years after Krapf had showed the way. Like
the famous Exeter Hall meeting in 1840, which Livingstone had
attended as a young man, his funeral drew together all kinds of
people keen to undertake 'a venture for Christ', not least his native
countrymen.

Among those standing round Livingstone's grave at Westminster
Abbey on 18 April 1874 was James Stewart of the Scottish Free
Church, who happened to be on leave from Lovedale, the Scottish
missionary institute in South Africa which enjoyed quasi-colonial

status as an industrial training centre. Stewart had already played, and was to play again, an equivocal role in the missionary drama. Like Livingstone, he had a complex character and was personally very ambitious. In 1861–62, at considerable risk, he had come out to the Zambezi to advise his Scottish co-religionists on missionary openings in the area Livingstone was working in, incidentally acting as escort to Mary Livingstone in circumstances which added to the atmosphere of intrigue and scandal surrounding that unfortunate expedition. Stewart was present at her death, an eyewitness to the difficulties encountered by the Anglican missionaries and himself a victim of acute depression brought on by fever and hardship. His report did not inspire his backers to commit themselves to central Africa and he eventually took up the post of Principal of the Lovedale Institute, whence he cast tentative looks towards the north as a field for personal achievement, a curious echo of Livingstone's ambition. 'I wish to be first,' Stewart wrote, 'I would not care to follow after the path had been opened.'

Returning to Scotland from Livingstone's funeral Stewart brought up again the idea of a mission to the Nyasa region, to be named Livingstonia in his memory. Not in response to a request from a chief or a tribe, but just because it was associated with Livingstone's explorations. The idea caught fire at once among the all-important Glasgow business-men with whom Stewart had good contacts; money for the mission was soon subscribed, and shortly afterwards they formed a limited company to trade in the area as well. Livingstonia was advertised as 'a great centre of commerce, civilisation and Christianity' – a missionary factory, as it were. In May 1875 an expedition was ready to leave Britain and in October the same year it was at Lake Nyasa. The man appointed to lead it, however, was not Stewart himself, but Young, the sailor and former colleague of Livingstone, chosen because of his previous experience of the area and knowledge of boats, a key matter in a lake-side settlement. Though Stewart played an important part in the early days of the mission, it owed its success to the genius of Robert Laws, like Livingstone a doctor and self-made man, who spent forty years in its service.

Associated with it was an Established Church of Scotland mission which was a more explicitly colonial venture, based on a nucleus of freed slaves, the pattern adopted at Zanzibar and Mombasa by English missions and advocated by the 'experts' in the area. As a result this Blantyre mission, which took its name from Livingstone's birthplace on the Clyde, ran into difficulties over questions of civil jurisdiction, difficulties which were exploited in the British press by a travel-writer who happened to pass that way, so providing a field day for critics. Despite this, the two sister missions were to form the nucleus of the future colony of Nyasaland (now Malawi), and were powerful influences in the development of the future Northern Rhodesia (Zambia) and Kenya.

John Kirk was also at that funeral in Westminster Abbey. A vain and dogmatic Scot, well known in Zanzibar for telling tall stories, Kirk had risen from being Agency Surgeon, the job Livingstone found for him, to Consul and Political Agent, in which capacity he was heir to Hamerton's policy of bolstering the Sultan's authority to further British interests in the Indian Ocean. He was a cool diplomatist, dedicated to his job, with powerful friends in England to defend him against Stanley's criticisms and the unmistakably sour feelings Livingstone expressed in letters about him.

On the face of it, Kirk's regime appeared to give Britain leverage against the slave-trade without the necessity of direct intervention in the government of East African peoples. To Kirk and the men of power in London and Bombay, most of them good Anglican churchgoers and friends of missions, this approach seemed justified on high moral principle. They could congratulate themselves that by merely threatening a naval blockade, the Sultan was brought to sign another treaty banning the trade at sea. He further agreed to close the official slave-market in Zanzibar itself. The date, 5 June 1873, could even be linked in history books in a mysteriously providential way with Livingstone's death a month before.

To the missionaries on the ground, however, and to all those who penetrated the interior, it was as much of a sham as in Krapf's day, well described by Charles New, one of the Methodists at Ribe, as 'an over-cautious policy and a long-winded diplomacy'. Nor was it fair to Livingstone's own last writings.

Livingstone could not be dismissed like Krapf for being a foreigner and a meddler in politics. But as Stanley was the only white man to have spoken to him during the last seven years of his life, the official mind retreated behind the pretence that the American reporter had whispered, Iago-like, into the older man's ear when he was at his most vulnerable, in order to stir up trouble between old friends. Livingstone's own complaints about the way things were done in Zanzibar – which meant by Kirk – were thus attributed to Stanley's prejudice.

The controversy was to continue long after Livingstone's funeral. But there could be no hiding the fact that the words inscribed on

Livingstone's tomb, to be read by countless visitors to Westminster Abbey, were prompted by Stanley's arrival at Ujiji and the new hope he brought with him: 'All I can add in my solitude, is, may Heaven's rich blessing come down on everyone, American, English, or Turk, who will help to heal this open sore of the world.' Claimed as Livingstone's 'last words', they were actually written fully a year before his death during his wait at Tabora in the letter, to which he referred in his journal on 1 May 1872, destined for the *New York Herald*. Hence Livingstone's priority – *American*, English, Turk.

It was Livingstone's final appeal to the world above the head of the British government, and beyond diplomacy, nationality and churches, beyond race and colour and empire, an appeal to that new public opinion with which Livingstone instinctively identified himself, and of which Stanley of all those at Westminster Abbey was the truest representative. It was Stanley who had inspired his epitaph.

6

With characteristic energy, Stanley was first off the mark to pick up Livingstone's work. He had returned to England to take a leading place as one of the pall-bearers at Livingstone's funeral. In June the same year he put to the London *Daily Telegraph* and his own *New York Herald* a scheme whereby they should jointly sponsor an expedition, led by himself, to clear up all the geographical riddles of central Africa which had so bewildered Livingstone. Both papers agreed at once. Before the year was out he had paid a quick visit to America, organised his expedition and returned to Zanzibar to set out once more for the interior.

He was not to emerge again until August 1877, a thousand days later, when he appeared on the Atlantic coast of Africa having achieved all his objectives. He had successfully traced the River Congo some 1,800 miles from the heart of the continent to its mouth, through territory which till then had been thought impenetrable, a journey which involved him in thirty-two fights and in negotiating fifty-seven cataracts, waterfalls and rapids. It was the most spectacular African adventure ever attempted, before or since. More than Burton, Speke or Baker, more than Livingstone even, he showed that Europeans suitably equipped in material and morale could master Africa as they were mastering all other parts of the globe. With one daring stroke he swept away the aura of mystery in which the giant continent had hitherto been enveloped, thus exposing it, for good or ill, to the new forces at work in the world.

The missionary societies of Britain followed hard on his heels. During the three years that he took to complete his work, they succeeded in planting themselves, or were on the way to plant themselves, on the shores of Lake Nyasa, Lake Tanganyika and Lake Victoria. It was not all Stanley's doing, of course, though undoubtedly his physical success contributed powerfully to the overall sense of new commitment. In the case of Uganda, however, it was as a direct result of his own activities.

In April 1875 Stanley arrived at the court of Mutesa, King of Uganda, of whom the outside world had first heard from Speke in 1862 as a bloodthirsty and neurotic despot. Technically he was only ruler of the Baganda, a large tribe strategically situated on the northern shores of Lake Victoria, but he exercised a wide imperium over what was loosely known as Uganda. Stanley's first impression of Mutesa was of overwhelming respect. 'I see in him the light that shall

22 *Mutesa, with his chiefs*, illustration from *Through the Dark Continent*

lighten the darkness of this benighted region. . . . In him I see the possible fruition of Livingstone's hopes.' Though he came to modify this view of Mutesa's character, Stanley was convinced that his kingdom was ideal for a Christian mission.

The change in Mutesa from the whimsical tyrant of Speke's description Stanley attributed to the influence of Islam, introduced by Arabs who had come to Uganda in ever-increasing numbers over the last two decades, dazzling him with their gifts and sophistication.

Mutesa's position and the supremacy of the Baganda were disputed by other powerful tribes to the north who stood between Uganda and the expanding Egyptian empire of the Sudan. Contact with Zanzibar gave Mutesa much needed material support, and his men had been travelling to the coast for support for the last decade. Livingstone had met a party of them when he was waiting at Tabora. They were returning with a large quantity of gunpowder which they had procured from the Arabs, but ran into difficulties due to the unsettled state of the caravan route.

But if Stanley was impressed by Mutesa, Mutesa was equally impressed by Stanley. The Expedition's leader lost no time in expounding those religious truths, soundly based on the Bible, which he had absorbed in his Welsh orphanage. Stanley's uncomplicated teaching captivated Mutesa's imagination. 'Now, Stamlee, tell me and my chiefs what you know of the angels!' He was strongly reassured also by the eleventh commandment which Stanley, on the authority of the New Testament, appended to Moses' ten: 'Honour and respect the Kings, for they are the envoys of God.'

By a strange coincidence, Stanley found that at the very moment of his own arrival another white man was on his way to Uganda. He turned out to be a Frenchman, Ernest Linant de Bellefonds, the son of an old White Nile explorer, who came at the head of a company of Egyptian soldiers. As luck would have it, de Bellefonds was a Protestant, so that when Mutesa questioned him about Christianity, he repeated Stanley's Bible stories in almost identical terms. That two white men should come at the same moment from opposite ends of the world to his kingdom, and be of one mind about the nature of God, made a powerful impact on Mutesa, indeed it seemed a miracle. He asked Stanley for Christian teachers. Stanley had brought with him from Zanzibar an ex-slave boy from the Anglican mission on the island. After some hesitation he agreed to leave him behind under Mutesa's protection to translate passages from the Bible and start a church. And in a famous dispatch, which reached Britain in November 1875, he broadcast Mutesa's appeal to the outside world:

'Oh! that some pious, practical missionary would come here! What a field and harvest ripe for the sickle of civilisation!'

Reading Stanley's report in a German newspaper, Ludwig Krapf wrote to speed his old society, the CMS, to action. He saw at once that it was a race with Islam. Krapf had been approached by an old supporter, the eccentric millionaire hermit of Leeds, Robert Arthington, with an offer to finance a mission to Uganda led by the veteran German himself and drawn from the continental societies Krapf was in touch with. Sadly, he could not do it. Meanwhile the CMS had received an anonymous offer of money on condition it moved directly to the interior – a policy which met with much head-shaking by those cautious men. But the offer was too good to refuse and within a month the new policy had been adopted. In June 1876 an advance party of the new mission was at Zanzibar; a year later they were in Uganda where, in November 1878, they were joined by the redoubtable Alexander Mackay, whose name is inseparable from the history of the church in Uganda.

In commiserating with his father-in-law over a piece of slander by his missionary colleagues Livingstone propounded a law: where a man thinks himself least vulnerable, there the world will attack most savagely. Moffat had just been accused of covetousness, though no man in Africa showed less concern over money; Livingstone himself was to be accused of cowardice in face of the Boers and Krapf of meddling in politics, both preposterous but hurtful charges. Now it was Stanley's turn. On this, the greatest of all African expeditions, he was accused of superficiality and sensationalism, of being a mere 'penny-a-liner' who laid on battles for the sake of his newspaper and was gulled by pagan rulers. Even Arthington wrote of him in quaintly reproachful terms.

Stanley's journalistic methods, his egotism, the frankness of his sentiments and the openness of his conduct have masked from later generations the sheer good sense of his reports and his breadth of vision. It was not an Anglican bishop and university-trained men that Stanley appealed for, but Christian doctors, agricultural experts and skilled workers; he did not ask for a mission tied to a sect or a home church, or even to a western power, but for a commitment by 'the entire white race' to receive Africa into world civilisation on equal terms.

Other travellers like Baker and Burton had dismissed the African as incapable of advancing in the world. Some, like Cameron, saw the continent largely in terms of meeting the requirements of European industry at a time of economic recession, that is, as a market for the export of cheap western products, the manufacture of which would give employment to Europe's industrial poor.

Stanley saw Africans as fellow members of the human race, capable of love, gratitude and nobility, and able to attain all the attributes of civilised man. They were therefore subject to the same moral law as himself. Because of his own stern childhood, his values were paternalistic and he placed greater emphasis, perhaps, on obedience than love, just as in his religion he dwelt more on chastisement by Jehovah than on the atonement of Christ. Though deeply degraded by centuries of barbarism – and Stanley pointed out that the same was true of the inhabitants of Ancient Britain before the arrival of Christianity – Africans were aware of their moral plight. 'It is, therefore, a duty imposed upon us by the religion we profess, and by the sacred command of the Son of God, to help them out of the deplorable state they are now in.' In writing like this Stanley showed himself to be more than a mere adventurer; he was, in the widest sense, a missionary like Livingstone. And though Stanley was never without critics in Europe, nevertheless wherever he went in Africa his name was respected and his methods endorsed by Europeans and Africans alike.

Stanley left Uganda without knowing how his dispatch would be received, or even if it would reach the outside world. The chance encounter with another white man had led him to break the sequence of his reports in order to send those relating to his first impressions of Uganda by de Bellefonds via the Nile route and Cairo; the remainder, dealing with his subsequent circumnavigation of Lake Victoria, went by Arabs via Zanzibar and actually reached their destination first, causing a momentary rift between his English and American sponsors.

Quite fortuitously, therefore, the public were prepared for the famous letter about Uganda through 'human interest' material gathered after it had been written. Furthermore, the Uganda letter came with a legend attached to it saying that it was only found by chance in de Bellefond's blood-stained boots after he had been killed on the Nile. This made good headlines which helped publicise the Uganda appeal and seemed to add to the providential nature of the case. Krapf, for example, said it was 'the most remarkable point in the whole affair'. The story was not properly disproved until many years later. These technical matters, connected with the mechanics of communication in Stanley's day, and analogous to modern techniques of processing newsreel material, add an extra dimension of fantasy to the historical record.

As Stanley advanced through Africa delays of nine or twelve months took place between the writing of his reports and their publication. Thus another famous dispatch, dated 29 July 1875, described how he had returned to punish a lake-side tribe who had almost killed him on his way to Uganda. It was published in August the following year and at once brought forth protests from his opponents, on the grounds, among others, that he was flying the British and American flags at the time and had no right to do so. The professional humanitarians in Britain, enraged at Stanley's earlier handling of Kirk, called for him to be hanged on the site of his exploits and would hereafter never lose an opportunity to denounce his methods. They would always contrast him unfavourably with Livingstone, forgetting that the Livingstone of *Missionary Travels* was fully prepared to 'cut his way through' opposition with his Makololo warriors and had written: 'the pugnacious spirit is one of the necessities of life'. Stanley's technique was to be regularly employed a decade or so later when colonial regimes asserted 'law and order' in their territories.

In October 1876 Stanley reached Nyangwe, the most westerly depot of the Arabs located on the great river which Livingstone called the Lualaba and believed, contrary to all geographical sense, to be the Nile. Some 300 miles west of Lake Tanganyika, it was the last point where contact with the outside world was possible. Beyond stretched the awesome rain forests of the Congo, a primeval world of unknown extent where the sun's rays never penetrated. 'Go and tell your kind you have seen silence,' Stanley imagined their tall grey shafts saying when he ventured alone into their shadows.

At Nyangwe Livingstone had been forced to turn back when his supplies ran low and his servants threatened mutiny. Cameron had followed his trail there after meeting the party bearing his corpse. But he too shrank from plunging alone into the forests and had turned south-west to reach the Atlantic at Benguela in Angola, a notable but rather pointless journey which left the riddle of the river unsolved.

What Stanley had accomplished was creditable enough. As far as East Africa was concerned there was little further justification for an expensive journalistic expedition. At Nyangwe he had to decide what to do next.

Had he chosen to return straight to Zanzibar, or make the detour southwards to the Zambezi which he contemplated, Stanley was certain of an honoured place as a geographer and missionary pioneer. Any of the societies then considering Africa would have welcomed his services.

23 *Heads for the North and the Lualaba; tails for the South and Katanga*, illustration from *Through the Dark Continent*

But he did not choose to do so. In a celebrated passage he later described how he tossed a coin with Frank Pocock, his surviving European assistant, heads onwards, tails southwards and back. Six times in a row the coin said back. They ignored it. Stanley would not let blind fate rule his destiny. If he was to be martyred, perhaps eaten by cannibals, it must be for a grander cause than geography. Where Livingstone imagined himself to be the Ancient Mariner, Stanley imagined himself, in retrospect at least, to be like Tennyson's Ulysses. He was resolved to go forward to the ocean or find death in the attempt. The beyond claimed him as it had claimed Livingstone, and his destiny, he was convinced, lay in the unknown, in those unexplored regions which were peopled, the Arabs told him, by cannibals, pygmies and gorillas. If he was to die in Africa, then it must be for Africa; die not for discovery for its own sake – that fatuous search for the source of a river or the top of a mountain 'because it is there' – but in faith that discovery was God's work and would lead to the redemption of Africa.

There was another factor. Stanley had left England before Livingstone's *Last Journals* were published. Although he must have seen the originals, he had not studied them properly, if at all.

Hitherto he had resisted the temptation to reflect overmuch on Livingstone, partly from discretion, and partly because as he retraced Livingstone's steps he came to feel that he really had been wandering aimlessly in the last years of his life, wasting his energies because of his religious mysticism and sacrificing himself in pursuit of a Biblical will-o'-the-wisp. It was a remarkably accurate assessment of Livingstone's condition as revealed in the *Last Journals*.

Even so, Livingstone's shadow had been with him everywhere. 'Was he not a good man?' the Arabs would say to him whenever he mentioned Livingstone's name. At Ujiji he found the hut they had shared burnt down and he wasted no time on sentimental musings. But at Nyangwe, as he paused to decide his own fate, his thoughts were dominated by memories of his predecessor and his mission.

It was at Nyangwe that Livingstone had witnessed the massacre by Arab slavers of scores of innocent Africans attending the village market. More than anything else this experience convinced him of his mission and gave point to his last journey, if not to the whole of his life.

Yet the outside world had not moved in response to Livingstone's appeal, apart from those diplomatic gestures at Zanzibar. In what he judged might be his last words to the world Stanley brought the account up to date. It would serve as his testament should he not return alive from the beyond. In a brilliant dispatch he exposed the whole Zanzibari system, from the 'small private retail dealings' which could be seen near the coast, and which civilised men found no reason to object to, to the wholesale business of the interior rarely witnessed by white men, where at centres like Ujiji and Nyangwe slaves were herded together in pens ready for shipment to the coast. Frank Pocock had been reduced to nervous despair when he had had to cross Lake Tanganyika in a slave boat. 'Here', he wrote home to his parents, 'I hear always the roar of the sea on the shore of wild Tanganyika, or some poor wretch screaming for mercy who is being beaten by a slave-dealer.' It was in the Manyuema country that Stanley now saw the crop being harvested. Morally speaking, he concluded, as Krapf had done thirty years before, it all depended on Britain's friendship with the tinpot Sultan of Zanzibar and his villainous subjects.

So Stanley paid off a final debt to Livingstone's memory. His decision to go forward from Nyangwe freed him at last from his predecessor's shadow. He felt like a prophet now, he wrote to his friend Edward King, but whether his destiny would be revealed to himself in his life or to the world through his death, he could not say.

Nor did he much care. The perspectives of Africa induced this spiritual vertigo, so that the 'eternal, dreamless rest' of death was at times to be welcomed as relief from the vexations of travel. Stanley was not a contemplative man and his writings in this vein, his 'thoughts from notebooks', are of a deadening banality. At Nyangwe, at the uttermost limit of contact with the world, he knew at last the futility of words, feeling, as Livingstone had done, that he must write his testament with his life – 'Joy's soul lies in the doing.'

Christmas Day 1876 was celebrated, out there in the back of beyond, with a great farewell banquet for the Arabs. There were games, speeches and presents all round. Stanley had made a contract with Tippu Tip, the most audacious of the Arab freebooters, to escort him part of the way into the rain-forests until his own men were clear of the temptation to desert. The Arab could not face completing his side of the bargain, and they were mutually relieved to separate. Tippu Tip certainly never expected to hear anything more of Stanley; nor could Stanley have foreseen how their paths would cross again in these very rain-forests when, fifteen years later, he was to return from the other direction to relieve Emin Pasha in Equatoria. Tippu Tip's treachery on that occasion finally convinced Stanley of the need for Europe to intervene forcibly in Africa.

'The unknown half of Africa shall be revealed,' he told his people as they launched their boats and let the current take them into mid-stream, though no one could tell who would live to see it.

Five months later he emerged at the mouth of the Congo after a series of adventures which to be fully appreciated have to be read in his own account, published under the title *Through the Dark Continent*. In all he had lost about two thirds of his force, including all three Europeans, Frank Pocock being drowned on the final descent, to Stanley's great sorrow.

Stanley had revealed that the highway to the interior which everyone had talked about for the last half-century and which had eluded all other explorers did exist after all. With extraordinary intuition Robert Arthington, hidden away in his bare room in Leeds, had guessed that the Congo would prove to be Stanley's river. Three months before Stanley reappeared, he offered to finance Baptist missionaries working eastwards up the river and across the continent from the Atlantic, so fulfilling Krapf's vision of a chain of stations across Africa meeting on Lake Tanganyika.

To use a phrase much abused by Stanley's profession, Africa would never be the same again. Nor, in a way, would Stanley. In December 1877 he settled all claims from the survivors of his party in Zanzibar and returned to Europe. Waiting for him was the subtle King of the Belgians, Leopold II, a skilled player of the game of secret diplomacy, aliases and bribes. Although in America both Houses of Congress hailed Stanley's feat with a unanimous vote of thanks, in Britain the public were largely indifferent to his urging that his work be followed up. Accordingly, in December 1878 he entered Leopold's service and a new life of official duties, exchanging the role of journalist for that of a maker of states.

Eight months later he was back at the mouth of the Congo on behalf of his royal master. For the next five years, with unstinting energy, Stanley then laboured to build up a communications and administrative system to exploit the resources of that part of the continent which could be reached by the mighty river. It meant blasting roadways, making treaties with native chiefs, supervising porters and undertaking arduous trips up and down its waterways. What is now the Republic of Zaire was largely Stanley's creation and it earned him his African name of 'Bula Matari', Breaker of Rocks. For some further years he remained under contract to Leopold, but was prevented from completing his work on the Congo by French diplomacy. He became an adviser to statesmen, appeared at international conferences and was seen in the company of the rich and the powerful. One stirring African adventure was left him, but it has no part in this narrative. So he passes into the wings. After that first descent of the Congo, his work was done, and the stage was set for a new protagonist, the Roman Catholic Archbishop of Algiers.

CHAPTER SIX

PRIMATE OF AFRICA

24 *Biskra, on the edge of the Sahara, Lavigerie's retreat in later years*, from Ormsby's *North Africa*, 1864

I

On the crest of a hill overlooking the bay of Algiers stands a strange legacy of French occupation. Outwardly Moorish in its domes and decorated tiles, Notre Dame d'Afrique is emphatically European inside. Unlike the great cathedrals of Europe, which rose directly out of the religious experience of the people who toiled and worshipped in their shade, this North African church was built by a conquering civilisation as a proud symbol. The French could have chosen no better site. The doors of Notre Dame d'Afrique open onto a breathtaking view of the Mediterranean, across which lies the homeland of the conquerors. What was once no more than a shrine of prayer for safety at sea became a Christian standard on a heathen shore.

Cool and serene Our Lady of Africa presides inside. She stands on a tall pedestal behind the great altar, clothed in a gorgeous robe of

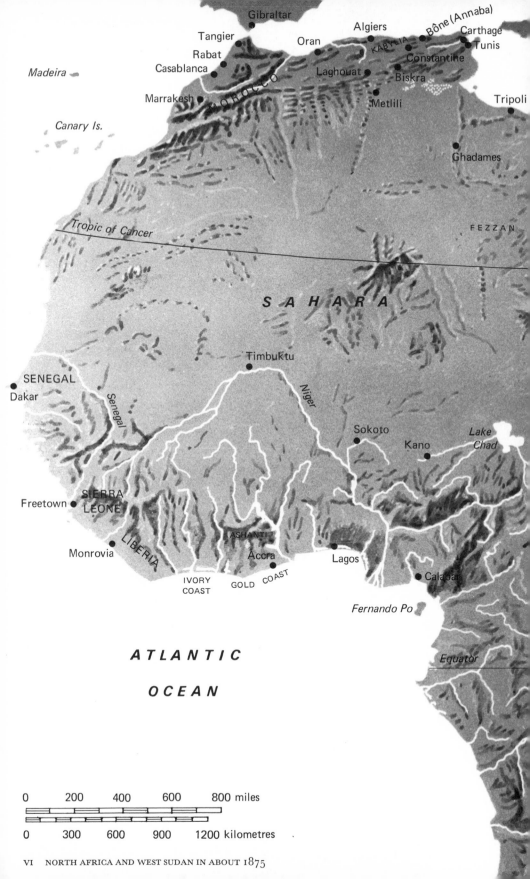

Madeira

Canary Is.

Gibraltar
Tangier
Rabat
Casablanca
Marrakesh
MOROCCO

Oran
Algiers
KABYLIA
Bône (Annaba)
Carthage
Tunis
Constantine
Laghouat
Biskra
Metlili

Tripoli

Ghadames

Tropic of Cancer

FEZZAN

S A H A R A

Timbuktu

Niger

SENEGAL
Dakar

Senegal

Sokoto
Kano

Lake
Chad

Freetown
SIERRA
LEONE

LIBERIA
Monrovia

ASHANTI
Accra
IVORY
COAST
GOLD COAST

Lagos

Calabar

Fernando Po

A T L A N T I C

O C E A N

Equator

| 0 | 200 | 400 | 600 | 800 miles |

| 0 | 300 | 600 | 900 | 1200 kilometres |

VI   NORTH AFRICA AND WEST SUDAN IN ABOUT 1875

blue and gold and crowned with a gilded tiara. Her skin is noticeably dark in colour. High above her head on the inside of the central dome a flamboyant painting depicts a group of European prelates imploring her aid at the consecration of the church. An inscription reads 'Our Lady of Africa pray for us and the Mussulmans'.

Notre Dame d'Afrique was begun in 1854, the year of the dogma of the Immaculate Conception, and finally consecrated in 1872. But it was in 1879 that it saw what was, on any account, one of the most extraordinary scenes yet played in the missionary drama.

On 20 June that year a new kind of missionary caravan was dedicated to the protection of Our Lady of Africa. It consisted of reinforcements to a pioneer band of priests which had set out for East Africa the year before, the Roman Catholic response to Stanley's great adventure. To discipline porters and fight off robbers, six former papal zouaves, four Belgians and two Scotsmen, had been enrolled to escort this new caravan on its long and perilous journey. The zouaves were France's Berber mercenaries, from which pious Frenchmen had taken the idea of organising a special European corps to serve in Rome. They were a kind of religious Foreign Legion, their uniforms being modelled on those of the Moorish cavalry. They had been disbanded in 1870, but when the need arose for armed guards to accompany priests into Africa, there had been no lack of volunteers. Now these six in their exotic dress came to make their last vows and to receive the final blessing of their church.

The Archbishop of Algiers conducted the service in person. A majestic figure, dressed in a great red and gold cope, he stood like a latter-day Joshua on the steps of the high altar to intercede with God for his missionary army, whose swords lay at his feet. As the ceremony reached its climax, one by one the volunteer soldiers approached him to receive back their swords from his hands. 'Use this sword', the Archbishop said, 'in God's service only and never wield it unjustly.' Standing in a shaft of sunlight he allowed its rays to play on the ornaments of his episcopal cross and on the steel blades of the swords, sending brilliant flashes of colour around the solemn assembly. The six men then knelt for his blessing. The Archbishop drew each man's weapon from its sheath and dubbed him on the shoulder. 'Be a soldier of peace,' he said to each one in turn, 'be courageous and true and devout.' Finally, he placed round every man's neck a small crucifix, to be worn until their engagements were ended, and sent them on their way with his kiss of peace.

It is in a series of magnificent set-pieces like this that Charles Martial Allemand-Lavigerie moves through history. He was a

Marshal of France, but in command of a religious order of his own making, a missionary statesman whom his contemporaries compared with Richelieu. Like Livingstone he was given a grand vision for the redemption of Africa, and it took him into the jungle of ecclesiastical politics and European statecraft. The solitary Protestant in the wastes of heathen Africa turned from the degradation that was all around him to the word of scripture; Lavigerie, facing spiritual degradation in the political arena in which he had to move, found the sacraments of his church as necessary and as consoling. Where Livingstone reached for publicity to further his cause, and found it in Stanley, Lavigerie reached for the power of the state, and found it in Republican France.

He was a man of many parts. Like St Paul he set out to be all things to all men, so that he might win all to his church. He was a great builder: of churches, seminaries, schools and hospitals; he turned his hand to history, archaeology and anthropology; he concerned himself closely with horticulture and was the first to introduce the muscat grape to North Africa, for which he was recognised as 'le premier colon de l'Algérie'. He was a successful educationist, social worker and propagandist. A stickler for etiquette, especially from French officials; an ascetic, who made a regular practice of contemplating death and who several times asked for the last rites; a sufferer from acute rheumatism which periodically took him off to European resorts for lengthy cures; a master of theatre, who never lost an opportunity to exploit the religious ceremonial of his church. Hot-tempered, moody, a stern disciplinarian, his outbursts more than once tested the faith of his subordinates and made his critics doubt his sanity. Ruthless in the affairs of state, he seemed outwardly a very worldly man, whose portrait suggests a crafty Venetian merchant, clothed in purple, but inwardly he was an utterly humble being who embraced poverty for his own person. Lavigerie paid for his human feelings in great spiritual suffering. Had he kept a journal it would almost certainly have become a classic, like the writings of David Brainerd and Henry Martyn in the Protestant world and Livingstone's *Last Journals*. But he was as reticent about exhibiting his most intimate spiritual life as he was forthcoming in promoting his church. The motto Lavigerie chose for his coat of arms was the single word 'Caritas'. It was the impulse by which he lived. Without it he would indeed have been but a clanging cymbal.

With Lavigerie the drama centres on General Headquarters rather than the front-line soldier. While his missionaries acted on his instructions at isolated posts in the desert or thousands of miles away in the centre of Africa, he had to remain behind to do battle on their behalf with European governments. He could be with them only in prayer and in the great mystery of the Mass.

It was, therefore, a great triumph of the imagination that Lavigerie was really celebrating in Notre Dame d'Afrique on 20 June 1879. Less than ten years had passed since all his hopes for France and his church had been rolled in the dust by the Prussians, less than five since he had thought his own work in Africa was over, and barely twelve months since this new commitment which was to have such momentous consequences. There would be setbacks again and moments of renewed doubts about the future. There would come a time when he would send an anguished message to his missionaries in the heart of Africa to be ready to pull out altogether. There would come a day in this very church when he would turn imperiously on Our Lady of Africa, striking the flagstones with his great jewelled cross, and accuse her before God and man of doing nothing for her black children. '*N'étès vous mère que pour oublier vos enfants?*' he thundered at her then. '*Il faut que çela finisse!*'

But for the present, history, it seemed, was vindicating his claims for western Christendom. The reports sent back by the first expedition of 1878 were encouraging; only one father had died on the road and the two parties had already started work among the people living by the two lakes. This new missionary campaign gave him hope for the renaissance of Catholic France. It gave him hope, too, that the walls of pagan Africa would at last be breached so that Christianity could come to grips with the ultimate evil of slavery.

'What remains, then, for us to do, is to make these tribes, sunk alas! in the deepest degradation, understand how great is their impiety; to teach them that all men are brethren; that in creating man, God gave him freedom, freedom of soul and body, a freedom which, when the whole world fell under the slavery of sin, Jesus Christ restored to him, not thinking it too dearly purchased at the price of His own blood.'

The commissioning service for the missionaries and their zouave auxiliaries had lasted the best part of the day. Exultantly the religious banners of the expedition were sanctified in the presence of a great throng of North African colonists, men and women of all nationalities who had made their home in Algeria under the French flag and in the Catholic faith. It was time for Lavigerie to say farewell to his missionaries – 'you, the purest honour of my ministry'. 'God speaks to you by the voice of Peter', Peter who in the person of Leo XIII was still virtually held prisoner in the Vatican by the new Italian

25 *Cardinal Lavigerie,* an official painting made for the White Fathers by Albert Weber

state. From his captivity in Rome, the Pope had called them to strike the last blow against modern slavery as another prisoner, Paul, had struck the first blow against the chains of paganism in the ancient world. Lavigerie was deeply moved by the historical parallel and by the idea of a captive pope sending out apostles to a heathen continent. He raised his arms to bless them, 'in the name of the faith whose empire you will spread', in the name of charity, of light and liberty, in the name of Christ.

At the end of that memorable day it was this missionary Archbishop, this prince of the church, who suffered most at the approaching separation. He was the one who would not be at the martyr's banquet. He longed for it himself, but God had not found him worthy. So be it. But perhaps their sacrifice would win him mercy and peace.

Slowly Lavigerie descended the altar steps. In full episcopal robes he went down on his knees in front of the small party of missionaries and gravely kissed each man's feet. It was what the early Christian martyrs used to do in the catacombs on the eve of entering the Roman arena. Before the year was out eight of them would be dead.

2

To Lavigerie, as to all Frenchmen, the sudden humiliation of France before Prussia in the autumn of 1870 was a terrible blow, all the more terrible for being so wholly unexpected. His ardent patriotism aroused, he had at once pledged his church bells for melting down into cannons and released half his staff of diocesan priests for service as army chaplains. Defeat brought chaos to Algeria, where the army was disbanded, most of its officers having already left hurriedly for their homeland. In Algiers itself there was mob rule; in the country-side the appearance of anarchy; in the Kabylia mountains a native uprising. The emotional shock to Lavigerie was doubled by the almost simultaneous occupation of Rome by Piedmontese troops who thereby secured the political union of Italy under the House of Savoy. The strain brought Lavigerie to the brink of despair. He was being rendered powerless to fulfil all his responsibilities. In stricken tones he confessed one day to one of his priests that he felt he could hardly carry on. He took off his ring and pectoral cross. '*Tenez, mon enfant,*' he cried, '*Je ne suis plus Archevêque.*'

But only he could initiate the work of reconstruction. It would mean endless appeals for funds and arduous and often dangerous journeys to defend the rights of his people; in all, a task as physically exhausting as any undertaken at the opening of a mission by a Moffat or a Krapf. For six months Lavigerie was away from North Africa and during this time he contested a seat in the new Constituent Assembly, in which he was rebuffed. When he eventually returned to his see across the Mediterranean, all his previous work was in ruins. His embryonic seminary was deserted; the priests he hoped would one day work among the native populations of North Africa were dispersed; his orphanages were threatened with closure through lack of funds. A fresh blow to Lavigerie and his fellow Catholics was the refusal of the Royalists to take over the government of France when the opportunity presented itself, despite a direct appeal from the Pope conveyed by Lavigerie in person.

Lavigerie was sustained by his historical imagination. France was not her rulers, nor even her soil; France existed wherever French men and women believed in her destiny. A regime had fallen but not an ideal. If this ideal of France could survive the storms of the world, so too could his own vision for Africa. Indeed he felt their destinies were linked more closely than ever. France's defeat by Prussia, Lavigerie believed, was God's chastisement on an impious nation; one that had abandoned her mission in the world and in Africa had even encouraged the heathen in their false gods. Now the penalty had been paid and a new start could be made.

Thousands of refugees had fled from their homes in Alsace and Lorraine, the two provinces which Bismarck exacted as the spoils of war. Many of them were members of Lavigerie's former see of Nancy, for whom he felt a particular sympathy. He appealed to them now to make new homes in Algeria. 'Algeria, *la France Africaine*, through me as bishop opens her doors and holds out her arms to you.' They would find, he said, a better climate, more fertile soil and land reserved for them on easy terms, an arrangement which Lavigerie had personally negotiated with the authorities. What this new France wanted was new sons. It was still a heathen country, but it could become Christian again as it had been in the days of St Augustine. 'You will be its true apostles!' he cried.

Ten thousand families from the lost provinces of Alsace and Lorraine accepted the offer and settled in Algeria, though not as the authorities had hoped as agriculturalists, most of them being town-dwellers. At the same time thousands of Catholics also turned their backs on metropolitan France, feeling betrayed by the Royalists and out of sympathy with the Republic. A true Frenchman, they felt, could no longer live in France itself where anti-clericalism and party politics were corrupting the soul of the nation; the true Frenchman could only express his nationality by emigrating, thus spreading his religion and civilisation overseas. Here lay one of the ironies of history. From the collapse of Imperial France in 1870 rose the imperialism of Republican France. Over the next two decades France acquired a colonial empire greater than any she had aspired to in the past. By the end of the nineteenth century 40,000 French men and women were to find themselves working in Catholic missions around the world, an extraordinary evangelical force comparable with that which had erupted in the Protestant world at the beginning of the century.

Lavigerie was one of the architects of this empire. Recovering his faith in the Catholic destiny of France, he set about establishing a missionary base in his North African episcopate. The congregation of priests, which in 1868, in Lavigerie's own words, 'arose of itself' to answer the immediate need of famine relief, had been put to a severe test. Now applications poured in. By 1873 numbers had risen to a hundred, many of the new-comers arriving with the refugees from France. Lavigerie reformed them into a regular missionary order with a proper constitution and rules. Their official title now became the Society of Missionaries of Our Lady of Africa or, alternatively, Missionaries of Algiers to distinguish them from a Lyons-based society. Popularly they became known as the White Fathers from their white habit, the *gandourah* and *bernous*, which was copied from the robe and hooded cloak worn by the Berber tribes of North Africa. Around their necks they wore rosaries in imitation of the Moslem beads for the names of Allah. They were to become 'Arabs by charity', Lavigerie said, when he presented the first two priests to the Pope. He planned to send them to the oases along the northern fringe of the Sahara and into the Kabylia mountains, where he hoped to find survivors of the original Christian church among the descendants of people who had taken refuge there when the Arabs overran Roman North Africa.

At the same time Lavigerie revived the ancient tradition of calling a North African provincial council, to which he submitted the rules of his new society. It was another deliberate appeal to history. After an interval of twelve centuries the customary acclamations of praise were to be heard once more in an African sanctuary:

'Long life to Archbishop Lavigerie!' cried the celebrant. 'To the Church of Africa brought back to life from the dead. Alleluia! Alleluia!'

'May she never die again!' echoed the crowd of worshippers.

'To the French Army whose matchless courage has triumphed in the name of the Cross and reclaimed these heathen lands for Christendom!'

This time the crowd replied in the words of the psalm, 'Some trust in chariots and some in horses, but we will trust in the Lord of Hosts!'

'To the missionaries who by the grace of God will carry the light of the gospel to the people of Africa who sit in darkness and in the shadow of death!'

'How beautiful are the feet of those who bring tidings of peace!'

'Mission work in Algeria', Lavigerie told his White Fathers, 'is far from being the chief, still less is it the exclusive, object of your ambition. The aim and end of our Apostolate is the evangelisation of Africa, of the whole of Africa, of that almost impenetrable interior

whose dark depths are the last hiding places of a brutal barbarism
where cannibalism prevails, and slavery in its most degrading forms.'

Livingstone's death and funeral obsequies had recently been in the
headlines. Lavigerie called the attention of his missionaries to the
scene in Westminster Abbey. Here was a man rewarded with the
highest national honour, said Lavigerie, but he spoke of Livingstone
only as an intrepid explorer, not as a missionary. It was not for such
human glory or the mere love of adventure that Lavigerie sought
recruits, but men ready for true martyrdom. 'My dear sons, you do
not seek such things as that. No thought of gain or glory impels you.
You will be without bread or shelter, you will die unknown to the
world, perhaps under some terrible torture. This is all I can promise
you. But you know, and it is all you need, who it is who can reward
those who serve Him, according to their merits.'

These great set-pieces left Lavigerie emotionally exhausted. It
was his vision for the evangelisation of Africa that had first brought
him across the Mediterranean. Having seen his missionary order
properly constituted he felt his work was over and death was near.
His depression was made worse by the difficulties he encountered in
administering his see under an anti-clerical regime in France. There
were doubts whether the Archbishop's face would be seen much
longer in Algiers.

In the summer of 1875, however, his voice once again resounded
through North Africa. The occasion was the ceremony in which
religious services were reintroduced into the French colonial army.
A French bishop could not withdraw from the world of generals and
colonial officials, but must carry the missionary crusade into their
ranks. At the height of his row with MacMahon Lavigerie had insisted on his being accorded the twenty-five gun salute of a Marshal of
France, which was his right as Archbishop; now, as of right, he would
address them as their spiritual head.

For three-quarters of an hour Lavigerie delivered a terrific speech
on the army's conquest of Algeria. He extolled its glory, its valour,
its battle honours, its generals. Names and deeds associated with
French heroes in North Africa passed beneath his review in a glittering parade of history. It was an astonishing performance for a priest,
and only a man with Lavigerie's imagination could have made it.
His audience was spell-bound. But suddenly he paused, to turn on
them the full force of his episcopal authority. Why, he asked, was
this victory given to France? In order that God's work might be
done. In order that Christian charity should follow behind the
armies. In order that truth should conquer, with peace and order.

'If ever France has received a mission from on high, when was it more obvious?' he demanded. '*O France chrétienne*, your mission is not to seize the treasures of the conquered for the sake of blood and glory, nor to drive them out to take their place. Your genius is to pass on to them light and truth, even in sacrificing yourselves.' And this mission, the Archbishop declared, did not end with Algeria; beyond lay Morocco and Tunisia, and beyond them Egypt and Syria, where the remnants of Christian people awaited their earthly liberator. To conquer in the name of the Cross was France's destiny, so that one day Africa would find light again and live. 'I will not live to see it,' he concluded, 'but I shall die confident that one day it will happen.' On behalf of a church which once had humbled emperors, Lavigerie commanded Caesar to give place to God.

He had his eyes on the Sahara where the French army was constantly in action against desert tribes who for centuries had lived by raiding the settled areas and making off into the sandy wastes where pursuit was impossible. It was a kind of warfare which a later generation would describe as romantic, a 'beau geste' world of forts, bugles and legionaries. Several commanders in this frontier region had welcomed Lavigerie's missionary impulse, though surreptitiously for fear of their military superiors in Algiers. One of the most famous of them was called de Sonis, a man of real piety, whose charity, courage and sense of justice were later upheld by Lavigerie as ideal French qualities. 'Our holy General de Sonis' the Archbishop called him. 'More would be done by the Cross than by the sword,' de Sonis had written when in command at Laghouat, before the White Fathers' arrival. Seeing de Sonis at his daily devotions, with his rosary and simple prayers, the Arabs would look at one another and say, 'We have at last got a good Governor, for he recognises the power of God!' The flag of peace, the sword of justice, and the Cross, they were all needed for Lavigerie's North African mission.

In the course of 1875 the most notorious of the robber bands was broken and a number of prisoners taken. Among them were men from the Tuareg tribe, those sullen, veiled camel-riders who were masters of the caravan routes and owed allegiance to no one. Lavigerie intervened with the colonial authorities to save these Tuareg prisoners for his White Fathers, and they gradually succeeded in coaxing them out of their reserve.

In return for their liberty the Tuareg promised to guide a party of three White Fathers across the Sahara to Timbuktu, some 1,500 miles distant. This legendary city of mud-huts, situated strategically on the most northerly point of the Niger, was thought to be the headquarters of slave-traders in the western Sudan. The way to it from the north also pointed to France's other African colony of Senegal, on the Atlantic. If Algeria and Senegal could be joined then France's destiny, and Lavigerie's missionary dream, would be fulfilled. How missionaries known to oppose slavery could exist so far from outside support was a question with which Lavigerie did not appear to concern himself. It was to be a 'venture for Christ', like Livingstone's, though the world might reasonably think it foolhardy in the extreme.

The natives of Metlili where the White Fathers were based begged them not to leave, and finally asked them to sign a paper taking upon themselves full responsibility for their actions. Early in 1876 the three priests set off under the protection of the Tuareg, full of faith and ardour. It was a journey that would take them at least seventy days and if successful would do for north and west Africa what Livingstone and Stanley had done for the east and the centre.

They were never seen alive again. Rumours that they had been murdered gradually reached the northern fringe of the Sahara, but what exactly happened to them has never been established. They left no record behind them and none was ever clearly brought to light. Various accounts spread of how they met their fate, it being generally assumed that their Tuareg guides betrayed them once they were clear of the settled areas, and either killed them themselves or allowed others to do so. At all events they never reached Timbuktu, and they rank as the first martyrs in Lavigerie's missionary society.

Lavigerie was deeply shocked by their fate. These men were his spiritual sons. He wept for them like a father, but with their brethren sang the *Te Deum* in their honour. At the same time he was faced with fresh disputes with the French government, following the massacre of a French military column in the Sahara. Though volunteers pressed forward – to make a 'beau geste' for Christ was how Lavigerie put it – he withdrew his men from the Algerian Sahara and switched them to Ghadames, where the roads south from Tripoli and Tunis converge. From here, in 1881, another party of three White Fathers made a second attempt to penetrate the desert barrier, making ultimately for Kano in northern Nigeria. But they too were murdered by their guides a short distance, only, from their starting point. This route to inner Africa remained effectively closed until French troops entered Timbuktu from Dakar in 1894.

The tragedy of the martyrs in the desert raised for Lavigerie a fundamental question relating to the missionary expectations of Christianity in the Moslem world. For Islam is a religion founded on human success; this is the essence of its message, the basis of its appeal in this world and for the next. Christianity, by contrast, is founded on human failure, symbolised by the cross. It is therefore scarcely surprising that Islam denies the historical fact behind this symbol, namely the crucifixion of Jesus. The Koran states that it is a Jewish fable and condemns it as 'a monstrous falsehood against Mary'.

The brilliant Frenchman Pascal summed up the contrast in a telling phrase. Rather than conclude, he wrote, that since Mahomet succeeded in the world, Jesus Christ could also have succeeded in the world, we must acknowledge that, precisely because Mahomet succeeded, Jesus Christ had to die.

Lavigerie had warned his missionaries that they must do nothing to arouse Moslem fanaticism. Conversion of individuals to Christianity was out of the question; it would take at least a hundred years, he once said, before any large numbers of baptisms could be expected. In the meantime, there must be no overt preaching of the gospel. The Christian was a missionary to the Moslem only as a neighbour might be, by tending the sick, helping the afflicted and exhibiting in his own person the truth of his religion. His missionaries would thus appear only as men of God, while to the French colonists in North Africa Lavigerie said: 'We leave God to carry on, in His own good time, His work in their souls. Our part is to do His will and fulfil His commands by showing them that in our labours of love we are obeying a law of charity higher than their own. Our greatest happiness, after all our sacrifices, is to hear the Mussulmans exclaim: " Really, what good people these French are!"'

Many of Lavigerie's contemporaries, following the evolutionary consensus of the age, held that Africans could not attain to the refined heights of Christianity without passing through an intermediary stage of religious life, like Islam. As a Christian, Lavigerie had no truck with this view; and as a political realist, he pointed out that it simply did not correspond to the facts of life. The Moslem justified his faith by its political success in this world; well then, said Lavigerie, what was actually happening in the world? With one notable exception, Islam was everywhere in full retreat, pressed back by Britain in India and South-East Asia, by Russia in Central Asia, and by France herself in North Africa and the Near East. Turkey was disintegrating. The one exception was in the interior of Africa where there was no political opposition.

When therefore his opponents accused Lavigerie of mixing religion with politics, citing the deaths of his missionaries in the Sahara,

Lavigerie turned the argument on its head. 'The true civiliser,' he wrote, 'the only effectual preacher at this present time, is the action of events which change the political aspect of the country. Unwittingly, unwillingly even, our Commandants, our soldiers are the chief factors of this change. They represent force, and force to the Mussulman is the hand of God. We see proof of this in Algeria, where, without any other apparent action, a general disintegration is taking place in Moslem society, from which religion is not exempted.'

Later, the full enormity of Islam's presence in Africa, referred to by explorer after explorer, would inspire him to call for a new crusade against the slave-traders. At this distance of time it is something of a puzzle to imagine where all the African slaves who passed

26 *I address myself to Christian England, because nowhere can I find a greater respect for liberty and human dignity. Punch* cartoon of August 1888, at the height of Lavigerie's campaign against the slave-trade

through Arab hands actually went to. There does not appear to be the same large negroid element in the populations of Asia and the Middle East as exists in America as a result of the European slave-trade. But as information accumulated from Lavigerie's own missionaries and other explorers, a new horror came to light. Many thousands of Africans captured as slaves were destined to become human sacrifices to the fetishes of West Africa. Thousands more were enrolled by the Arabs to form their own slave-trading forces. After a time, the system fed off itself. Lavigerie quoted Livingstone's experiences and agreed with him that it was impossible to exaggerate the horror of what Islam had meant in practice for Africa. 'The Mussulman religion is the very masterpiece of the evil one', concluded Lavigerie, and he went on to call for armed intervention by Europe to suppress the traders still at work in the centre of Africa. The earthly city had its responsibilities under God. 'Force is absolutely necessary', he cried. 'Charity, however great, will not suffice to save Africa', and if governments would not give a lead ('I am no politician, I do not want to encourage complications') 'why then, we will appeal to the people'.

3

On the first day of January 1877 Lavigerie startled his missionaries by announcing that he had written to the Pope resigning his see. He wanted to become a simple missionary like them. The deaths of the three men in the desert weighed on his mind and he felt he could no longer direct undertakings without sharing in them himself. He was a shepherd without love, he told them.

Lavigerie's burden was the public responsibility of his office. The truth was he was hurt by his inability to get France to follow his lead overseas. He was sickened too by French politics and the superficiality of French society. 'In France, everything seems to be finished,' he said wearily, while in Africa there was so much to be done. From 1875 he had been urging the French government to take over Tunisia, whose Bey, nominally subordinate to the Sultan of Turkey, was an ineffectual ruler. His polyglot subjects, said Lavigerie, needed rescuing from the blight of Islam. The Italians were represented in Tunis by the Capuchins and looked on it almost as an extension of their own country, as the French looked on Algeria; but France had a stake in Tunis too in the shrine to St Louis which had been bought by Mathieu de Lesseps, the father of the canal builder, on behalf of Charles X to commemorate his illustrious ancestor. Lavigerie longed to resurrect the ancient see of Carthage and restore the memory of France's saintly king, which had fallen into disrepute among Tunisians through a gaffe perpetrated by the French government. Asked for a statue of St Louis, Paris had sent instead one of Charles the Fat, confusing the various effigies which had been dumped in the basement of the National Assembly during the French Revolution. By then, however, the Bourbons had quit the stage altogether and no money was available to maintain the shrine.

Carthage had been one of the greatest cities of the Roman Empire, the headquarters of the Christian church in North Africa and glorious in the annals of the church through the names of Cyprian, who was martyred there, and Augustine, who preached some of his greatest sermons within its walls. But the past lay buried under mounds of earth and rubble outside the Turkish city of Tunis. Only a broken column and an occasional fragment of sculpture or mosaic gave a clue to the magnificence of the Roman city. Lavigerie dreamed of piecing them together so that the church could be seen to rise again from the ruins of history. He succeeded in ousting his ecclesiastical rivals, taking over responsibility for the Catholic community himself, and he acquired for his own use the hill of Byrsa, an acropolis which overlooks the plain of Carthage.

The Eastern Mediterranean was changing beyond recognition since Lavigerie's visit to the Lebanon after the Druses' massacre of native Christians in 1860. As a result of the Crimean War (1854–6) France and Russia had each obtained special interests in Palestine. The Protestants now had their bishop there, a joint Anglo-Prussian appointment. With the building of the Suez Canal distinguished tourists like England's Prince of Wales and Prussia's Crown Prince had begun visiting the Holy Places, so much so that the Turks were obliged to construct a new road from Jaffa to Jerusalem to accommodate the growing numbers of pilgrims from the west, the first real change in communications since the end of the Roman Empire. There was talk, even, of colonisation by German and American Jews, the first intimations of modern Zionism.

Looking at all these happenings from his North African vantage point Lavigerie's imagination was fired by the belief that God, through human history, was making a stupendous offer to his people. If Algeria could be incorporated again within Christendom, why stop there? France in his eyes was the heir to ancient Rome, the very stones revealed it! Concern yourselves with these ruins, he instructed his White Fathers, so that the poor barbarians of Europe may see that the church is not an enemy of science. Her priests must also be archaeologists so as to proclaim in museums as well as in churches the promise of the resurrection.

But the politicians of the French Republic were enmeshed in Bismarck's diplomacy and lacked their Archbishop's vision. The spectre of further wars haunted their councils, if not with Germany, then with England; if not with England, then with Italy. Russia also claimed to be the heir of Rome, of the Byzantine Empire; the Sultan was bankrupt, and Ismail nearly so; but Britain preferred the Turk to be in residence at Constantinople rather than the Slav. In 1875 Disraeli bought Ismail Pasha's holding in the Suez Canal Company under the noses of the French to give England a commercial stake in Egypt, the prelude to physical intervention. The following year Gladstone told the Turks to clear out of Bulgaria, 'bag and baggage', following a horrific massacre of the Christian population by bashi-bazouk commandos. The British Foreign Office contemplated proclaiming a protectorate over Turkish Anatolia, while the new imperial Germany was leading an ideological campaign against the Papacy. The diplomats operated behind an elegant façade of Offenbach and chinoiserie, of picnics on the Bosphorus and drawing room charades. It was a world in which the Sultan's astrologer was known to be a key figure, though no one could say whose pay he was in. Meanwhile, Europe was in the process of forming itself into an alliance system which could only end in catastrophe.

So at the beginning of 1877 Lavigerie felt frustrated and in despair. Perhaps too he felt he was overstretched and failing in his priestly duties. But a man with his energy and ambition could not be down for long. The Pope refused to allow him to resign, and suddenly his vision for Africa appeared in a new and more brilliant light.

It was Stanley who was responsible. Stanley's progress through Africa had become a world event. Among those whose interest was awakened was the astute King of the Belgians, Leopold II, a cousin of Queen Victoria and related to half the royal families of Europe. Ambitious, well-travelled and bored with his role as a constitutional monarch, Leopold was fascinated by the world of African adventure opened up by Stanley's writings. One of the original shareholders in the Suez Canal Company, he had disposed of his stock at a handsome profit, leaving him with a personal fortune. In September 1876, while Stanley was still in Africa, he was host in Brussels to an impressive gathering of African experts who, in the name of science and humanity, and quoting Livingstone's reference to an 'open sore', drew up a plan for an international association to co-ordinate schemes for opening up Africa to western civilisation, rather as the United Nations sponsors relief work in our own day.

In June the following year, the association held its first meeting in Brussels. Ostensibly it was still international in character, but many of its national committees hung back, uncertain of their own governments' objectives in Africa. Leopold pressed ahead, drawing on his own resources, and the association thus became largely a Belgian royal concern. In December 1877 its first representatives arrived in Zanzibar, as it happened the day before Stanley finally sailed back to Europe after discharging the survivors of his epic journey to the mouth of the Congo.

Lavigerie could not remain an inactive bystander. He too was fascinated by Stanley's dispatches from Africa. Was Mutesa's appeal for missionaries to be met only by Protestants? In the course of 1877 Lavigerie wrote urgently to the Pope warning him that the Protestants were dominating the Brussels association. He also wrote to warn his own government that France was in danger of finding herself excluded from influencing the future of the continent unless she acted quickly. 'France must be represented in these vast mysterious regions,' he insisted, and not just by solitary pioneers, but by an effective organisation.

In this critical situation Lavigerie saw a striking opportunity for his White Fathers. In great secrecy he worked out a plan whereby his Catholic missionaries could move rapidly into the interior of Africa and establish themselves in small colonies of freed slaves in the same way as they had started work in Algeria with the orphans of the cholera epidemic. Leopold had declared that his objectives were wholly secular, but that he would welcome missionaries of any denomination who followed the same path. The Roman Catholic church, Lavigerie argued, could not let this offer pass, or it would be denying its claim to be the one true church. Moreover, it would be denying to the Africans what was the one essential element of civilisation. Balked by the Sahara from reaching inner Africa from the north, his mission to the Western Sudan was for the time being non-viable. Let the White Fathers' area, therefore, be exactly the same as that mapped out by the Brussels association. In effect, Lavigerie challenged the Catholic church to fulfil its missionary duty in the unexplored regions of Africa.

By the beginning of February 1878 Lavigerie's agents were in Rome. Pius IX was dying, but the Vatican regarded Lavigerie's scheme with such importance that between the death of one pope and the election of his successor the cardinals met in Consistory to give it their approval. Within four days of his election Leo XIII was able to announce the setting up of four new mission fields in Central Africa, two in the Congo region, one based on Lake Victoria and one on Lake Tanganyika. The whole of this vast area he entrusted to Lavigerie and his White Fathers, allocating some initial money from a special Vatican welfare fund. All this was in addition to Lavigerie's existing responsibilities for the Western Sudan.

The Archbishop had already made careful preparations, down to the gifts which his missionaries should bring to Mutesa. Having learnt from Stanley of the African ruler's fondness for European uniforms he toured the second-hand clothes shops in Paris to buy up the cast-off court dresses of the former imperial regime. It was to prove a masterly stroke. Before becoming Pope Leo XIII had served in Brussels where no doubt he had been involved in Lavigerie's secret soundings. Lavigerie was also in close touch with the French Foreign Office about his plans, which included a visit to Jerusalem at the Pope's request to take over the shrine of St Anne which France had acquired after the Crimean War, but which had lain neglected for the last twenty years.

Once the papal decree was announced, therefore, Lavigerie was able to move fast. By the end of March, no less, ten White Fathers were on their way to Zanzibar, so that when a month later a roving spokesman of English Protestants turned up in Algiers to ask Lavigerie not to compete with their societies in East Africa, he was already too late.

In June the same year the first Catholic missionaries to enter that part of Africa set out from Bagamoyo with an impressive caravan of 500 porters. In their white robes and hip boots, with large cork hats on their heads and rifles and canteens of water slung round their shoulders, the White Fathers brought a new touch to the East African scene. At Tabora they divided into two parties and by early 1879 they were at Lake Tanganyika and Lake Victoria respectively. They were marching, one of them said, to the great rendezvous of humanity and civilisation, while far away in Notre Dame d'Afrique Lavigerie was praying for their mission and preparing whatever they might need in the way of reinforcements.

4

That Rome was anti-Christ was a plausible theological proposition widely held by Protestants. Newman for a time believed it provided the only valid basis for the Anglican church. Under the old Dutch

East India Company Roman Catholic priests were banned from the Cape and, though the English removed the restriction in 1830, the Roman Catholic church made no missionary impact in South Africa during Moffat's fifty years at Kuruman. The few priests there catered mostly for Irish Catholics among the colonists. Krapf had run up against Roman Catholics in Ethiopia where he believed they had been responsible for his expulsion from the Kingdom of Shoa. Coming from a Protestant German state, he used the language of Luther and the Reformation. Rome was the 'dragon-head', the 'mother of harlots', and its propaganda 'the infernal efforts of the man of sin'. He urged his English patrons to be cautious about releasing information about East Africa, as the Jesuits were 'everywhere in ambush'. Though Krapf was impressed by the Austrian Catholics he met on the Nile, he firmly believed that Rome was a political church and that she was represented in Africa by Portugal to the detriment of Christian missions and civilisation.

Livingstone shared this view. He would refer disparagingly to the Pope as 'auld Nikey ben' when writing to his family, and he too feared the influence of Rome on Portuguese policy towards British attempts to enter Africa via the Zambezi and Mozambique. Hence his desperate search for a highway to the interior open to the world. He had nothing but respect for the first Jesuit missionaries in Africa, in the days of Portuguese supremacy: 'How the Jesuits prayed,' he once wrote, 'and what missionaries they were! I am not a missionary compared to them.' But he had little good to say for their successors. The Portuguese priests in Angola were notable only for the fine beards they sported and the many bastards they spawned, and at Zumbo, the furthest point reached by the Portuguese from Mozambique, Christendom's only legacy to Africans appeared to be the ability to distil spirits from a gun-barrel.

He was haunted by the desolate ruins of Zumbo. They challenged his view of history. Why had those earlier missions in Africa failed? Livingstone gave two answers. As far as Angola was concerned, the Portuguese had failed to translate the Bible into Negro languages, so the faith of the first African converts had soon given way to superstition and fetish worship, even though many of them were able to read and write. As for the interior, Livingstone concluded that the underlying cause must be the involvement of Portugal with the slave-trade. For both these reasons, therefore, he was led into advocating what amounted to a spiritual dual mandate, to bring the elect to the knowledge of God and to spread western civilisation.

The Roman Catholic rejoinder was that, in St Augustine's terms, the church can only exist in those conditions of orderly government which it is the proper end of the earthly city to secure. The church must therefore seek the support of powerful and sympathetic states. Portugal and Spain had at one time provided such support, even at the expense of the Jesuits, but the role had then been taken over by France under the Bourbons. The fleur-de-lis, chosen by Clovis as an emblem of his baptism into the Christian faith, was not an inappropriate symbol of mission.

Whatever the consequences, Lavigerie's decision to switch the White Fathers from the Africa of the Sahara to the Africa of the Great Lakes was true to this tradition. Writing in 1880 about the progress of the mission, he made no secret of the fact that it was fear of losing the continent to the Protestants that was the main factor in the decision. He described the Catholic mission as the logical fulfilment of God's purpose for the church in history. Livingstone and Stanley had their part to play in this as they had paved the way for the Brussels association. This openly secular body, Lavigerie wrote, merited 'immortal glory' for being the instrument by which the gospel was at last able to enter the continent. Leopold's 'crusade against barbarism' was praiseworthy in itself in an age of progress, but it would be incomplete if the church herself did not march alongside. Brushing aside the Protestant missionary impulse of the previous half-century Lavigerie quoted Pius IX's uncompromising words on the subject: 'It is to the truth of which the Church is depository, and not to error that the great command was given: "Go and teach all nations . . .".'

The totalitarian claims of the Vatican excluded any other view of history, just as Livingstone's idea of progress determined his attitude towards the past. Since the Pope had been deprived of temporal power in Europe, with the loss of his Italian states, it became more necessary from the Catholic standpoint to assert his mystical authority as Vicar of Christ. The dogma of papal infallibility, promulgated by the Vatican Council of 1870, had strengthened the Pope's position within the Roman Catholic church (in the preliminary discussions Lavigerie had supported the Pope against his fellow French bishops). So far as the rest of the world was concerned, Pius IX modified the dogma of 'no salvation outside the church' in order to embrace a wide number of souls who did not partake of the church's sacraments.

The reawakening missionary conscience of the Catholic church could be seen elsewhere in Africa. In the very year (1877) when Lavigerie was urging the Vatican to move into Central Africa from east and west, an English Jesuit, Alfred Weld, also urged that a mission be sent northwards across the Limpopo into the Zambezi valley, into the regions made famous through Livingstone's explorations with the Makololo. Weld was the assistant to the general of the Jesuit Order, and he based his plan on a Jesuit seminary which had been established at Grahamstown in 1875 on the initiative of the Roman Catholic bishop of Natal. There were still only a handful of priests in the whole of South Africa and the mission envisaged by Weld had perforce to draw on Jesuit fathers from many different provinces of the Order in Europe. But his plan went through with the same speed as Lavigerie's. In December 1878 the Belgian leader of the mission, whose previous experience was in India, had a farewell audience with the Pope and sailed for Africa with five priests and five lay brothers. Helped on their way by traders and Catholic sympathisers they all trekked north along trails blazed years before by Moffat and Livingstone and the ill-fated Makololo mission of Helmore and Price. For nine years these Jesuits struggled heroically, but fever coupled with their inexperience defeated them, and they had to wait for Cecil Rhodes' armed pioneers before they were able to establish themselves in this part of Central Africa.

Sectarian rivalries have existed within the Christian church since the earliest times, as among the Corinthians in St Paul's day. They constitute, it could be said, a fact of history and they could not therefore be kept out of Africa, unless Africa was to be kept permanently out of the world. Lavigerie had instructed his missionaries not to set up in areas already occupied by Protestants, and with the notable exception of Uganda the White Fathers were able to co-operate with their denominational rivals in the field. On reaching Lake Tanganyika, for instance, they agreed with the LMS to work in different spheres. The Jesuits entering Matabeleland also had amicable dealings with the Protestants who had preceded them and who, thanks to Moffat's reputation, had the ear, if not the soul, of Moselekatse's son Lobengula. They remained spiritual competitors, of course, and suspicious of each other's methods. 'To show we were Catholics not Protestants . . . we showed them the Crucifix as the book from which we taught,' wrote the English Jesuit Augustus Law at Lobengula's kraal. But whether it was a book or a crucifix, a substance or a symbol, a declaration or a sacrament, a phrase or a gesture, it was faith and not theory that carried conviction. Protestants and Catholics each made many converts in Africa, but it was in the love they showed, and not in statistics, that the truth of their claims was made known.

Uganda proved different for a number of reasons. One was that Mutesa insisted the rival parties should remain close by him at his capital, which brought into sharp conflict the incompatible personalities of the two leading missionaries involved, Alexander Mackay, the Scotsman serving the Anglican society, and the French priest, Lourdel. Another reason lay in Uganda's strategic importance in that part of Africa, which of course was what had caught Lavigerie's attention in the first place, and Stanley's before him. The pressures of the outside world would inevitably bear down on Uganda, as on the Matabele, and the religious factor was an additional complication to Mutesa's situation.

What was momentous about Lavigerie's move into Central Africa was that it was the first explicit assertion of European nationalism in support of the missionary cause. Hitherto the Roman Catholic establishments in Zanzibar and Bagamoyo had been warmly recommended by British officials. Their typically French neatness made a strong impression on Stanley. The fact that the Jesuits in Matabeleland were of many different nationalities also aroused no adverse comment; while in South Africa French Protestants worked harmoniously with their British colleagues, and one of the most outstanding of their number, François Coillard, was to be largely responsible for seeing that Barotseland was incorporated within the British Empire.

Lavigerie was not thinking himself of the benefits that would accrue to France in a commercial or military sense, but of what France had to offer as the civiliser of the world; and he was not thinking of France as she then existed under the Republic, but of the France that exists in the imagination of her worthiest sons and daughters. Not the France of the Enlightenment, of Voltaire and Talleyrand's 'douceur de vivre', but the France of a St Louis, the King who died in Tunis on a bed of ashes on his way to a crusade, the France of a de Gaulle, but not of the Gaullists.

English Protestants like Alexander Mackay could hardly be expected to sympathise with this view; nor was it always held in such exalted terms by his own missionaries, like Lourdel, who, being younger men, were more attuned to the new nationalism of the age. Ultimately the White Fathers would become an international body, but it was only natural for outsiders to see them in the early days as forerunners of French imperialism.

Perhaps Lavigerie did not realise how his action would be interpreted in the new Europe which had come into being as a result of Prussia's victory over Napoleon III. 'My map of Africa lies here,'

Bismarck is reported to have said once, pointing to Alsace-Lorraine. His one constant preoccupation was to prevent France from trying to reverse the decision of 1870. To this end colonial ambitions must be encouraged and the eastern ulcer, as Turkey's future in the Balkans was called, must be kept open. In 1877 Russia attacked Turkey again, and again the other European powers had to intervene to shore up the Sultan's ramshackle empire. Bismarck called for a Congress in Berlin to arrange matters where France was secretly promised Tunis and Britain settled for Cyprus. His next move would be to stir the colonial pot himself by advancing Germany's newly discovered claims in Africa. At the same time France was backing her own exploration in the Congo, using for this purpose an Italian-born adventurer called de Brazza, and relying on French missionaries of the Holy Ghost Society to support her national ambition.

In East Africa France had always been more aggressive in her dealings with the Sultan than Britain. Early in 1878 it happened that the French Chamber voted a large sum of money for a French expedition to attempt to cross Africa from east to west, with no specific objective except to 'show the flag'. A new expression for new times. The expedition was entrusted to an obscure French priest, Debaize, who had volunteered too late for the Brussels association. Debaize led his men courageously to Ujiji and there died, the Protestants on the lake kindly seeing to the disposal of his effects and the return of his porters to the coast. Next the French consul in Zanzibar asked the Sultan for a sweeping concession over his mainland dominions, much to Kirk's chagrin who had seen a British attempt in the same direction fail. German explorers on the Tana River were also making treaties with local rulers, unknown at the time to anyone but the German Chancellery; while the Brussels association was also active in the interior.

Against this background Lavigerie's action in switching his White Fathers to the same area was certain to be interpreted in terms of European national ambitions. What is the news? the Africans might ask themselves in Uganda and on Lake Tanganyika. And the answer would now be, no news but alliances, congresses and spheres of influence, and soon protectorates and white settlement, together with European flags in profusion and taxes and punitive expeditions, plumed hats, brass bands and tea parties. Africa had entered the modern world.

5

In May 1881, acting on confidential information supplied by Lavigerie, the French army marched into Tunis to claim openly what had been promised secretly. 'Please God,' said Lavigerie, 'may this French triumph be the final victory of Christendom in Barbary.' It must be a victory of charity, he insisted, and he demanded money from France to support the work of the church in the new territory. In October he left Algiers to take up residence in Tunis. On the way he stopped at Bône (now Annaba, Algeria) and bought the hill which overlooks the ruins of Hippo, the small Roman port where Augustine had been bishop. Another church to be built, another piece of the grand mosaic of history to be restored. The past, Lavigerie believed, was coming to life again, thanks to Catholic France.

In March the following year he was at last made a Cardinal. The honour was long overdue, but it had been held up while Marshal MacMahon was President of the French Republic. Lavigerie stage-managed the ceremonies personally. He chose Carthage as the venue, where the ruins of past civilisations were a reminder of both the grandeur and the vanity of human achievements. The purple, he said, would soon be his shroud; and it was not his own humble person that was being honoured, but Africa, till then the only area of the globe unrepresented in the sacred college of the Roman church. 'What are the ghosts of Hannibal and Hamilcar saying?' Pius IX had once teased him. Go tell the Pope, Lavigerie now instructed his messengers, that the voices of Cyprian and Tertullian, of the great Augustine himself, would soon be speaking again as the cross raised itself once more in the primatial see of Africa, alongside the French flag.

Who was fooling whom? Was Lavigerie the dupe of the French politicians, or were they his dupe? It is the question the world always asks, and from his point of view was the least important. What happened was that the most anti-clerical of French governments inside France was also the most ardent supporter of her prelate overseas. Lavigerie wanted to turn the French foothold in Palestine, the shrine of St Anne in Jerusalem, into a missionary base, as much French as Catholic, for work among the Greek and Arabic speaking communities of the Near East. The Pope endorsed the ecclesiastical and Gambetta the political arrangements in a famous saying: '. . . anticlericalism is not for export'. Lavigerie wanted priests for Tunisia, they were accounted for in the French military budget as army chaplains; he wanted to build religious schools, they were paid for by the state as municipal works; the Arabs had grievances and threatened to make trouble, Lavigerie received them in church with great solemnity and had them eating out of his hand. He said later that he was able to do more in Tunis in eighteen months than in Algeria in eighteen years. France consulted him over appointments in Tunis. Paul Cambon, a famous French diplomat, was selected to be consul-general on his recommendation. He told Lavigerie that the French minister, Jules Ferry, who was noted for his anti-clerical laws, 'considers you as one of the most active and powerful agents of France abroad. He would do anything for you.'

Lavigerie returned the compliment. When he received his red Cardinal's biretta from the President of France, 'in recognition of the signal services you render to your country', Lavigerie replied that the missionary's greatest joy, in serving God and man, was to honour the name of France. They were not empty words. He knew that the greater his own prestige and responsibilities as a missionary bishop, the greater was France's influence overseas. When the Latin Patriarch in Jerusalem (an Italian) obstructed his school in Jerusalem, Lavigerie had it removed from his jurisdiction. When the Archbishop of Malta had the temerity to call himself Primate of Africa, prompted by England according to French historians, Lavigerie went straight to Rome to get the Pope to threaten him with dismissal. He claimed the title for a Frenchman, himself.

In due course a French protectorate was proclaimed over Tunisia and Lavigerie became Archbishop of Carthage (and Primate of Africa) in addition to his see of Algiers. The hill of Byrsa which he had acquired in 1876 for a seminary was chosen as the site of a new cathedral dedicated to St Louis and replacing the dingy shrine of earlier years. Lavigerie designated the location of his own tomb while the foundations were being laid.

In the same year, 1884, the leader of his first band of White Fathers to Central Africa, Livinhac, was made a bishop and competition for influence in Uganda intensified. Having failed to act with Britain in Egypt, France had lost the position she once enjoyed of being the dominant European power on the Nile. After the battle of Tel-el-Kebir (1882) the Union Jack flew highest in Cairo and an English banker, Evelyn Baring, gave the orders on behalf of Britain. But if France had failed to control the Nile where it reached the sea, she might still control it at its source in Central Africa. The elusive goal of Burton and Speke and Grant, of Livingstone and Stanley, now became a matter of military strategy and armed expeditions, as well as of denominational rivalry. Lavigerie spoke of establishing a

Catholic kingdom in the middle of Africa with its own Catholic army trained by his zouaves. In 1884, also, the Anglicans appointed their own bishop for Central Africa, with Uganda as his prize, who tragically was to be speared to death as soon as he arrived there.

Lavigerie was now at the height of his fame; but, as had often happened with him in the past, he was seized with melancholia. Once again he thought death was near, and some time towards the end of 1884 he drew up his spiritual testament. He dedicated it to his church and to France, the two loves of his life. He had done everything, he said, to preserve the historic bond between them. For France was only great in that she was Catholic; she owed her glory, her very life, to keeping faith with the Holy See. His own recent labours to prevent his beloved country ('*ma pauvre et chère patrie*') from breaking that faith had now brought him to the point of death. Yes, in a way, he had worked more for France than for his church. Because the church belonged to eternity and France, like all earthly cities, belonged to time. His was a dual citizenship, and though he owed his first allegiance to the heavenly city, he longed also to see his earthly one blessed among the nations of the world, as Augustine, his great predecessor in North Africa, had prayed for Rome. But man had God's warning that a city divided against itself could not stand. Rome fell; Carthage fell; was France now also finished? Sorrowfully, bitterly, he had watched her slow decline from her past glory, from the time when faith and virtue were the watchwords of her citizens, and her rulers were ready to defend truth and justice in the world. Had God now taken away from France her mission on earth? He prayed that it might not be so. But what was the prayer of a man before the judgements of the Almighty!

Then there was Africa, for whom he had given up everything when seventeen years before he felt God calling him to her service. Since then, what burdens, what weariness, what pains! He had given his life to bring the ancient Christian church into the light again and to rescue her people from the shadow of barbarism. And he had achieved so little, a voice only calling on others to make straight the way of the Lord, his one reward, to suffer.

The document makes melancholy reading. But Lavigerie did not die that year. Eight years still lay before him in which he continued to labour for France, for Africa and for his church. But in January 1885 an event took place which transformed the situation in North Africa and spoke louder than any words of his to awaken European concern for Africa. At the end of that month, the forces of the Mahdi, fanatical worshippers of the prophet of Islam, took Khartoum and challenged all that Lavigerie stood for. The repercussions were felt at once in Uganda, and soon throughout tropical Africa. But in taking Khartoum, the Mahdi had had to kill a man whose name counted for more in the world's headlines than that of a French Cardinal.

CHAPTER SEVEN

LIKE IRON

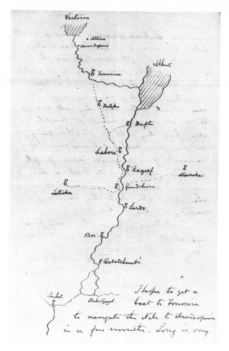

27 *Gordon's approach to Uganda*, sketch map from a letter from Gordon in Rhodes House Library

I

Enter Charles George Gordon, Royal Engineers, a veteran of the Crimea and comrade-in-arms of Garnet Wolseley, Queen Victoria's most successful general; known also as Chinese Gordon for his daring deeds on behalf of the Emperor of China for which he was honoured with the Order of the Bath by the British government; a blue-eyed self-contained man, born in 1833 to a General of the Royal Artillery; a friend of street urchins, who 'slaved at prayer' and 'saw if Jesus did really die He must have died for some greater result than that

seen in the Christian world'; a mystic, to whom it was suddenly revealed one night, with 'a palpable feeling', that God lived in him to give point to his life beyond any the world might claim. Most people thought Gordon was eccentric for holding such views and for trying to apply them in his own life. Eccentric or no, he takes his place in the climax of this story because of them; indeed, without them his life would hold little interest for posterity.

Gordon first came to Africa in 1874 as Governor of the Equatorial Province of the then expanding Egyptian empire, succeeding Baker as an employee of Ismail Pasha. His brief was to extend the frontiers of Egypt southwards to the Equator and the Great Lakes – as far south, in fact, as he could – and he pursued the task with an energy that astounded everyone. Within three years he had surveyed the upper reaches of the Nile, put a boat on Lake Albert, corrected the geographical errors of others and set an administration working. South of Gondokoro a line of forts manned by Egyptian troops marked the way to Uganda. Their names – Dufile, Fatiko, Foweira, Mrooli – appear fleetingly on maps to authenticate this strange episode in African history.

It was in the course of this work that Gordon sent Ernest Linant de Bellefonds, one of a number of foreign adventurers who came his way, to Uganda where he coincided with Stanley. Loyal to his brief Gordon was cool towards Stanley's activities. His was the only 'government' in that part of Africa; anyone claiming otherwise was an impostor. Gordon was sceptical also of what Stanley said about Mutesa's interest in Christianity, and he advised his friends in England to be cautious about sending missionaries there. In all probability, he wrote, Uganda will soon be part of the Egyptian empire and in its present state of fetish worship would profit more from Islam than Christianity. With de Bellefonds Gordon sent a Mullah to instruct Mutesa in the Koran, and de Bellefonds had to help the holy man out when he grew embarrassed at the African's questions. Stanley, for his part, was sceptical of de Bellefonds's military posture in a situation where his few men stood no chance against Mutesa's army.

Claiming Uganda for his master, the Pasha, Gordon prepared to annex Mutesa's kingdom. He sent a detachment of soldiers under a Sudanese officer to Lake Victoria to receive the African potentate's submission, only to find Mutesa quite capable of standing up for himself. His bluff called and de Bellefonds having been killed by some natives he was trying to punish shortly after returning to the Nile, Gordon then sent a German doctor, Eduard Schnitzer, otherwise known as Emin, to negotiate a withdrawal of his men. For the time being Uganda remained independent, and Emin, who in the course of a mysterious career in the Near East had become a Mohammedan, stayed on in Gordon's service to become in his turn Governor of Equatoria. When Khartoum fell in 1885 he was still in his remote province, cut off from the outside world but happily adding to his collection of stuffed animals, until rescued somewhat reluctantly by Stanley in 1888.

As Governor of Equatoria Gordon soon came to the conclusion that his 2,000-mile line of communications with Egypt via Khartoum and the Nile was unsatisfactory. For supplies and the execution of his orders he depended on Egyptian officials down river who were active in the slave business themselves. But only 400 miles separated his province from the Indian Ocean and if access to Equatoria could be gained from there it would cut out the corrupt Egyptian administration of the Sudan altogether. He therefore persuaded Ismail to mount a military expedition through the Red Sea to occupy part of the East African coast, set up a base there and march inland to join him. Gordon selected Formosa Bay as the best site, a deep-water anchorage where the River Tana debouches into the ocean close to Lamu. Mombasa was also spoken of as a reasonable Egyptian objective.

The force was commanded by a British naval officer, Captain McKillop, on loan to Ismail to train boys for the Egyptian navy, but it ran out of coal, oil and water, lacked any system of transport, lost some officers and men at the mouth of the Juba, and got into a muddle over its orders. Kirk at Zanzibar was naturally incensed at this invasion of his protégé's preserves, and Sultan and Pasha nearly came to blows before the expedition retired as ineptly as it had arrived. Gordon had originally planned to march through Uganda to the sea, but he abandoned the idea when Mutesa blocked his way and the McKillop episode was soon dismissed as a piece of Egyptian folly. Gordon's strategic intuition, however, was right, though it took his own death at Khartoum to prove it.

Gordon hated Africa. He was deceiving the natives, while the Egyptians, he felt, needed civilising more than the people they were attempting to conquer. Concluding there was little point in his work, he tried to resign from Ismail's service. In another strange might-have-been of African history there was a chance he would lead an expedition from Zanzibar to Uganda, financed by a consortium headed by William Mackinnon, a Scottish industrialist interested in the Indian Ocean, who was at that time negotiating for a concession from the Sultan to his mainland dominions. The Pasha of Egypt, however, persuaded Gordon to remain and take on even greater responsibilities as the Governor-General of the Sudan, a vast area of North Africa stretching from the Red Sea to Darfur, and from Wadi Halfa to within a hundred miles of the Equator. Between 1877 and 1880, as the viceroy of a viceroy, Gordon exercised more power than any other white man in Africa. During this period he earned his reputation as the scourge of the slave-traders, whom he confronted personally in a series of spectacular camel rides across the desert, often arriving in their lairs in full uniform ahead of his small escort and relying only on the force of his moral authority.

Thanks largely to Gordon's efforts and to the appearance he gave of civilisation's advance into Africa, Lavigerie was able to send his second missionary caravan by the Upper Nile route after that impressive send-off in Notre Dame d'Afrique, as did the CMS with their reinforcements for Uganda. In Gordon's time, too, Catholics struggled to revive the missions which the Austrians had pioneered so bravely earlier in the century. But they were still dogged by famine, drought and disease; their death-rate was fearful and they encountered antagonisms as a result of Gordon's own activities against the slave-trade. Gordon himself took no part in missionary activities, believing in an absolute distinction between secular and spiritual work. For the man of action, there was no place, let alone time, for tracts for the heathen; there were no prayer meetings or preaching to his entourage, no personal evangelism at all. That he was a man with strong religious convictions was obvious to all who came near him; but, as a Roman Catholic bishop shrewdly pointed out, he probably owed his moral ascendancy over Arabs more to his chastity than to his faith, an aspect of his character which made him an uncomfortable companion to those who possessed neither. The fact is, Gordon was in Africa as the mercenary of a Moslem prince and his only motive in carrying on was to use the position which God had given him to break the slave-trade. 'Were it not for the very great comfort I have in communion with God, and the knowledge that He is Governor-General, I would not get on at all.' Meanwhile as a ruler, he was free to execute and flog men whenever his passions were roused. Not that he liked doing it, but there were moments when he was stirred by more than legal form: 'I have hanged a man for mutilating a little boy, and would not ask leave to do so', he said in a letter. So it came about that no man in his day rendered unto Caesar more faithfully the things that were his, because no man of power in that age had less use for Caesar's rewards. 'I have a Bank,' he wrote on coming to Africa, 'and on that bank I can draw. He is richer than the Khedive and knows more of the country than Baker. I will trust Him to help me out of this and every difficulty.' And when it was all over and he was looking forward to peaceful self-effacement: 'To attain the closest union with Christ is certainly to follow Him and forsake all positions of rank and honour of this world; all other things belong to Satan's kingdom.'

In June 1879 Ismail's bank at last ran dry. He had become so entangled in financial difficulties he was forced to abdicate in favour of his son Tewfik, a sad come-down after the brilliant show he had mounted at Suez ten years before. Gordon had remained in Africa only out of loyalty to the Pasha, giving him moral support to the end, but with his patron's disappearance there was nothing to keep him in Egypt. He undertook a last hazardous foray into Abyssinia as Plenipotentiary for the new Khedive and then resigned.

The departure of Ismail and Gordon from Egypt brought an era to a close. They were a strangely matched pair, the Pasha so sensual and worldly, his Governor-General so austere, so detached. Within a few months the house of cards they had built together collapsed. In September 1881 the underpaid and disgruntled officers of the Egyptian army, led by Arabi, rose in protest at the way their country was being run by infidel outsiders. A flurry of diplomatic activity resulted in the bombardment of Alexandria by British warships and the landing of British troops under Garnet Wolseley, who routed the Egyptians at the battle of Tel-el-Kebir in September 1882 and installed British hegemony over Egypt.

A month later saw the beginning of the fateful year 1300 in the Moslem calendar in which the Mahdi, or Expected One, was due to appear. A Mahdi had already declared himself in the person of Mahomed Achmed, an ascetic living on an island on the White Nile some miles south of Khartoum. Almost at the same moment as Arabi's rebellion (the two movements were probably in touch with each other) this son of a Dongolese shipbuilder emerged from his island retreat to raise the standard of revolt in Kordofan, a wild mountainous region of the Sudan, west of the Nile, which was the haunt of slave-traders and fierce Bedouin tribes smarting under Gordon's chastisement of two years before. A Holy War was proclaimed to purge Islam of the corruptions seen in Cairo, in Constantinople, in Mecca even. The desert tribes of poor men, known as 'dervishes', flocked to his banner welcoming the chance of throwing off Egyptian and Turkish rule and resuming their age-old activities of plunder and slave-trading – the *razzia*, as it was known. El Obeid,

capital of Kordofan, fell after a bloody siege. An Egyptian army of
ten thousand men commanded by a retired British officer, Colonel
Hicks, was annihilated to a man. The revolt spread to the Red Sea,
where the Egyptians suffered further defeats. Khartoum itself was
threatened, and with Khartoum, Sennar and Berber.

After quitting Egypt in 1880, as he thought for good, Gordon
mooned about the world at a loss to know what to do. He wanted
rest, but was bored with it, turning for consolation to a more intense
study of the Bible: 'I see lakes and seas of knowledge before me'. He
began taking Holy Communion regularly, a practice which seems to
have made him grow gentler and more positive in his religious views.
He accepted the post of secretary to the Viceroy of India, but
resigned it within a week of arriving in Bombay; he revisited China;
served as Engineer Officer in command of the garrison in Mauritius;
then as special commissioner in South Africa, where he got on well
with Cecil Rhodes and won the respect of the Basutos, but fell out
with the Cape government. Finally, he was drawn to Palestine and
the Holy Places in a self-imposed exile from life which was not very
fruitful for his spirit. He thought the Egyptians deserved all that was
happening to them and that the Sudan would be better off independent. In any case, it was too late to do anything there.

But inactivity also irked him. Trials and afflictions were preferable
to doing nothing: 'I prefer life amidst sorrows, if those sorrows are
inevitable, to life spent in inaction.' The truth was, Gordon was a
soldier and needed to be given orders so as not to feel his own will or
desires were involved in the circumstances in which he found himself
in the world. He came to believe that God's purpose for him would
be revealed in his death, probably in action, but how could he best
fulfil this mission?

Late in 1883 he agreed to take up a post under Stanley in the
Congo, redeeming a promise he had made to King Leopold of
Belgium. It meant resigning his commission. On New Year's Day
1884 he was in Brussels and made the final arrangements as to his
terms of service and pension.

The day after he got back to London there was a knock on the door.
It was W. T. Stead, editor of the evening newspaper, the *Pall Mall
Gazette*, a man with a nonconformist conscience and a flair for
popular journalism. For two hours he interviewed Gordon about the
situation in the Sudan and next day published the text of it under the
headline 'Chinese Gordon for the Sudan'. At once *The Times* and
other influential papers joined the chorus. So did the Queen. Headlines now made their own news and the popular cry of 'Send Gordon!'

was more immediate copy than accounts of the actual state of affairs in the Sudan. But what Gordon was expected to do was not very clear to anyone.

Gordon was excited at the prospect which suddenly opened before him. It was what he really wanted all along. Samuel Baker came to press him to agree. When he had gone Gordon confessed to a friend who had been with them that the demon of self had taken possession of him again. 'Yes; you saw me – that was myself – the self I want to get rid of.'

On 18 January Leopold and the Congo were set aside and Gordon accepted the job of evacuating the Egyptian garrisons from the Sudan and handing over the region to its traditional rulers. He left England the same day. 'I go to the Sudan tonight,' he telegrammed his friend, 'If He goes with me, all will be well.' A week later he was in Cairo where the Khedive appointed him Governor-General with full executive powers. On 18 February he reached Khartoum to a tumultuous reception. 'I come', he said 'without soldiers but with God on my side, to redress the evils of the Sudan. I will not fight with any weapons but justice.' He was Gordon Pasha, and that should have been enough.

What followed is well known. Gordon alone provided the defence of Khartoum. Evacuation was impossible and the city was soon cut off, except by river. He had several thousand troops well supplied with ammunition, but they would have meant nothing without his presence in the Governor-General's palace. One man was enough to keep off the Mahdi's army. 'I am here like iron,' he wrote when called on to surrender.

The dervish forces, swelling in numbers daily as tribe after tribe joined, sprawled across the desert. Gordon learned that the Mahdi put pepper under his finger nails so that he could weep whenever he wanted by scratching his eyes. It was apparently an old trick among fakirs, and it rather depressed Gordon. 'I had hitherto hoped I had to do with a regular fanatic, who believed in his mission,' but the pepper business ended his interest. Meanwhile the official system of communications confused the sequence of his own messages out of Khartoum, so adding to the fantasies of government diplomacy. In the end, after he had sent his cypher down-stream, Gordon did not know what was contained in the last incoming telegrams. It hardly mattered to him. 'We can keep a continual telegraphic communication with Him,' he had once written. 'That is our strength.' Now he noted in his journal: 'I am deeply grateful for those who have prayed for us.'

Both Gordon and the Mahdi looked for a way of settling matters at Khartoum without fighting, but none presented itself. Gordon could have saved himself, of course, by accepting the Mahdi's terms, which meant turning Mohammedan (as Slatin, the young Austrian Gordon had made Governor of Kordofan, had done), or by sailing away down river again with his steamers, or even retreating southwards to join Emin. He chose to remain with the people to whom he had pledged himself, making their fate his own and seeking his destiny in theirs. His last message to the Mahdi ran: 'It is impossible for me to have any more words with Mahomed Achmed, only lead.' And from across the Nile the Mahdi's men hurled back at him: 'Know, O thou enemy of God, there is no escape from death at our hands and from death by lack of food.'

Gordon always thought of death as being a release; living in the world he said, was like being at school, and leaving it like going home for the holidays. 'Death is the glorious gate of eternity . . . there is a vast void in us unfilled while here below.' In all his African escapades, as earlier in China and the Crimea, he took no thought for his personal safety. On earth, his duty was to act as a soldier, but his life was in God's hands to preserve or destroy according to a wider, deeper, purpose than winning battles or relieving fortresses. Occasionally he would feel a pain in his heart when his military training warned him against being caught unprepared, for to fail in his duty as a soldier would be failing to respect the gifts God had given him. But for a soldier like Gordon to try and live in complete faith in God's omnipotence produced moments of great tension, as when he feared he was trapped by King John in Abyssinia: 'I do try and think, and try to put into practice, that God is the supreme power in the world, and that He is Almighty; and, though "Use-your-judgement" people may say, "You tempt God, in putting yourself in positions like my present one", yet I do not care. I do not do it to tempt Him; I do it because I wish to trust in His promises.'

So in the last critical weeks in Khartoum there was a conflict between the experienced soldier, desperately in need of help, and a man who trusted God: ' "Is My hand shortened?" and "You have no possible way of escape," are continually contending with one another,' was how he put it. In one of his last letters, he wrote: 'I always felt that if we got through it would be a scramble. There would be no glory to man . . . He is not unfaithful if we fall; for it may be for His greater glory and He does not promise everything we ask if it is not good for us to have it. I am content He will enable me to keep my faith and not deny Him.'

28 *General Gordon: The Last Photograph*

Soon after daybreak on Monday, 26 January 1885, the dervishes at last found a way through the defences of Khartoum. Surging through the city to the Governor-General's undefended palace, they killed the solitary white man they found there and cut off his head to present to their master. The Madhi showed it to his prisoner, Slatin. Gordon's blue eyes, Slatin wrote later, were half opened, his face composed, his hair and his short whiskers almost white. 'Is not this the head of your uncle, the unbeliever?' his captors exulted. 'What of it?' replied Slatin. 'A brave soldier who fell at his post; happy is he to have fallen; his sufferings are over.' The nearest British forces were still two days away down river.

So Gordon's defence of Khartoum, a brilliant defence in military terms, ended abruptly in a wild outburst of violence which claimed some 10,000 victims. With the fall of the capital of the Sudan,

Egypt's pretensions as an imperial power in Africa also came to an end, which in turn rendered futile Gordon's own body-breaking work of previous years.

Gordon dead, however, proved a more potent symbol of militant Christendom that Gordon alive, potent enough to topple Gladstone and put Liberalism out of effective action for twenty years. Public opinion wanted a hero, not a failure. The only role that fitted the dead Gordon was as a martyr of Empire, even though the strident note of imperialism was everything Gordon hated. 'I hate all the boasting of our papers,' he once said, commenting on the risks men ran for what he called 'paper distinction'. Cecil Rhodes saw it differently. When he heard of what had finally happened at Khartoum he kept repeating 'I am sorry I was not with him! I am sorry I was not with him!'

By his death, then, Gordon provided the British Empire with a moral alibi. 'I have done my best for the honour of our country,' ran the final message of his journal. His country would certainly do its best to honour him. Thus, in Africa, all kinds of men came to feel they were walking in Livingstone's footsteps, or ruling in Gordon's shadow; a Rhodes, a Mackinnon, a Goldie of the Chartered Companies, a Lugard or a Harry Johnston among the adventurers, each one dreamed of colouring the map red. Britain, France and Germany, even Italy, advanced particular claims to a civilising mission and within a matter of ten years had divided up Africa between them. By the time Britain was able to avenge Gordon's death at the Battle of Omdurman in 1898, the scramble for Africa was over and Africa had been given its present shape.

Gordon's death was also an inspiration to a whole new generation of missionaries, as Livingstone's had been in the previous decade. They would have a different role to play from the pioneers, finding in the colonial era their greatest opportunity to propagate their beliefs. The cultural gulf, of course, led to an assumption of racial superiority among many of them, yet they were able time and again to mitigate the arrogance of imperialism, and more than colonial regimes they could claim to have the real interests of Africans at heart. As things turned out, they would come into sharp conflict with colonial governments over many issues and help pave the way for eventual independence.

Indeed, the ultimate message of the missionary church was freedom, the freedom of Christ's empty tomb. This is what the gospel, the 'good news', meant. It implied freedom from the ignorance of past centuries; freedom from the thraldom of malign spirits; freedom from the barriers to human progress raised by tribal custom; freedom from the limitations on social and economic well-being imposed by untamed natural forces. Such a liberating of men's minds and spirits was bound to lead also to a demand for personal and political freedom. The missionary gospel carried with it a challenge to the very assumptions of the colonial state.

CHAPTER EIGHT

INSTEAD OF VICTORY, TRUTH

29 *Battle of Omdurman, 1898*

I

After leaving East Africa Ludwig Krapf settled in the pretty village of Kornthal in southern Germany, where he rejoiced over the revival of missionary interest in the interior which followed Stanley's travels. His impulsive nature made him long to join the new men at the scene of his old labours, but he had to content himself with translation work and a wide correspondence with the men in the field, encouraging, warning, urging them on, his own scheme for a chain of stations up the Nile, called the Pilgrim Mission, having run out of funds.

Krapf's second wife died soon after his return from the Magdala campaign, leaving him with a little daughter, and he then married his housekeeper to provide a home for her. In 1875 he welcomed his old colleague Rebmann back to Europe after an absence of thirty years in East Africa. Rebmann had gone blind and suffered greatly, but he was more hopeful of missionary openings than when they last met. He died the following year and was buried at Kornthal. Two years later Krapf took an affectionate farewell of the eighty-year-old Bishop Gobat, who had returned to Europe to visit his numerous grandchildren before dying in Jerusalem in 1879. Then Krapf grew weaker himself. He spent a happy afternoon with his friend from Abyssinia, Martin Flad, whom Napier had rescued from Theodore's clutches. The following morning, 27 November 1881, he was found dead by his bedside, kneeling in an attitude of prayer.

By then the Zanzibar regime appeared strongly consolidated. A new Sultan, Barghash, had succeeded Majid in 1870. In 1875 he visited England and was received by Queen Victoria's ministers; England helped him recruit a native army on the mainland and provided a naval officer, Matthews, to command it, together with 500 Snider rifles. Talks took place with Mackinnon and his friends for a concession to exploit the commercial potential of the mainland. It was called philanthropic capitalism in the nineteenth century, today it is known as development aid. A road inland was begun from Dar-es-Salaam which saved that site from reverting to the jungle. But it led in the wrong direction and advanced only seventy miles in four years. A 'tramway' was really needed, said Stanley. The offer of Robert Arthington, the hermit of Leeds, to pay for a boat on Lake Tanganyika brought the LMS to East Africa and with them those two opinionated seamen, Edward Hore and Alfred Swann. Roger Price, survivor of the ill-fated Makololo mission and veteran of Bechuanaland, was brought in to experiment with ox-travel in the vain hope that the tsetse fly might not prove a barrier to the interior, as it was on the Zambezi. Inland the Arab colony at Ujiji was growing apace and boasted its own tradesmen, apprentice craftsmen and boat-builders; but with the arrival of the LMS men, the White Fathers and miscellaneous members of the Belgian association, the numbers of Europeans also greatly increased. There were certainly too many of them for Kirk's liking.

But Krapf's intuitions about East Africa soon proved correct. The Mahdi's victory dealt a resounding blow to the white man's prestige, especially to Britain's. Repercusions were felt throughout Africa as the Arab colonists and their native allies, ably led by men like Tippu Tip and Rumaliza, made a determined bid for physical control. In the interior, from Lake Nyasa to Lake Victoria, missionaries of all societies, English, Scots and French, had to fight for their own and their converts' lives, initially without much support from outside. Joubert, one of Lavigerie's earliest zouaves, displayed particular coolness with an African militia he had trained, keeping order over a wide area on the western shore of Lake Tanganyika. (He was sometimes described as an African Gordon, but unlike Gordon he married an African Christian woman, settled in the Congo with a large family and survived until 1927.) In Uganda, the first Anglican bishop of East Africa, Hannington, though warned against attempting it, chose this moment to appear from the east of Lake Victoria, which the Baganda believed to be an ill-omened direction. He was stopped at the border and murdered, probably through Arab instigation, and a savage persecution of African Christians in Uganda followed. On the coast, Krapf's Wesleyan protégés, now on the River Tana and at last in touch with the Galla, were attacked by Masai, again through Arab instigation. The Houghtons, husband and wife, were speared to death as they stood defenceless in front of their new home.

Perhaps the Sultan himself lay behind it all, perhaps his waning authority was responsible. In either case his sham empire could not continue much longer. At Bismarck's prompting the Germans suddenly discovered an interest in Africa and made a bid for Uganda. In the absence of French political interest, Lavigerie was inclined to back them, as much to curb the Arabs as to outmanoeuvre the British. Spheres of influence were agreed on, Laws on Lake Nyasa, Mackay in Uganda and the White Fathers all coming to the same conclusion. It was essential that Europe intervene on behalf of the Africans, if East Africa was not to go the way of the Sudan.

Kirk's presence at Zanzibar was now an embarrassment to everyone and in 1886 he left, ostensibly to consult in London, never to return. His retirement was said to be on health grounds; but he lived on until 1922, his ninetieth year, to be held up to another generation as a model of diplomatic correctitude.

In 1887 Mackinnon obtained his concession to the British sphere and formed the Imperial British East Africa Company to promote it, with Mombasa as his base and Kirk an interested party. But in trying to compete with the Germans the company went bankrupt. After what had happened at Khartoum, however, British public opinion would not sanction the lowering of the British flag once it had been raised over Uganda. In 1894 and 1895 Britain declared protectorates over Uganda and the future Kenya, and Germany satisfied herself with Tanganyika. Nyasaland (Malawi) became a

British protectorate in 1891. Leopold's independent Congo state took responsibility for territory west of Lake Tanganyika and the king ran it personally until 1908, when public opinion forced him to hand it over to the Belgian government. With Joubert's forces incorporated in the new state, Lavigerie formed a special Belgian contingent of his White Fathers to take up work there. But he refused Leopold's offer of financial support, which was conditional on the White Fathers' flying the flag of the International Association over their mission stations. Lavigerie said that he would not allow his name and his cause to become involved in human interests.

Anti-slavery forces were converging on the Arabs of the interior from east and west and their day was over. A last fight was put up against the Germans on the coast, but it was quickly smashed. Missionaries of all societies were now free to enter the field and assist in the process of 'development'. Noteworthy among them was a Scottish industrial mission, which was led by James Stewart, now aged sixty, and which was originally financed by Mackinnon and his friends as a private venture. It began at Kibwezi, on the Yatta Plateau, where Krapf had tried to start his mission, but with the appearance of the railway it moved to a site close to the future Nairobi where it played an important part in the political life of Kenya.

2

Robert Moffat was in his seventy-fifth year when he retired from Kuruman in 1870. Within six months of their return to England his wife Mary died, leaving him to face life alone in what was for him a strange land.

For a time he was afflicted by restlessness, but public opinion recognised him as the doyen of Britain's African missionaries. In the new popular journalism he was famous as Livingstone's father-in-law. He was much sought after for missionary meetings and civic receptions, at which he picked up the role of publicising Africa for which Livingstone had died. Moffat's tall, manly bearing, his eagle eye and white patriarchal beard, gave him an impressive appearance, but it was, as always, his personal magnetism that told with people. In Africa, he had so embodied the spirit of truth that the Bechuana, who were habitual liars, found it impossible to tell lies in his presence. So in England, churchmen found their habitual sectarian prejudices dissolving in his presence. He became a kind of prize exhibit of

Victorian religiosity. He was introduced to the Queen, and invited to dine with the Archbishop of Canterbury at Lambeth Palace; he breakfasted with the Prime Minister at Downing Street, received university degrees and the freedom of cities, was shown to the seat of honour and preached in Westminster Abbey. All this left him unmoved. 'When we think of the glories of eternity how small the mites of power in this world are,' he said once after leaving Gladstone's company.

In 1879 he settled into a cottage at Leigh, near Tonbridge in Kent, which was on the estate of Sam Morley MP, one of a group of wealthy non-conformists who contributed at various times to his support. It was a peaceful retirement, though men destined for Africa still sought him out, and he kept abreast with happenings there, protesting at the British government's handling of the Zulus in 1879, welcoming the take-over of the Transvaal in 1877 and dismayed at its return to the Boers in 1881 after Majuba.

It was a time of disaster for Bechuanaland, with tribes fighting among themselves, the Boers setting up more independent republics and English liberals unwilling to interfere. Kuruman eventually became a colony of poor whites and land speculators moved in with bogus claims and sharp lawyers. From the wreckage Khama obtained British protection over what was considered mostly desert and is now known as Botswana. When Moffat knew them the Boers were so poor they sometimes had to pay their officials in postage stamps. But diamonds and gold changed their prospects and brought in many thousands of diggers who cared nothing for their queer society. As far as the British Empire was concerned it would take another war, the last of Queen Victoria's reign, to unite the white people of South Africa.

Partly because of this unsatisfactory situation Robert Moffat's eldest surviving son, John Smith Moffat, gave up missionary work to join the colonial service, in which capacity he played an important part in the agreement between Lobengula and Rhodes on which the British South Africa Company's take-over of Matabeleland was based. It was an understandable human response to a changing world, though it brought him no peace of mind. But he and other Moffat descendants were respected for the enlightened racial attitudes they displayed.

It was not Robert Moffat's way; he never allowed secular considerations to cloud his idea of mission. At Kuruman he and Mary used to make a point of watching the terrific thunderstorms that pass across the skies of Bechuanaland. 'Eh Mary!' he would exclaim as the lightning revealed a face lit up in ecstasy, 'it makes me think of what we shall see on "that day".' On 9 August 1883 he died, words of scripture on his lips to the end, and so passed according to his own beliefs into that eternal ecstasy of which he had caught such vivid glimpses.

3

In the merry-go-round of congresses which European statesmen called to decide the fate of Africa, Cardinal Lavigerie won honour and respect. Politicians sought his advice and hesitated to incur his wrath. Paris, Brussels, London rose to him when he preached a great anti-slavery crusade, citing 'your great Gordon', and calling for a new military order like the Knights Templars of old to drive the Arabs out of Central Africa. In his support Leopold spoke of establishing a papal colony in Africa, guaranteed by everyone. Then, suddenly, at the behest of the Pope, Lavigerie called for his countrymen to rally round the Republic. To French Catholics his act seemed a betrayal of all that he had lived for, and scorn and contention became the companions of his last years.

He was infinitely saddened too by news of the civil war which finally broke out in Uganda after years of political turmoil, following Mutesa's death in 1884. In these years the numbers of African Christians in both the Anglican and Roman churches had grown rapidly, despite – one might almost say, because of – cruel persecutions. Unhappily, their sectarian loyalties coincided with their own internal tribal rivalries, a situation which has had tragic consequences elsewhere in Africa, as in Ireland. In Uganda the Arabs and their converts, much encouraged by the Mahdi's successes, added a third element of discord, while the French and English missionaries naturally sided with their co-religionists, each of whom could put 2,500 armed men in the field. Matters were brought to a head by the appearance of Captain Lugard on behalf of Mackinnon's short-lived Imperial British East Africa Company.

In the so-called scramble for Africa Uganda became a focus for all the different forces converging on the continent – commercial, political, strategic – and the missionaries could not avoid being caught up in a situation which involved, as much as anything, appealing to their respective public opinions at home. Though near to death, Lavigerie responded to his White Fathers' version of events by publishing an open letter in which he accused England of religious partiality and called down divine retribution on 'those Christian societies who shall henceforth shed blood or carry destruction into places where missionaries are seeking to implant the Gospel'. To allay nationalist feelings the French White Fathers, in 1894, invited English Catholics of the Mill Hill Order to share work in Uganda with them. By this time spheres of influence had been decided on in Europe and Uganda was definitely allocated to Britain. Lavigerie had foreseen the situation. 'Undoubtedly we must love our own country,' he said towards the end of his life. 'That is the law of nature. But we must rise above that law and merge all nations in one love. That is the law of the Gospel.'

Lavigerie died soon after midnight on 26 November 1892; not, as his romantic nature would have liked, a martyr in heathen lands, but prematurely aged, racked with rheumatism and suffering from a stroke. Ten days before his death he learned that his last great plan for a body of armed lay missionaries to guard the caravan routes across the desert had been vetoed by the French government for fear of displeasing others. So at the end he felt obscurely let down by history, his last days were clouded with depression and he sought consolation in reliving his childhood in the Basque countryside of France.

Many of Lavigerie's targets turned out to be windmills, and with his theatrical gestures and French rhetoric he often cut a somewhat ridiculous figure. As his Spanish biographer says, a Quixote, but what a Quixote! The scale of his vision, like his ambition, meant that failure like success claimed the whole of him; not for him the luke-warm way of the church of Laodicea, but a passion that took him to the heights and plunged him to the depths. He suffered, finally, from this sense of failure when it seemed that God had forsaken him, as perhaps Livingstone felt dying alone in the middle of Africa. 'Failure,' says the Roman Catholic, 'is a form of grace'. When he heard of his faithful Cardinal's last illness, the Pope went to his private chapel and remained alone in long drawn-out prayer.

France accorded him a state funeral. His body was drawn through the streets of Algiers on a gun-carriage to the harbour where a war-ship was ready to carry it to Carthage, there to be laid to rest in the vault he had prepared for himself in his new cathedral. As the vessel pulled away from the shore what caught the eye was the figure of a solitary priest, bare-headed and buffeted by the wind, holding up Lavigerie's great episcopal cross in the prow. It was fitting imagery for the new era Lavigerie had done so much to bring into being.

30 *Stanley, after his last great African expedition, in 1890*

4

Stanley died in the early hours of 10 May 1904, listening to the chimes
of Big Ben in London. 'How strange! So that is Time!' were his last
words. He had said once that his ambition was to be more than a
consul. Perhaps President of the United States? The circumstance of
his entering the world made it an impossibility. What then? A
martyr to progress? But he survived Africa and after Gordon's death
at Khartoum the role was no longer available. No wonder he com-
mented so captiously on Gordon's fate, for what was left for Stanley?
The relief of Emin in 1887–90 proved indeed to be a superb feat of
courage, organisation and leadership, but by then such daring deeds
were being presented more effectively by writers of fiction, men like

Henty, who had been with Stanley on the Ashanti campaign, and Rider Haggard, whose *King Solomon's Mines*, published in 1885, was the most popular book of the year and has continued in print ever since. Emin's own sordid end at the hand of Arab slavers some months after his relief by Stanley passed unnoticed.

For Stanley there was marriage to a famous society hostess, a seat in Parliament and a Knighthood in the Order of the Bath. But the man who had been congratulated by Mark Twain for his very American qualities had to deny them to obtain these English rewards; he still travelled in style, lectured and interviewed, but his utterances were trite echoes of a jingoistic age; he who once prided himself on being the master of his fate found himself double-crossed by Leopold and exploited by others. Forgeries, scandal and truths told with bad intent dogged him to the end of his days and he was tainted with what he himself called the 'moral malaria' of the Congo. Although he was married in Westminster Abbey, he was not to be buried there, beside Livingstone, as he wished.

Instead he was laid to rest at Pirbright, Surrey, near the country house which he had bought as a home for his wife and adopted son. In the village churchyard his widow erected a six-ton granite stone from Dartmoor over his grave. She completed his unfinished autobiography and did all she could to preserve her view of him in the world's memory. Let hers be the last words about him, the words she chose to be engraved on that six-ton megalith: 'I desired to record simply his name, "Henry Morton Stanley", and beneath it, his great African name, "Bula Matari". For epitaph, the single word "Africa", and above all, the Emblem and Assurance of Life Everlasting, the Cross of Christ.'

5

When the European war of 1914–18 broke out there was an outside chance that the participants would keep it out of Africa, as they had agreed to do in theory at Brussels in 1890. 'What would Livingstone think of such a foolish fight?' wrote an anguished German missionary to Dr Laws in Nyasaland, appealing to him to use his influence to keep peace in their part of the continent. It was to no avail. Instead, the belligerents enrolled their African dependants in their armies, mostly as carriers, to take part in campaigns far from their own villages and in conditions for which they were quite unfitted. Thousands died of disease, exhaustion and hardship, thousands more from epidemics which raged at the war's end. Thereafter the colonial state had no moral basis for its continued existence in Africa and it was not long before the European empires of the nineteenth century themselves dissolved. So a Kikuyu herdboy born in Queen Victoria's reign in what was then called British East Africa could live to become President of an independent Republic of Kenya and the mission schools in which he, along with many others, first learned to read and write became seed-beds of a whole generation of leaders in modern Africa.

But, in Augustine's terms, earthly cities rise to fall, and fall to rise again, while the City of God draws its members from every time and place, from every nation, race and class of people. Lavigerie's intuitions about history and his insistence on adaptation to local customs, 'in everything compatible with Christian and priestly life', go deeper than perhaps even he realised. In Africa today, in thatched huts in the bush as well as in new concrete buildings along each 'Church Road' in each new township, multitudes of African Christians, young and old, come together to worship in their own languages and in their own ways, led by their own priests and elders, and ready to send out their own missionaries. South of the Zambezi some 2,000 independent churches acknowledge Christ quite apart from white men's liturgies, dogmas and disciplines. In 1964 twenty-two of the Uganda martyrs of the last century were canonised by the Catholic church, an example to Christians of all denominations who, in that country and others, have had to withstand similar onslaughts by similar regimes.

What of the future? 'I exercise no authority but that of love and kindness', Livingstone had written when slave traders fled at his approach; 'I see nothing in the world worth looking after if it has not a direct reference to the glory and extension of the Redeemer's kingdom', Moffat reflected once about his work; 'I would rather learn that you were dead than see you lose the spirit of your vocation and become some kind of African adventurers,' Lavigerie instructed his White Fathers. The faith of these men, like that of the African martyrs of Uganda, is a world away from the ideologies of violence and revolution which are now being preached in Africa, ostensibly in the name of Christian churches.

Indeed the appearance in history of a Livingstone, a Stanley or a Gordon, challenges all such secular interpretations of man's destiny. Likewise the work of Moffat, Krapf and Lavigerie. The strength of their beliefs and the drama of their lives are themselves a repudiation of the materialist view of the universe. What made them unique was their inner life, which is not to say that they were every one of them saints or even very likable people. But to understand the source and quality of that inner life takes the enquirer beyond the range of technical history.

As Henry Martyn, that saint of missions, neared the end of his brief but glorious life, he came to see how impossible it was to convince worldly minded people, whether Christian or Mohammedan, 'that what they call religion is merely a thing of their own, having no connection with God and his kingdom'. 'Oh! when shall time give place to eternity!' were almost his last recorded words. His situation, alone in Persia and close to death, gave him great clarity of mind. 'How senseless the zeal of churchmen against dissenters, and of dissenters against the church!' he wrote. His own experience confirmed that of countless others before and after, namely that 'the kingdom of God is neither meat nor drink, nor anything perishable; but righteousness, and peace, and joy in the Holy Spirit.'

ACKNOWLEDGEMENTS AND SOURCES

The literature on Africa is vast and growing, as modern research adds new information every year. I do not claim to have unearthed any sensational and hitherto
unpublished material, but I have concentrated my reading on those areas most
relevant to the central theme. Where the evidence is conflicting I have interpreted
it from a declared standpoint.

A starting point has naturally been the works written by the principal characters
and published during their lives, or, like Livingstone's *Last Journals*, which were
edited by Waller, to meet public response to his death. I have mentioned the
relevant works in the text. Most of them now fetch high prices and libraries have to
guard their first editions carefully. One could wish for cheap re-issues.

In this context everyone must be grateful for the publications undertaken in the
Oppenheimer Series and by the Van Riebeeck Society, which have made primary
sources so much more accessible. From the former I have drawn extensively on the
Matabele Journals of Robert Moffat, edited by J. P. R. Wallis – for example, for the
quotations on pages 87, 94 and 95 and on *Apprenticeship at Kuruman*, edited by
Professor I. Schapera; from the latter I have used *The Diary of Andrew Smith*,
edited by Professor P. R. Kirby, and *Letters of the American Missionaries, 1835–1838*,
edited by D. J. Kotzé. Likewise, the several volumes of Livingstone's letters and
journals, edited by Professor Schapera, have brought that extraordinary man much
closer to the student of the period. I have quoted frequently from them. The
introductions and annotations to these works and others in the two series are of
immense value and I acknowledge my debt to them.

The problems connected with different versions of these primary sources are well
discussed by their editors. Early missionaries were asked by their societies to keep
regular journals to assist in missionary propaganda at home. This often led to the
appearance of various accounts of their activities, some copied, some in précis
form, some in private letters, some for publication. 'I have an aversion to journalis-
ing,' grumbled Moffat on more than one occasion. He felt it was a distraction from
the main task in hand. His reluctance may also have arisen from the competitive
use made of his material by others, for example by Philip and Thompson. What he
marks as being only for his wife's eyes has a quaintly strait-laced quality, in keeping
with his character. But one cannot help being struck by the integrity of all Moffat's
writing. Discrepancies of substance never occur nor did he ever descend to the
cheap or the mawkish.

The archives of the old London Missionary Society, with which Moffat was
connected all his life, are incorporated with those of the Council for World Mission
and lodged at the Library of the School of Oriental and African Studies, London,
and I am grateful for permission to use them. I have quoted Moffat's account of the
Battle of Lattakoo from this source. It is contained in a letter to his wife's parents
and copied from his journal, being virtually identical with that printed in *Apprenticeship at Kuruman*, except for one sentence. Where Moffat's journal has 'the firing was
slow but extremely irregular, from a most irregular and undisciplined corps', his
letter, in which he presumably corrected the journal, has 'the firing was slow but
extremely regular . . .'.

On pages 80 and 90 I have put into a simplified dialogue form Moffat's various accounts of his conversations with Moselekatse. He recorded these in a rather cumbersome manner, possibly because he had been using an interpreter.

Cecil Northcott's *Robert Moffat: Pioneer in Africa*, published in 1961, and *The Lives of Robert and Mary Moffat*, by their son J. S. Moffat, new edition published in 1886, are both essential reading. Moffat's farewell sermon which I have quoted on page 70 is taken from the former (p. 171). On page 259ff. Northcott also gives in full Moffat's important letter to Livingstone, written from Moselekatse's head-quarters in October 1857.

In his *Matabele Journals* (Vol. 2, pp. 234/5) there is a moving passage in which Moffat reflects on the place occupied by the Bible in his life. Although he was by then an old man and had spent much of his life translating the Bible into a vernacular language, he could still write, 'When is the mind to conceive or the pen to write, the undying unfading and ever refreshing wonders of the Bible, the Book of God . . . I read the Bible today with the same feeling I ever did, like the hungry when seeking food, the thirsty when seeking drink, the bewildered when seeking counsel and the mourner when seeking comfort.' From this passage and many others it can be seen how important a part scriptural texts played in the lives of men like Moffat, as I have tried to show. But it is perhaps worth adding that those of them who were English-speaking used the Bible in the King James, or Authorised, Version, so that readers accustomed to modern translations may find themselves missing Biblical allusions which constantly occur in their thoughts and writings. For example, on page 147 I have quoted a famous scene in which Livingstone uses the phrase 'and should such a man as I flee?' which he took from the Book of Nehemiah. The New English Bible rendering is 'should a man like me run away?' Whatever the translation, however, the Bible is itself a primary source to help elucidate other sources.

In the case of Ludwig Krapf I have drawn mostly on the letters he and his colleagues wrote in English which are preserved in the archives of the Church Missionary Society in London. They were handled very discreetly by CMS officials at home when it came to missionary propaganda for fear of political repercussions. I have not been able to compare them extensively with the letters Krapf wrote in German to his continental friends, but where I have done so they do not suggest any fundamental difference in emphasis nor do they contain vital additional matter. They perhaps reveal rather better his spiritual state and dependence on Lutheran tradition. The quotation on page 120 is taken from one of them, and I am grateful to Erika Grothe for her help in translating. I am most grateful, too, to Miss Woods at the CMS library for her patient advice, for drawing my attention to other CMS publications and for loaning me biographies of such men as Gobat and Isenberg, Charles New's *Life, Wanderings and Labours in Eastern Africa*, and *Thomas Wakefield*, by E. S. Wakefield, a most interesting account of the Methodist mission at Ribe.

Livingstone bluntly refused to oblige his society in the matter of a journal, though his output of words in letters and private notebooks was prodigious. 'My thoughts run on a book of travels' he wrote once to his brother, preferring no doubt to do the job of publicising Africa himself rather than leave it to men in London for whom he had little regard. The success of his books certainly justified this attitude. His skill as a propagandist can be seen in the way, time and again, he hit upon a striking phrase to catch the public eye. We can imagine him turning them over in his mind as he plodded along until he felt he had them right, and then releasing them in different quarters where they would be sure to make their mark.

The lengthy quotation which appears on page 137 is taken from *Livingstone's*

African Journal, 1853–1856, edited by Schapera, Vol. 1, p. 58. I have included this in the hope that it may convey something of Livingstone's unique and compelling style and be of interest as an illustration of how he used the Bible and applied it to his own situation. The famous scene which I have quoted on page 147 comes from Vol. 2, pp. 373–4 of the same journal. The passage quoted on page 146 is from *Livingstone's Private Journals, 1851–1853,* edited by Schapera, p. 167. I have consulted Livingstone's letters in the British Museum for his impression of Stanley. They and the Waller Papers at Rhodes House, Oxford, give his views on Kirk and the set-up in Zanzibar.

The literature surrounding Livingstone's activities is large, particularly on the Zambezi Expedition, which he wrote up himself jointly with his brother Charles in *Narrative of an Expedition to the Zambesi and its Tributaries,* which was published after he had left England in 1865 for the last time. There are some interesting points made in *Livingstone: Man of Africa,* essays edited by Bridglal Pachai, especially those contributed by Professor George Shepperson and his friends at Edinburgh.

A recent biography, *Livingstone,* by Tim Jeal, may be read alongside the classic *Personal Life of David Livingstone,* by Blaikie, first published in 1880. Among the best accounts is *Livingstone the Liberator,* by James MacNair, first published in 1940 and for many years available at the Livingstone National Memorial at Blantyre, Scotland.

The problem with Stanley, as his recent biographer Richard Hall puts it, is to sift fact from fantasy and falsehood. Hall's *Stanley, An Adventurer Explored* is excellently researched as to many of the facts and falsehoods of Stanley's life. But many uncertainties remain, especially over the details of his activities; nor is the question of fantasy so easily disposed of, because it lies at the very heart of Stanley's profession of journalism. That is to say, what the public read and believed is as much an historical fact as what actually did or did not happen.

For example, did Livingstone say 'How is the world getting along?' as Stanley records in *How I Found Livingstone,* published in 1872, or 'Pray tell me how the old world outside of Africa is getting along?' as appears in Stanley's *Autobiography,* published posthumously in 1909? And does the different phrasing matter?

What is more to the point, did Stanley actually ever say 'Dr Livingstone, I presume?' or was this just a journalistic device which he did not take seriously when he wrote it, but bitterly regretted afterwards since he could never then disown it? Curiously, in what would appear to be Stanley's original record of that historic meeting with Livingstone, his diary entry ends with the words 'As I saw him, I dismounted.' The next page, which would presumably have carried a note of their first words to each other, has been torn out – when or by whom is not known – leaving the inquirer in doubt as to the very nature of this kind of historical evidence. But, after all, what is in question is the essential veracity of the reporter, not his method of working or the details of his copy. There is much in Stanley's original diary which certainly vindicates his reporting – for example, his note on what Kirk said about Livingstone in Zanzibar – and yet there is so much else missing as to raise new puzzles. Are we to regard his extensive dialogues with Livingstone which were subsequently published in various forms to be entirely fanciful? Or are they acceptable historical evidence? For myself, I am impressed by the manner in which at many points Stanley's account is corroborated by what was later to appear in Livingstone's *Last Journals.* Thus on pages 600–1 of *How I Found Livingstone* Stanley describes how the two of them came across a skeleton in the 'forest of Ukamba', which prompted Livingstone to reflect on the kind of quiet

African grave for which he longed himself – a remarkable duplication of Livingstone's own mention of the subject in the *Last Journals* (Vol. I, p. 307).

The problem, then, with Stanley is one that looms even larger in our own day, with our more advanced techniques for processing news through film and videotape to meet the ever increasing demands of mass communication. As Livingstone's Africans would say, What fables! What lies! I am most grateful to Mr R. M. Stanley of Furzehill Place for letting me see his grandfather's notebooks and I conclude, with him, that it would be unwise to speculate further until full-scale research can be completed on the Stanley archive.

As things stand, and as far as Stanley's real beliefs are concerned, his own books, his posthumous autobiography and the authorised life by Frank Hird, published in 1935, remain the essential basis for insights into the man and his trade. *My Early Travels and Adventures* (1895) includes a full description of the opening of the Suez Canal; extracts from Stanley's 1874–7 notebooks are published in *Exploration Diaries*, edited by R. M. Stanley and A. Neame. Norman R. Bennett, of Boston, U.S.A., has provided a masterly commentary to *Stanley's Despatches to the New York Herald*, which he has edited, and in which he touches on the problems mentioned above. All Bennett's work on East Africa is worth reading. His introduction to the second edition of Alfred J. Swann's *Fighting the Slave-Hunters in Central Africa*, 1969, is a notable piece of scholarship in this field.

The material on Lavigerie, including official Catholic records, is at present more elusive. Goyau's biography is probably the best, though dated. Clarke's *Cardinal Lavigerie and the African Slave Trade* gives a contemporary English view, while Arteche's *The Cardinal of Africa* is a lively Roman Catholic portrait with typically Spanish hues. William Burridge's *Destiny Africa* stresses the modernity of many of Lavigerie's missionary ideals, and I am most grateful to Father Burridge for reading my text and helping me over a number of points. *Gubulawayo and Beyond*, edited by Michael Gelfand, is the poignant story of the Jesuit mission of 1879–87 told in their own writings.

On Gordon, I find Lord Elton's biography the most convincing. It may be supplemented by *Colonel Gordon in Central Africa*, a volume of Gordon's letters edited in his life-time by George Birkbeck Hill, by Bernard M. Allen's masterly *Gordon and the Sudan*, and by *General Gordon's Khartoum Journal*, edited by Lord Elton. Lytton Strachey's wicked but witty portrait in *Eminent Victorians* need not be taken very seriously, but James Morris has a brilliant chapter on Gordon in *Heaven's Command*, a book that gives a glittering panorama of the British Empire over the whole period.

Among general works a special mention must be made of *The Missionary Factor in East Africa*, by Roland Oliver, while a useful standby is the *Concise Dictionary of the Christian World Mission*, edited by Stephen Neill and others. Langer's standard works, *Bismarckian Diplomacy* and *Diplomacy of Imperialism*, give the international political background for the end part of the story. In addition, due acknowledgement must always be made to the writings of Reginald Coupland. In his 1968 introduction to the re-issue of Coupland's *The Exploitation of East Africa, 1856–1890*, which was first published in 1939, Professor Simmons rightly points out that, although Coupland's approach to Africa was profoundly affected by the times he lived in, we can still admire his historical craftsmanship. It will have become clear in this book, however, that seen through the eyes of Ludwig Krapf, the history of East Africa appears in a very different light from that thrown upon it by Coupland. I should also like to mention the four-volume work by C. P. Groves, *The Planting of*

Christianity in Africa which, though necessarily condensed, seems to contain every important fact connected with its subject. Groves pays tribute to the help he received from Edwin W. Smith and I certainly endorse his assessment of the high quality of Smith's works. His biography of Roger Price, *Great Lion of Bechuanaland,* and his *Life and Times of Daniel Lindley* are most instructive.

Admirable bibliographies giving the titles of books and articles for wider reading may be found in Jeal, Hall, Northcott and E. W. Smith, to name no others. The catalogue in the Library of the Royal Commonwealth Society is also extremely useful in this respect. Two articles by Sir John Gray, out of many, may be mentioned: in the *Uganda Journal* No. 1 (1934), 'A precursor of Krapf and Rebmann' describes the activities of Lieutenant Emery, Owen's Governor of Mombasa, 1824–6; *Uganda Journal* No. 28 (1964) discusses in detail Ernest Linant de Bellefonds's trip to Mutesa. *Tanganyika Notes and Records* Nos 56, 57 and 60 (1961 and 1963) carry Norman R. Bennett's exhaustive studies of the Americans in Zanzibar. Finally, two books that I must note are *A Memoir of Henry Martyn*, by John Sargent – my edition was the twelfth, published in 1835 – and *Suez: De Lesseps' Canal*, by John Pudney. I have used material from both in Chapter One.

I acknowledge gratefully the help received from librarians and archivists at: Association for the Propagation of the Faith, British Museum, Catholic Central Library, London Library, Public Record Office, Rhodes House, Royal Commonwealth Society, School of Oriental and African Studies. I must also thank Mr M. I. Baldwin of the Weapons Department and members of the Reference Section of the National Army Museum in Chelsea.

I am greatly indebted to Mr John Messenger, who prepared the maps, and to the following for their kind permission to reproduce illustrations: Africana Museum, Johannesburg: nos 2, 8, 9, 10, 11, 13; Compagnie Financière de Suez: nos 1, 3; Council for World Mission: nos 5, 7, 12, 20; The Institution of Royal Engineers: no. 28; National Army Museum: no. 29; Rhodes House, Oxford: no. 27; Royal Commonwealth Society: nos 14, 16, 17; Mr R. M. Stanley: no. 21; The White Fathers: no. 25; Dr H. F. Wilson: no. 19.

INDEX

Jeremy Murray-Brown

FAITH
and the
FLAG
The Opening of Africa

'Sunday, September 24, 1854, saw the climax to this extraordinary duel of wills between the men of God and the men who embodied all earthly power in that remote fastness of Africa. Moffat stood up, Bible in hand, in front of his wagon; he was white-haired now, but as erect as on the day he first set foot in Africa thirty-seven years ago. Beside him sat the king, naked, obese, a cruel tyrant for all his outward geniality. In rows on the ground squatted his warriors, old men and young, all professional killers, all quite naked. The temperature rose into the nineties, but no one stirred, and as Moffat began to speak a profound silence fell as though all creation had paused to listen.'

In these words Jeremy Murray-Brown describes an historic moment in the lives of Robert Moffat and Moselekatse, king of the Matabele.

Following the success of his biography of Jomo Kenyatta, Jeremy Murray-Brown now looks at the history of Africa in the last century. He presents it through the lives and beliefs of six notable figures: Robert Moffat, the outstanding pioneer of southern Africa; his more publicised son-in-law, David Livingstone; Ludwig Krapf, the first Protestant missionary in East Africa and forerunner of Burton, Speke and Grant; Henry Morton Stanley, illegitimate son of a Welsh farmer, who became the most celebrated explorer of his time; the flamboyant French Archbishop of Algiers, Cardinal Lavigerie, founder of the Catholic White Fathers; and General Gordon, the enigmatic hero of Khartoum.